Ann Naymie

D IS FOR DARING:

The Women behind the Films of Studio D

—NFB ARCHIVES

"DARE TO BE FEMINIST; DARE TO BE OUT; DARE TO FIGHT BACK;
DARE TO BE DIFFERENT; DARE TO SPEAK OUT"

Cover, Studio D Twentieth Anniversary Booklet

D IS FOR DARING

The Women behind the Films of Studio D

To Ann
with all my best
wishes
Gail

GAIL VANSTONE

Feb. 27, 2008.

WOMEN'S ISSUES PUBLISHING PROGRAM

SERIES EDITOR BETH MCAULEY

LIBRARY AND ARCHIVES CANADA CATALOGUING IN PUBLICATION

Vanstone, Gail
D is for daring : the women behind the films of Studio D / Gail Vanstone.

Includes bibliographical references and index.
ISBN 978-1-894549-67-7

1. National Film Board of Canada. Studio D — History. 2. Women motion picture producers and directors — Canada — Biography. 3. Feminist motion pictures — Canada — History and criticism. 4. Documentary films — Canada — History and criticism. 5. Feminism and motion pictures — Canada — History. 6. Women in motion pictures. I. Title.

PN1999.N37V35 2007 791.43082'0971 C2007-904466-2

Edited by Beth McAuley
Designed by Liz Martin

Cover photo courtesy of Signe Johansson
Whistle image courtesy of Ginny Stikeman

Sumach Press acknowledges the support of the Canada Council for the Arts and the Ontario Arts Council for our publishing program. We acknowledge the financial support of the Government of Canada through the Book Publishing Industry Development Program (BPIDP) for our publishing activities.

ONTARIO ARTS COUNCIL
CONSEIL DES ARTS DE L'ONTARIO

Printed and bound in Canada

Published by

SUMACH PRESS
1415 Bathurst Street #202
Toronto ON Canada M5R 3H8

info@sumachpress.com
www.sumachpress.com

To Lily and Linnea
in anticipation of your daring.

CONTENTS

ACKNOWLEDGEMENTS

BEHIND THE UNDERTAKING of preparing this book for publication — performed in solitude and in company — stands a body of colleagues, family and friends to whom I owe a debt of gratitude for their guidance and unflagging support. This book is drawn from my doctoral thesis and for that I thank my supervisor Brenda Longfellow whose own documentary film work fired my imagination. Brenda guided me through the territory of feminist film theory, urging me to approach my subject from multiple perspectives while according me the space to draw my own conclusions. I want to thank Janine Marchessault and H.T. (Tom) Wilson for their insights and scholarly inspiration, particularly to Tom for his singular and valued encouragement; Caitlin Fisher for urging me on with her marvelous spirit and her creative engagement with ideas and with feminist undertakings; Dyan Elliott, deeply cherished friend, for her infectious energy and inimitable wit, for impeccable scholarship and invention with footnotes as forms of storytelling and whose careful reading of my work strengthened and refined its ideas; Catherine Swanson, for her insistence that scholarly work *must* be tempered with good friends, good food and "theory retreats" to Florida; Leslie Sanders for always asking the right question; Laura McLauchlan for her inimitable brand of incitement and for hospitality in Nova Scotia; my esteemed "Montreal connection" for hospitality while I conducted research; Reesa Winer for her special brand of warmth and humour; and Joan Barfoot, my greatly valued friend from childhood who helped set this process in motion and for her utterly true fictions about women's lives.

Of course, central to the writing of this book is Sharon McLeod, Butler, Bogart and the inestimable Oscar who invited me into their space, offering me a "room of one's own" to write and who lifted my spirits more than words can describe. A particular debt of gratitude is owed to Beth McAuley, vastly gifted editor, whose skill has taught me much and given me great pleasure, as well as to Sumach Press for pursuing Studio D's story to such a fine degree. Many thanks to my colleagues and students in the School of Arts and Letters at York University for ongoing generosity and for generating the intellectual climate where work of this nature can flourish. Many thanks to Kay Armatage for her wisdom.

Embedded in this work is a fabric of memories and fragments of inspiration I prize: Bernard Lutz, recently retired archivist of the National Film Board, who not only assisted me in finding the necessary Studio D records when I began this process but also graciously and delightfully invited me to lunch in the legendary NFB cafeteria, allowing me to retrace the footsteps of the women of Studio D and who *always* found useful answers to my questions; Kathleen Shannon who spent an entire day with me when I only expected a two-hour interview and for later surprising me with a copy of the cartoon that graced Studio D's walls for a time; Terre Nash who gave me copies of Kathleen Shannon's papers uncollected elsewhere; Signe Johansson for her perceptive insights and the box of personal Studio D photographs she handed to me as she cleaned out her office in the midst of retiring from the NFB; Gerry Rogers for her surprise phone call in the middle of winter and for sharing hilarious insider stories; Dionne Brand and Jennifer Kawaja for their marvelous gift of feminist stories in the eleventh-hour of my writing that seasoned and clarified my analysis; Miriam Waddington who trekked up the Sunshine Coast with me in search of Bonnie Sherr Klein and to Annie for her welcome when we arrived. I am indebted to the Studio D filmmakers — Dorothy Todd Hénaut, Bonnie Sherr Klein, Terre Nash, Gerry Rogers, Beverly Shaffer, Ginny Stikeman and Margaret Westcott — who shared the details of their experiences with me and allowed me to film them as we spoke.

In response to Constance Backhouse's exhortation to recognize the supportive men behind any feminist undertaking, I must name my film-loving partner Kevin Karst, who proofread my work and firmly believes in the value of women's stories and in their telling. Finally, a mother's thanks to my children — my cohorts — Arron and Scott Best for their inimitable company and to Cathy, treasured daughter-in-law, for her spirited and resolute self. Anterior to all of these resonates the voice of my much-loved father who urged me to "get a good education" — a sentence that still rings in my ears.

INTRODUCTION

STUDIO D'S REPRESENTATION OF WOMEN'S LIVES, 1974-1996

The point was not so much to make films but to make a difference.

— SIGNE JOHANSSON, STUDIO D PRODUCER (1974–1996)

Representing women on film? ... Experience validated is terribly important [and] very empowering.

— KATHLEEN SHANNON, STUDIO D EXECUTIVE PRODUCER (1974–1986)

... the essential thing was to make films from our experience, passionate, emotional films. It was a way of looking at the world.

— TERRE NASH, STUDIO D FREELANCE FILMMAKER (1975–1996)

A SCANT TWO YEARS BEFORE IT CLOSED IN 1996, THE NATIONAL FILM Board of Canada's Studio D adopted the slogan "D is for Dare." A brochure announcing "20 Years of Making Films, Breaking Stereotypes"[1] set out its film releases for 1994 along with a list of "daring" accomplishments claimed by Studio D on the occasion of its twentieth anniversary. "We have to dare as we have in the past to be different, to be feminist, to be 'out,' to fight back," proclaimed Ginny Stikeman, then executive director of Studio D (1991–1996), marking the occasion. "Our films dare to be different by challenging the way in which women's lives are depicted by the mainstream media. Our goal is to make films that encourage discussion and dialogue among women, and that promote action aimed at improving the status of women in society."[2] Daring to be different and daring to provoke discussion that would lead to feminist activism, indeed, marked the entire body of work credited to Studio D throughout its lifetime.

Unfortunately, this assertive stance did not protect Studio D from dissolution. In January 1996, the federal government published the findings of the Juneau Report, officially entitled *Making Our Voices Heard: Canadian Broadcasting and Film for the 21st Century.* Prepared by Pierre Juneau, Dr. Catherine Murray and Peter Herrndorf, the report, in essence, conducted a review of the mandates of the CBC, the NFB and Telefilm Canada to determine "whether these institutions continued to be essential, how they had to change, how they could reduce costs and how they should reform structurally."[3] The report reaffirmed the "traditional" core strengths of the NFB — to act as a centre for nurturing new and emerging filmmakers; to provide opportunities for filmmakers not feasible outside the NFB; and to support development of documentary films where the market had failed to provide these in sufficiently large numbers. In addition, the NFB was enjoined to "clarify its *raison d'être*; focus its scarce resources on production; make its films available to a greater number of Canadians; decentralize its operations; and make greater use of freelance talent"[4] (the federal government had reduced the NFB annual grant of $80 million to $56 million, roughly a 25 per cent cut).[5]

One year after launching its "Dare to be Different" publicity campaign and two months after the release of the Juneau Report, despite a series of collaborations and the implementation of several internal reinvention strategies, Studio D received word of its demise. After making feminist documentary films for over two decades and garnering an unprecedented number of awards, Studio D learned officially that it would be closed within a matter of months. If Studio D came into being as a significant component of the Canadian women's movement in the 1970s, existing within an institution celebrated for its creation and promotion of national culture, its disappearance represented a lamentable official retreat from women's issues, signalling a new chapter in the struggle of Canadian women nationally to have their voices heard and their stories taken seriously.

The fact that a studio, underwritten by the state[6] and producing documentaries about women's lives, was dismantled raises questions about the larger issue of agency and citizenship for women in Canada. The closure of Studio D signals, I suggest, an official retreat from a commitment to considering women's issues and making their voices heard at many levels of government throughout Canada during the 1990s. Certainly, a wide range of government budget cuts at the federal level, magnified by trickle-down cuts to provincial and municipal levels, impoverished the material (and cultural) lives of many women in Canada. This phenomenon has recently returned to the spotlight with the Harper government's announcement in September 2006 of a $2-billion budget cut to social programs (Aboriginal programs, women's groups, initiatives for people with disabilities, literacy programs, among others), despite a $13-billion surplus accrued by the previous Liberal administration. Perhaps the most shocking of these cuts is the one directed against Status of Women Canada — in the September 2006 announcement, the Conservatives signalled "their intention to close 12 of the 16 Status of Women Canadian offices, following the decision to cut 40 percent of the equality group's operating budget."[7] For feminists who remember its establishment in 1972, the recent proposal represents an unthinkable retreat from what had come to be regarded as an unassailable mechanism of equality rights.

As a feminist film studio, Studio D's collective imagination was directed towards placing women's issues at the centre of national interests. Its closure, in retrospect, should not have been a surprise given the prevailing "neo-con" political climate. Indeed, its documentary film production and operation as a feminist film unit mounted an implicit critique of the gendered bias inherent in the official national narrative. Further, it articulated a dynamic feminist construct of the term "national identity" through its documentary production, challenging the "rhetorical 'inclusiveness' and 'unity' of the mandate"[8] of the NFB.

The reality of Studio D needs to be understood in the context of Canadian women's larger struggle to secure better rights for themselves; its fate, the result of a sea change in attitude on the part of a political regime that began to withdraw significant benefits from its female citizens, signalled a diminishing of entitlement of their "citizenship" on multiple levels. Judy Rebick, political commentator and former president of the National Action Committee on the Status of Women, identifies the loss of voice as one of the serious outcomes of such cutbacks in the Canadian social fabric:

> What concerns me now, though, is that we are getting so used to the absence of a feminist voice in public discourse, we barely protest anymore ... Not only is the absence of feminist voices in the public discourse letting governments off the hook on crucial public policy issues it is also leading to backsliding on hard-won gains.[9]

One reading of the historical record suggests that Studio D came into being without much institutional forethought or fanfare on the part of the NFB. It was formed in response to the local demands of a small group of women headed by Kathleen Shannon, a long-time National Film Board employee and a filmmaker in its *Challenge for Change* series. The women were inspired by second-wave feminism, which ascribed to the Canadian version of the American Women's Liberation Movement of the late 1960s and early 1970s. This small group wanted to create an official mechanism that would allow women's voices to be heard and their stories told. Their demands, coming on the heels of the release of the recommendations of the Royal Commission on the Status of Women in 1970, constituted one thread in the fabric of women's activism across Canada. However, some feminist historians suggest that official responses to women's demands for change are fragile at best and more likely to be politically expedient accommodations that are seldom carefully thought through.[10]

Studio D, then, stands as an intriguing study, a site of contradiction, an official instrument of feminism notable for its ability to contribute to the development of an ongoing feminist culture, although its abrupt closure yields scant evidence to indicate that its creation was ever any more than a spur-of-the-moment impulse on the part of the state. In light of this official retreat in the last decade of the twentieth century, it seems fruitful to examine the implications of Studio D as a particular "voice of, by and for women" — a phrase drawn from its mandate — as a cultural producer mediating between the state and its women as citizens/constituents.

This book examines the feminist film studio in what I hope represents, as Sheila Rowbotham suggests, a "look[ing] back at ourselves through our own cultural creations, our action, our ideas, our pamphlets, our organization, our history, our theory."[11] Studio D leaves behind it a complex legacy and a collection of films that documents a social movement — from its early "realist" documentaries that were classic instruments of feminist consciousness-raising to more complex films that explored deeper issues of women's sexuality and identity. As a body, this collection of documentaries captures many of the landmarks of and tensions arising from feminist activity in the 1970s through the 1990s, offering a unique, though not uncontested, account of the Canadian women's movement in English-speaking Canada.[12] Studio D existed as a particular example of second-wave feminism that organized both its institutional structure and its documentary film production around the process of consciousness-raising that was linked to the concept "the personal is political." Its films continue to furnish a provocative and instructive model for understanding feminist challenges today. In order to appreciate this account fully, Studio D needs to be examined within the context of three relationships: its relationship within the National Film Board; its mediated relation with the Canadian state; and its relationship to English-speaking feminist communities.

Despite a range of conflicting opinions made by commentators, feminists, film and culture theorists as well as members of the popular press, Studio D was most often criticized for projecting a homogeneous account of feminism. The principal focus of such criticism is captured in Elizabeth Anderson's view that Studio D documentaries were made by mainly white "middle-class filmmakers needing to come to terms with their race and class bias [and needing to] learn to broaden their focus on gender identity to include other forms of identity."[13] This is, of course, the classic critique of what has been labelled second-wave feminism.[14] More precisely, it is a veiled complaint against liberal feminism for operating within existing power structures, making Studio D a predictable target.

Feminist activity in the 1970s originated from many sites — student union groups, peace activists, voices from the New Left, grassroots feminists associated with women's liberation politics. However, the "launching" of the Canadian second wave that originated in the Royal Commission on the Status of Women (1970) is often attributed to professional women and middle-class housewives who were dissatisfied and critical of inequities they perceived in their lives. They embraced inequities as their main focus, consequently identifying and analysing the oppressions experienced by women as an undifferentiated sisterhood, assuming somehow that every one was universally the same. Later feminists would analyze the implications of sexual orientation, race and other forms of difference and point out how "universalizing" women in this fashion overlooks the particular problems of women who are not white and middle class. In fact, the role that feminists of privilege played as breakers of new ground has received little scrutiny thus far, a function, likely, of the magnitude and complexity of studying feminism as a complex and far-reaching social movement. However, I see the historical moment that gave birth to Studio D as a moment in Canadian feminism that deserves to be scrutinized by the historical contingency of ongoing feminist debates. And so, the historical context *must* be considered if Studio D is to be revealed in its full complexity. Is there a way, I ask, that we might productively analyze Studio D and its documentaries differently and, in so doing, assess the efforts of liberal feminism more generously?

This book, then, makes a fresh case for Studio D. While a number of Studio D documentaries have received extensive critical scrutiny by feminist film theorists and others, the story of Studio D as a component of the women's movement has received little examination. I reconsider and reassess Studio D and its documentary oeuvre as a feminist formulation that flourished for more than twenty years and do so from a vantage point that has thus far remained unexplored.

BUILDING COMMUNITY/BUILDING NATION

Studio D was located within the NFB whose mandate was "to initiate and promote the production and distribution of films in the national interest, in particular to produce and distribute and to promote the production and distribution of films designed to interpret Canada to Canadian and to other nations."[15] Within this framework, Studio D perceived women as both a national group and, at the same time, as an interrelated international community. In its early years, Studio D filmmakers operated from a position of shared ideology. Decisions were arrived at by consensus; strategies and proposed subjects were shared and debated in a community forum that displayed the defining characteristics of the 1960s consciousness-raising focus groups. Certainly, Studio D documentaries were understood to function as unproblematic windows onto women's various experiences, vehicles for achieving positive social and cultural change. Although some labelled it a "woman's ghetto,"[16] Chris Scherbarth characterized it as a "women's room" intent on conducting its affairs as an

NFB film unit in a different fashion, "deriving its identity from the specific purpose and 'social change' philosophy behind its film production rather than from its geographical location or the form of its films."[17]

As I researched the Studio more extensively, I concluded, along with Scherbarth, that Studio D had operated by "an unorthodox 'separationist' strategy aimed towards achieving equal opportunity for women,"[18] informed by the vision of Kathleen Shannon, its first and longest serving executive producer. Her vision animated and sustained the Studio from beginning to end, although other executive producers made significant contributions. Within the Studio, Shannon's strategy was used to design increased training and career possibilities by placing in women's hands "a certain degree of programming autonomy — therefore [making provision] for affirmative action *on the screen.*"[19] Strategies to engage the public were suggested through Studio D's production format of addressing "women's needs" by focusing on "women's experience" through the medium of film, admittedly from the Studio's perspective. This approach enacted "a necessary — albeit rare — alternative within a publicly-funded cultural institution to create the opportunity for women to work together … to express their previously unspoken perceptions and to tap their female visions."[20] Studio D documentaries are not, then, an isolated body of work but are embedded within the historical and material relationships and processes that formed them. They also constitute a singular account of Canadian feminist engagement.

When I began my research, I discovered that very little work had been undertaken on the subject of Studio D. At that time, the most recent work was Elizabeth Anderson's 1996 PhD dissertation, "Pirating Feminisms: Film and the Production of Post-War Canadian National Identity" (University of Minnesota, 1996). Anderson explores "the problem of defining and re-defining the culturally plural nation in the late twentieth century" by examining the NFB as a state-funded agency producing films that represent the Canadian nation. Examining Studio D through the intersections of gender identity and national identity, Anderson, then a scholar working in an American studies doctoral program, demonstrated that when a feminist film collective and a federal cultural institution are allied, resulting tensions complicate the production of a unifying Canadian identity. She construes Studio D as both complicit in and potentially disruptive of dominant discourses of nationhood, national identity and national unity, concluding that this inherent contradiction, in the end, restricted the project of Studio D overall.

However, while other scholars may have turned their attention to Studio D, they have examined it without my particular and multiple questions in mind. Chris Scherbarth's MA thesis, "Studio D of the NFB: Seeing Ourselves through Women's Eyes" (Carleton University, 1986), completed a decade before the Studio's closure, offers perceptive and valuable insights into its early history and inquires into its documentary distribution and audience reception. Zoë Druick, in her PhD dissertation, "Narratives of Citizenship: Governmentality and the National Film Board of Canada" (York University, 1999), explores more expansively how NFB films depicting "everyday lives and identities" are tied to shifting social policies. Drawing on material from 1939 to 1999, Druick includes issues of biculturalism, multiculturalism, housing, and the status of women and First Nations people. Aiko Ryohashi focuses on the Studio D documentary *To a Safer Place* (1987) to examine the functioning of government and the democratic use of film as a medium enabling culturally marginalized people to find their own voices in her MA thesis "The Progressive Philosophy of Studio D of the National Film Board of Canada: A Case Study of *To a Safer Place*" (McGill University, 1987). While I found their collective work useful, none contains the breadth of primary research material that I collected for this project.

In order to value the relevance of Studio D, I look at a number of interrelated themes: the ability of feminist documentaries to promote a model of identity politics at the same time capturing the nuances of women's various realities; the intersection of feminist activism and theorizing in documentary film, the shifts and debates within feminist film criticism. Within this framework, I explore what happens when a feminist film studio as an apparatus of state ideology engages in feminist cultural production on behalf of Canadian women. And why is this exploration significant? One possible answer to the question is suggested by feminist film theorist Teresa de Lauretis who argues that women's expression through film entails "both self-expression and communication with other women, a question [concerning] at once the creation/invention of new images and the creation/imaging of new forms of community."[21]

Inherent in this form of "imagining"[22] is the fact that some communities are created while others are not, which raises questions around issues of omission or distortion; thus, it may prove instructive to think the questions through. This is a key reason I am not interested solely in the films that Studio D produced; crucially, I am interested in why Studio D matters in a broader sense — how and why and to what extent its filmmakers created and imagined feminist communities, under what kinds of constraints, and with what lasting influence.

In this book, I interrogate and discover the contours of what I have come to understand as a very complex story — a story that involves Studio D in foundational relationships with the Canadian state, the National Film Board and the women's movement, including feminist film practices and aesthetics that emerged during this same period. I do so through personal interviews, through reading archival materials and the films' texts and through theoretical reflection. In the end, I am most interested in making a case for the lasting value and importance of Studio D as a feminist instrument of change.

This work, consequently, focuses on the value of women's stories as history, or more precisely, as counter-history, raising the issue of power and agency as contradictory forces in the formulation and production of Studio D. By locating the story of Studio D within the social and political narratives of Canadian life, I attend to women's stories and emphasize their centrality to the Studio's feminist practice and philosophy.

THE PERSONAL AS POLITICAL

The series of interviews I conducted with some of the principals and freelancers at Studio D offers a unique view of its feminist project. I concede, however, that interviews, while attempts to capture information, are influenced by personal and political investments. In fact, the ideological implication of the personal interview as a tool of research has received useful critical scrutiny. Trinh Minh-ha, for one, probes the politics of the interview in her documentary *Surname Viet Given Name Nam* (1989). Arguing that speech is always "staged" or "tactical," she notes, "To a certain extent, interviewees choose how they want to be represented in what they say as well as in the way they speak."[23]

The use of and constrictions surrounding personal storytelling form a significant theme in bell hooks's *Talking Back: Thinking Feminist, Thinking Black.* hooks's deployment of anecdotes of lived experience to provide an alternative to patriarchal rationalism is helpful in understanding Studio D's position.[24] Nonetheless, Sara Suleri cautions that accounts of lived experience "cannot function as a sufficient [theoretical] alternative [in and of themselves],"[25] noting that without careful analysis, personal accounts may be wrongly accorded "an iconicity that is altogether too good to be true."[26] Indeed, an analysis of power relations, more generally, allows us "to understand how we have been trapped in our own history."[27] As Michel Foucault argues, analysis (in this case, of Studio D's position) becomes a form of resistance and an advance towards a new economy of power relations that is "more empirical, more directly related to our present situation, and one that implies more relations between theory and practice."[28]

In a similar vein, historians such as Ruth Roach Pierson argue that a study of women's experience constitutes a form of resistance. Drawing on traditions of feminist historians working in European-derived cultures, Pierson challenges the very universality of the "grand narratives" embedded in Western history. She champions both a theorization of gender *and* an interrogation of experience, implicated as it is in concepts of "difference," "dominance" and "voice."[29] Even so, Pierson recommends the value of considering these women's stories about themselves:

> If contemporary feminism has contributed to the modernist and post-modern undermining of enlightenment certainties by invoking "women's different experience" to challenge the "grand narrative" of western history, feminism, as we have seen has also "heavily valorized" women's own narratives, women's stories of their own experience. Indeed this valorization has urged women's historians in the direction of oral history as the methodology, next to autobiography, promising to bring the researcher to the "reality" of women's lives. We have valorized oral history because it validates women's lives.[30]

To proceed into the territory of individual memory and oral testimony as revelatory texts, of course, raises key questions, To what extent are women competent witnesses to their own lives? How useful is it to draw on experience as a source of knowledge? Any evidence regarding Studio D, whether drawn from oral testimonies, official documents from NFB archives or elsewhere, cannot necessarily be taken at face value, of course. Rather, such evidence should be considered as revelatory texts inviting "deciphering and decoding for which critical and social contextual knowledgement are necessary."[31]

Pierson emphasizes the need to rethink the concept of "experience" and this, I argue, is particularly fruitful in an analysis of Studio D. Pierson contends that historians tend to operate on two collective hunches with respect to sources: the first, ontological, that there was a reality out there in the past; and the second, epistemological, "that reality is knowable, albeit imperfectly and incompletely."[32] Central to this book's storytelling are the memories of some of the women pivotally involved in Studio D. The recollections I collected and recorded between 1996 and 2006 illuminate a particular set of events and issues that constitute a stratified version of the "truth" about Studio D and its intellectual, political and aesthetic place within the larger North American women's movement.

In fact, much of my material has remained uncollected until now and, hence, underanalyzed, representing a fresh opportunity for theorizing the experiences of this particular group of "women in the trenches."[33] The stories I collected afford a behind-the-scenes picture of the official version and reveal a fabric of privilege, paradox and contradiction, perhaps a predictable consequence of a venture organized around the widely ranging and shifting concepts of "nation" and "feminism." Further, the stories are valuable feminist vehicles that highlight "alternative patterns of resistance to cultural and political hegemony."[34]

Indeed, one of the powerful legacies of the women's movement has been the recovering of women's voices "hidden from history."[35] By embracing this legacy and echoing Studio D's own strategies, my own project becomes implicated in these debates and examines the story of Studio D, in part, by recovering some of the voices of its members which may have been obscured over time and silenced since its closure. We need to contextualize such oral accounts, as Pierson suggests, but we also must allow the voices to sound.

The use of personal interviews documents a unique story about Studio D as a government-created but feminist-run film studio, facilitating a particular kind of historical excavation. In conjunction with a series of official Studio D documents and mediated by other theoretical frameworks, these recorded conversations illuminate the far-reaching potential of the Studio's philosophical stance and praxis. Recent feminist scholarship agrees that the autobiographical voice offers a fresh means of consolidating and establishing the legitimacy of women's voices holding forth a certain promise for building fresh communities. As Françoise

Lionnet points out, women's voices have sounded globally in a state of greater or lesser tension with other points of view throughout history. "Always present everywhere but rarely heard, let alone recorded, women's voices have not been a dominant mode of expression or a legitimate and acceptable alternative to ... dominant modes."[36] I am drawing on the formulation of Linda Carty's charge that Canadian feminist thought would be enriched if it were to link theory and experience more closely by attending to the first-hand accounts of some of the Studio D women. Indeed, in the case of Studio D, fruitful linkages need to be made between theory and accounts of the lived experience of women if we are to better understand the larger political and social implications.[37]

WHY STORYTELLING?

In this book, different kinds of stories — stories of Studio D principals, stories of the documentaries themselves (both at the level of the documentary narrative itself and in the wider sense of the underlying "feminist story"), stories of critical responses to the Studio and its work, institutional stories told in budgets and internal power structures — become pieces of a larger puzzle about institutional feminist ventures where each single story is mediated through many levels.

My use of personal interviews mirrors Studio D's own insistence on the importance of listening to women, recording and "understanding" women's individual accounts and interpretations, believing women to be credible witnesses, albeit witnesses whose access to memory is never unmediated. It is my own attempt at making feminist counter-history that is grounded in "a process-oriented, interview-based documentary method — a collaborative, supportive style of feminist work that has its own history and politics."[38] My emphasis on women's stories to "suture the work together in the absence of ... a linear story-line"[39] mimics the use of "talking heads" in feminist documentary films. Stories in the films as well as stories by those working on the films provide useful insights, helping to illuminate practices within the Studio as well as shedding light on its documentaries. The documentaries themselves tell stories of women's lives and experiences and reflect developments in feminist activism and thought in Canada, all of which, if considered from a current feminist stance, encourage a reassessment of the whole.

What brings me to a study of Studio D is a fascination with women's lives that embraces two often-related areas. I am compelled by the stories that women tell about themselves and their lives and, secondly, I am intrigued about the process leading to the gaining of a feminist consciousness. Not surprisingly, this book is bound up in my own journey and its own stories. A haunting thread throughout this book is a personal reflection on the events of my adult life, a life I measure as beginning sometime in the mid-1960s.

Although I lived through much of the second wave of feminist activity in Canada, it was not until certain formative events in my own life had been lived and reflected on in relation to the stories I heard other women tell — a number of these revealed in Studio D documentaries — that I would begin to avow a feminist consciousness. Studio D documentaries were instrumental in this germination. Pre-dating my interest in Studio D and documentary filmmaking is my lifelong fascination with literature and pleasure in the ability of fiction to "perform" lived experience, particularly the power of fiction to disclose and explore social and political concerns affecting women's lives. In my academic studies in French and English literature, I was introduced to life-writing. Then when I began work on this book, I became intrigued by many of Studio D's documentaries for their ability to illuminate the particularities of women's lives and realized there was a relationship between the documentaries and life-writing. I began to see the potential in these films and the stories they tell to revitalize the feminist process of consciousness-raising. This notion is somewhat reminiscent of Jennifer Horseman's argument in her study *Something in My Mind besides the Everyday*,[40] in which she expounds on the ability of newly gained literacy skills to engender an empowered sense of the self. This brings me to another thread of my own story — one of engagement and curiosity with Studio D.

As the women's movement gained momentum in Ontario in the early 1970s, I was a young woman, married and a mother of two small children. Educated as an elementary school teacher and a vocal music specialist, I returned from a two-year stay in Montreal to an arid job market in Toronto. By chance, I found employment in a major Canadian corporation, a job I soon found both enervating and diminishing. My life was ordered by lean economic circumstances and a burning desire to return to university. One day, I had an epiphany on the subway as I rode home from the office. I happened to be reading Margaret Atwood's recently released novel *The Edible Woman.* In one scene, the central protagonist, Marion McAlpine, emerging from a beauty shop to prepare for a party she has no wish to attend, suddenly understands her "being" is somehow being devoured slowly but inexorably by forces beyond her. Her fiancé Peter, a promising young lawyer, is a petulant, self-centred tyrant with a penchant for violence. All of the women she knows are trapped by their circumstances. Only dimly aware of the dangers the traditional cultural role holds for women, Marion has slowly become immobilized, relinquishing her authority to act on her own behalf. At that juncture, Marion's plight and my own merged — at least in my imagination — with Atwood's fiction providing the framework within which I could measure and begin to make sense of my own life.

For the first time, I remember daring to think about living my life differently, controlling its direction — a radical and unorthodox thought given my strict upbringing. I would not, at that moment, have named myself a feminist. I was too worried about the immediate censure from my family — parents, husband, children (too young to register protest) — if I were to strike out in the direction I was contemplating, and I was too lacking in knowledge of feminism as political action to claim the title feminist. Around the same time I read Kate Millett's *Sexual Politics* and Anne Sexton's *Transformations,* again using them as tools of self-examination.

Shortly after, I returned to university studies, by then a single parent, continuing to read literature written by women. An attraction to feminist literary criticism and, later, to feminist theory was a predictable development. Life experience and academic encounters led me closer and closer to Studio D. When *Not a Love Story* (1981) was released, I was a graduate student and watched it in a large lecture hall. Later, as a member of a women's studies teaching team, I reviewed a number of Studio D documentaries and used them in courses I taught. *A Writer in the Nuclear Age* (1985) illuminated the work of Margaret Laurence, and *Firewords* (1986) helped me to explore the concerns of such Quebec women writers as Louky Bersianik, Jovette Marchessault and Nicole Brossard in my own course, Images of Women in Modern Canadian Literature.

Realizing that doctoral studies would allow me to expand formally into the area of feminism cultural production in film, I enrolled in a

PhD program, balancing my teaching career with my new life as a part-time graduate student. I began to think more deeply about the intertwining themes of identity construction, the precariousness of the "emerging" female subject and the power of feminist documentaries to foster consciousness-raising. In short, I began to think seriously about the relationship between theory and practice in the understanding and shaping of women's lives. Attendance at the Feminisms in the Cinema Conference at York University in November 1990 and encounters with such luminaries as theorist Teresa de Lauretis and Canadian filmmaker Brenda Longfellow (who became my thesis advisor) ignited a fresh interest in feminist film criticism.

My interest in Studio D also grew out of a long-standing love of documentary films as a genre. The first documentary I ever saw was screened in the church of my childhood — a feature of the evening service which replaced the sermon with a documentary film, a radical move for a minister in small-town Ontario. I sat in the dark, probably about eight years old, experiencing what Sigmund Freud labelled "scopophilia," that visceral pleasure of "looking" and entering into the private cerebral one-on-one relationship with a film. This was my first experience with what theory, I have since learned, describes as "spectatorship." When I began to watch Studio D documentaries, I wanted to learn more about what was behind the operation of a feminist film unit within the NFB. I had heard it described as "a hopelessly blinkered collection of dull, privileged, white, middle-class filmmakers" but also as a "national treasure" and "the only government-sponsored feminist film studio in the world."

Fostering a particular form of spectatorship was a big part of Studio D's raison d'être: to create films that would reach out, inform and create a vibrant dialogue between the Studio and its spectators — in this case, a feminist audience. I had been among those Studio D spectators and I became intrigued, and so I began to formulate a series of underlying questions: What were the politics of operating a feminist unit such a Studio D within a national institutional setting? How did it negotiate with the state? How did it negotiate its path within the women's movement and in relation to other feminist filmmakers?

What I expected (naively) to find was a feminist utopia — a group of feminist innovators working within the National Film Board with state-of-the-art, state-sponsored equipment and an established international distribution network connected to a wide range of Canadian feminists in universities, in community-centred groups, in artistic communities, and producing documentaries that tracked and documented feminist debates of the time. But what I found instead was a series of issues and circumstances that dispute this myth of privilege — and herein lies, I hope, the contribution of this book. It is framed around drawing attention to Studio D's attempts to achieve feminist change that are found in conversations with some of the women who made up Studio D, news reports and articles, film reviews, NFB memos and internal documents, minutes of meetings and, of course, the documentary films themselves, which recommend a more sober but sanguine understanding of such institutionalized ventures if Studio D's feminist legacy is to endure.

TELLING STUDIO D'S STORY

Chapter 1 sets a context for the formation of Studio D, delving into the ideological territory of "second-wave" feminism in English Canada. I think of this period as a renaissance for women because it attended to women's demands for fairer social and political treatment, the inclusion of their demands becoming valid voices in the larger socio-political climate of the civil rights and liberation movements that were reshaping North American society. The creation of a women's studio within the organizational structure of the National Film Board was one instance of this renaissance. Taking advantage of the momentum for women's rights created by the *Report of the Royal Commission on the Status of Women* (488 pages long and containing 167 recommendations), Kathleen Shannon advanced a revolutionary idea — that women could make their own documentary films *and* form their own studio. This chapter sets out how Studio D came together as the result of her initiative and two key impulses: women wanting to become involved in feminist filmmaking and the federal government and National Film Board acting on Canada's commitment to meet the goals of the United Nations' International Women's Year (1975).

Chapter 2 examines the politics of establishing a feminist film studio within the NFB as a national cultural institution. If the Canadian state was bent on implementing nationalism, promoting the "Canadian nation" through its cultural institution, Studio D became a form of "élite accommodation" as the state responded to women's demands for greater autonomy as citizens. However, as Studio D began to take shape, it became evident that the state's cultural institution and the women in Studio D had differing notions about the question of national identity and national culture. Arguing that women made up more than 51 per cent of the Canadian population, Shannon stressed the "otherness" of the female voice and the urgency for women as a majority group to have their voices heard, an argument that fell on deaf ears institutionally. Undaunted, Shannon drew on the notion that Studio D was encouraged *as an instrument of the state* to make films for women, and she set out to make feminist documentaries that would both empower women by showing them they had a history and would "validate women's experiences in their own eyes." However, Shannon's argument for equitable funding in keeping with the NFB mandate to make and distribute films designed to interpret Canada to Canadians and other nations and the meager start-up funding Studio D actually received mark the beginning of years of struggle.

Chapter 3 looks at the early days of Studio D and the excitement of mounting a kind of "women's room" for feminist film, an indirect reference to Virginia Woolf's notion that if women had a room of their own they would be able to "develop the habit of freedom" and speak (create) in their own voices. From this location, the Studio projected a vision of "women as nation," an international sisterhood joined (un-problematically) by gender. While budget problems continued and Studio D found itself at ideological odds within its institutional setting, its documentaries began to reflect feminist issues in Canada, making Studio D a major voice for English feminism. As Studio D moved into the 1980s, it began to be criticized by other feminists as "a white, middle-class group of liberal feminists," likely unaware that Shannon's requests for a more diverse staff had been denied for budgetary reasons. Thus, some of the contradictions that were to plague the Studio began to surface. Following a soul-draining fight to save the feminist studio from closure in 1986, which incidentally attracted the support of a number of high-powered women and feminist groups across the country, an exhausted Shannon turned over the reins to Rina Fraticelli, Studio D's second executive producer. Unfortunately, the prevailing political climate in Canadian society, coupled with continuing budgetary restrictions, deepened the contradictions under which Studio D struggled to exist.

Chapter 4 argues that while Studio D was an important component of Canadian feminist cultural production and used two well-known features of second-wave feminism in its documentaries — the notion that "the personal is political" and that a process of "consciousness-raising" could achieve social change — it became a target for criticism within the Film Board and outside in the critical film community. It traces how Shannon used tenets of consciousness-raising to pioneer a unique approach to audience relations organized around a politics of giving women voice, particularly audience members and subjects of the films themselves. Recently, contemporary feminist film scholars like Alexandra Juhasz have expressed a certain admiration for the "social realist" feminist documentary, which is identified with the socialist feminism of the North American second wave. But towards the end of the 1970s, a "turn" in film theory to a more theoretical approach, associated with a new branch of British feminist film criticism with such figures as Claire Johnston and Pam Cook, opened up Studio D's position to criticism.

Chapter 5 examines how Studio D documentaries as "women's stories" championed the value of women's narratives as an important format for telling their stories. By combining notions derived from life writing as a genre *and* from consciousness-raising as a feminist praxis, a fresh appreciation of such feminist narratives emerges, offering insights that make Studio D's work relevant for feminists today.

Chapter 6 considers events leading up to the closure of Studio D, as the "national treasure" found itself embroiled in a series of internal struggles in an era of increasing cutbacks. In many ways, I argue, the problems Studio D grappled with reflected struggles that had divided the women's movement over questions of difference and race. Drawing on ideas from Audre Lorde's essay "The Uses of Anger," I argue that (intelligent) anger and struggle among feminists are inevitable and necessary for feminist change, suggesting that Studio D leaves a valuable and many-layered legacy for feminists today and for those still to come.

1. Studio D — the "would-be collective"

2. Kathleen Shannon

3. Nesya Shapiro

FOR FULL CAPTIONS, SEE PAGE 223

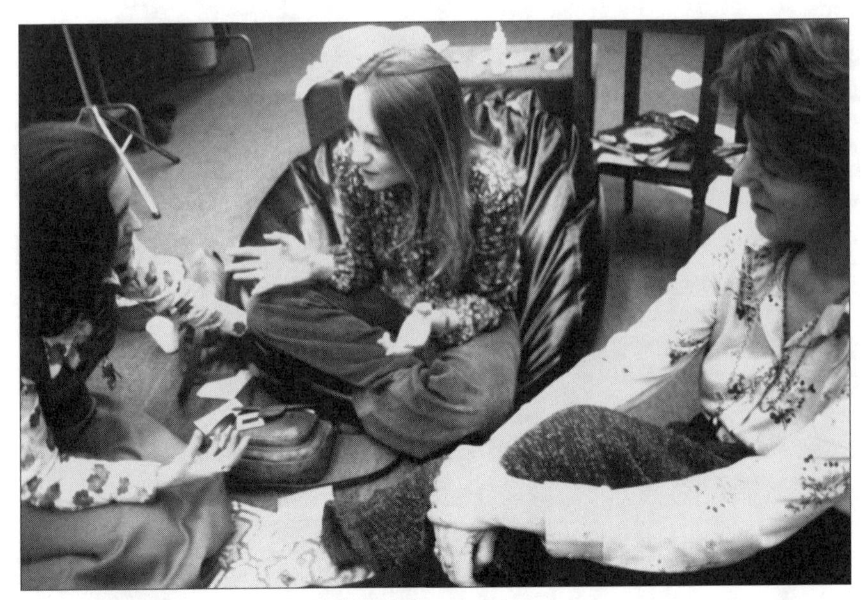

4. The "collective" discussing daycare

5. Pioneer animator Lotte Reiniger (left) with Nesya Shapiro (right)

6. Studio D in 1987

7. Anne Henderson (foreground) and Irene Angelico

8. Esther Auger

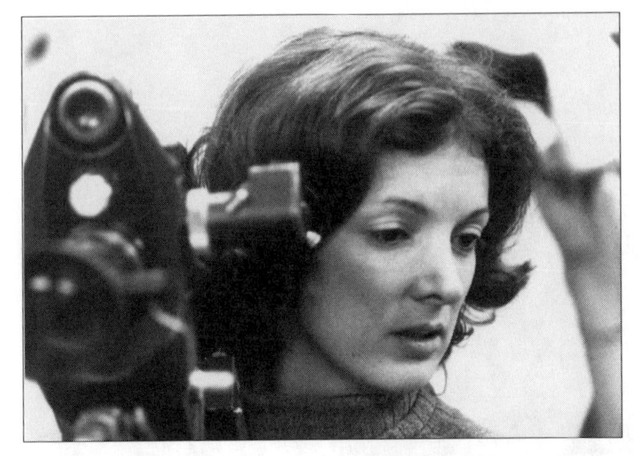

9. Animator with camera

10. Tiina Soomet

11. Aerlyn Weissman filming

12. International Women's Year (1975) workshop

13. Studio D sound technician

14. Ginny Stikeman

15. Susan Trow

16. Irene Angelico

17. Signe Johansson (left) and Doris Mae Oulton

18. Judith Sanderford

19. Anne Wheeler

CHAPTER 1

LAYING THE GROUNDWORK FOR A FEMINIST RENAISSANCE

The Government has no fixed ideas on what the "Women's Program" consists of ... they are looking for some convincing evidence that the NFB considers [it] important. That, too, is walking on eggs ...

— NFB MEMO (22 MAY 1974)

Movies make magic. They change things.

— BELL HOOKS, *REAL TO REEL*

Interim report from a pumpkin: ... we may have wheels by the time you receive this ...

— KATHLEEN SHANNON (NFB MEMO, 6 AUGUST 1974)

STUDIO D CAME INTO BEING AT APPROXIMATELY THE SAME TIME FEMINIST poet and theorist Adrienne Rich proclaimed feminism a renaissance "far more extraordinary and influential"[1] in shifting perspectives than the move from theology to humanism in the European Renaissance. Her use of the term is well placed since it evokes the notion of a sweeping cultural shift, a protracted period of evolving thought and cultural advances generally associated with progress and enrichment, for which feminism certainly has been responsible. Skeptical feminist scholars have pointed out that such accepted "schemes of periodization"[2] fail to capture the complexities of any historical period, foregrounding instead advances of the dominant members of that society. Nonetheless, it is tempting and useful to revisit the 1970s as a site of the rebirth of women's interests — a time when North American society was struggling to come to grips with questions surrounding the oppression (and liberation) of a number of groups, including, of course, women. In this context, Studio D emerged as a significant component of the "feminist renaissance" in Canada and an important, if contested, example of feminist cultural production.

Although its feminist filmmakers were proud to claim Studio D as the first and only government-funded film studio in the world dedicated solely to producing feminist documentaries,[3] Studio D's relationship with the state, the National Film Board and the women of Canada was negotiated on both complementary and contradictory ground. At first glance, its story is simply told: the three executive producers who led the Studio — Kathleen Shannon (1974–1986), Rina Fraticelli (1987–1989) and Ginny Stikeman (1990–1996) — produced over 150 documentaries that explored issues of national and international interest to women and that were directed mainly by women, both in-house directors and freelance filmmakers. Its two most popular films, *Not a Love Story* (1981) and *If You Love This Planet* (1982), unleashed international debates at the time of their release and continue to attract critical attention today. Overall, Studio D documentaries won more than 100 international awards, including three Academy Awards for *I'll Find a Way* (1977), *If You Love This Planet* (1982) and *Flamenco at 5:15* (1983), surpassing any other NFB studio in this respect

From the outset, Studio D established two main objectives: to project women's perspectives in its documentaries and to create filmmaking opportunities for Canadian women in a field traditionally dominated by men. The Studio's documentaries captured emerging feminist debates, shadowing such topics as women and work, pornography, sexuality, identity, female spirituality, peace initiatives, the colonizing of race and the celebration of feminist artists. Together, these documentaries provide one version of the women's movement in Canada, spanning a time frame of close to three decades.

Looming over this story of Studio D is a single figure, that of Kathleen Shannon, its chief instigator and ideological backbone. From the Studio's inception, Shannon had an inclusive vision that subscribed to principles of democracy and second-wave feminism. The fact that women made up roughly 51 per cent of the world's population entitled them to a majority voice, Shannon believed, an argument she raised again and again in their collective defence. Very much an activist, Shannon spurned theory as elitist, understanding women as a community joined worldwide by two main categories, both rooted in experience: motherhood and work.

The ideological territory Studio D occupied was fraught with contradictions. Over time, Studio D would be celebrated *and* attacked, both for its product — twenty-two years worth of (mainly) realist documentary films — and for its approach to feminist filmmaking. Its collective composition as a women's film unit has been understood both positively and negatively. Positively as embodying empowering feminist ideals that nurtured its full time, freelance and independent filmmakers. Negatively for imposing the Studio's self-conceived fiat that was driven by its own definition of feminism and feminist approaches while located in a protected inner sanctum deep within a national cultural institution, the National Film Board. While Studio D's philosophy has often been characterized pejoratively as one grounded in a "liberal feminist perception of unity in difference that exerted a reductive pressure on the shifting definitions of feminism,"[4] its films are indisputably valuable historical documents, marking key moments in the development of feminism in Canada.

Given such complex territory, I draw on several related theoretical approaches and intersperse these with the voices of some Studio D women in an attempt to decipher the Studio's vexed position. In marshalling these ideas, I suggest a set of conclusions that redeems Studio D from the charge that it was a rigidly white, middle-class, feminist operation and, hence, unforgivably "narrow" in its scope. Instead, by exploring some of the disjunctures that plagued Studio D as it engaged in producing feminist films "by and for" women of Canada, I have discovered an increasingly uneasy fit between the feminist politics of the Studio and the politics of the Canadian state over gender identity, national identity and feminist cultural production.

Kathleen Shannon, the first executive producer of Studio D, forged a major landmark for feminist filmmaking in Canada when she insisted that the NFB create a women's film unit. A respected figure at the NFB since 1956, Shannon was one of a handful of women working in film production in the country. Although Shannon was more experienced than many, having earned an excellent reputation as a gifted sound, music and picture editor, she witnessed with frustration several of her male colleagues (some of whom she had trained) receive promotions and handsome raises while she was overlooked. Shannon advanced a revolutionary idea — that women could make their own documentary films *and* form their own studio. In fact, through her experiences in the Film Board, Shannon was acquainted with a number of women in Canada who had expressed a desire to make their own films, as she noted in her proposal:

> I have been contacted by an astonishing number of women who have some training in filmmaking skills, but nowhere to apply them and gain further experience and professional credibility. Ideas for films by women are flooding in. Women have much to express, and need to control the means by which they express their concerns.[5]

Establishing a feminist film studio would mean a lot of hard pioneering work. First of all, there was no blueprint. Men dominated film as artists and industry figures at every level while women were employed as secretaries, stenographers, librarians and negative cutters.[6] Secondly, as Shannon often claimed, the NFB had no real wish for a women's studio and no financial commitment, establishing it only in compliance with a federal directive. Such suspicions are borne out by a memo circulated between NFB executives André Lamy and Bob Verrell detailing a telephone conversation with government officials:

> The government is considering proposals for International Women's Year … They said that we should be expected to "reorganize our priorities" and provide a special program that would be "really special." They are looking for some convincing evidence that the NFB considers a women's program important … [I]f we consider it important are we prepared to assign some of our 1974–75 unprogrammed funds to research and script [it]? Since we've insisted on unearmarked money in 1974–75 so we can respond to new priorities, I expect that it would test their credulity to say that we couldn't assign money to this now … [W]ould we be prepared to assign the necessary funds to the continuing costs of a women's studio? That is what they are looking for![7]

From its earliest days, almost without exception, the NFB had excluded women from formal filmmaking, following NFB founder John Grierson's philosophy that women should not assume prominent roles, prompting one film critic to observe, "Grierson's sexism was at least the equivalent of his British paternalism."[8] In fact, the "'monastic' discipline Grierson imposed on his film units during the 1930s meant that even filmmakers' wives were barred from the premises."[9] Although a number of talented women (Evelyn Spice Cherry, Judith Crawley, Sally MacDonald, Jane Marsh, Marge McKay, Gudrun Parker, Margaret Perry and Beth Zinkan among others) rose to prominence in the NFB during the mid-1940s when talented men were scarce, those holding positions of prominence all but disappeared once the war ended in 1945.[10] As film scholar Barbara Halpern Martineau notes:

> [Women] indeed played vital, central roles in the astonishing output of documentary films by the NFB during the war. It is also indisputably clear that this extensive participation by women at key levels in NFB production and administration diminished rapidly after the war ended … and that the next twenty years of film board production were heavily male-dominated, with almost no participation by women except at menial levels.[11]

Kathleen Shannon was a notable exception. Later, as its executive producer, Shannon would return to NFB films from this era, overseeing the release of *How They Saw Us* (1977), a series of eight short films featuring archival footage from documentaries shot in the 1940s and 1950s and interpreted through a feminist lens. In Shannon's acerbic view, the old films were nothing more than feminizing propaganda, revealing the extent to which images of women had been manipulated — popularized and stereotyped — to serve society's perceived needs during and following the war years. This patriarchal bias of Film Board documentaries, personified by authoritative male voice-over narration (referred to laughingly as the "voice of God" by irreverent feminists) and reinforcing the all-too familiar romanticized representations of women, rankled the articulate steel-willed Shannon. *How They Saw Us* was a sharp and often hilarious feminist retort. Later, speaking about the feminist acts of filmmaking and representing women, she claimed that "… to have your experience validated is terribly important and very empowering."[12]

Between 1971 and 1973, pre-dating the creation of Studio D, Shannon had already gained a taste for feminist filmmaking because she had "almost single-handedly produced, directed and edited a set of ten consciousness-raising documentaries"[13] known as the *Working Mothers* series, one of the series within the NFB's *Challenge for Change* series. The documentaries explored the plight of working mothers across Canada. In fact, Shannon's vanguard films explored many of the problems that *still* plague working mothers nearly forty years later, capturing the diversity among women in their portraits that would later be theorized by feminist thought. Spurred on by a set of feminist aspirations and a certain daring, Shannon decided that the androcentric balance within the Film Board should change, setting for herself a challenge that would test her imagination and her tenacity: the instigation of a women's studio, an all-woman studio that would produce self-consciously women-centred films.

Indeed, the *Working Mothers* series fit seamlessly into the simple but politically powerful "consciousness-raising" format employed by the generation of feminist filmmakers working in the late 1960s and early 1970s. Using the aesthetics of *cinéma verité*, Shannon structured her films around the ordinary details of women's lives, literally opening a new space "for women in women's terms."[14] The narrative voice was now female, as were the "talking heads," testifying to the particularities of mothers' varied experiences and conditions of inequity. Shannon directed the cinematographer to concentrate on the "ordinary" woman revealing conditions of her own life, while she, the adept interviewer, remained in the background.

However, in spite of the revolutionary call for women's rights issued by the *Working Mothers* series, Shannon was only too well aware that the NFB itself was guilty of perpetuating gender inequality. Taking as ammunition a comment by Sylvia Gelber, the director of the Women's Bureau in the federal Department of Labour, Shannon charged that "the tradition of defining certain tasks as masculine and others as feminine persists in the minds of many men — and many women" was still heartedly embraced by the NFB, even though times had changed:

> Women have been accepted where the job demands attention to detail, responsibility to others, a strong capacity for carrying out orders: editing, research, script writing, negative cutting, inking and "in-betweening," props and wardrobe, assistants of all sorts. They have been excluded from areas where self-affirmation and decision making take priority. Technical areas have been restricted in the mythical sense that women "don't understand electricity," or "don't have the physical strength." Those of us who have done both can attest to the fact that it is no harder to lug a camera case or Nagra than 20 pounds of groceries in a splitting paper bag plus a 35 pound squirming toddler in a slippery snowsuit.[15]

To reinforce her argument for a women's studio, Shannon cited a commitment by the Canadian government "to promote the improved status of women as citizens and as employees"[16] as "moral ammunition"[17] to lobby within the NFB, noting in her 1974 report:

> It has occurred to some of us that the NFB has not had a very good record in the past of fulfilling its mandate of "interpreting Canada to Canadians and the rest of the world, etc." when we consider that 53% of the population is female, and that [women's] point of view has hardly been expressed. Women have a different approach to society, and we must be our own spokeswomen.[18]

In her laying out of plans for what was originally labelled "Unit D" in NFB memos,[19] Shannon envisioned a radically different organizational structure that departed from established models in other studios. Ever the strategist, Shannon agreed in principle to the Film Board's position that the new unit be "just like any other unit,"[20] while at the same time resisting the notion that the organizational structure of the Unit be identical. In her defence she quoted the NFB's freshly articulated stance promoting women and equality: "It is heartening that the N.F.B. has realized that women ... have long been denied the opportunity to develop professional skills, the opportunity to express their points of view and the opportunity to participate in decision-making."[21] Writing for the NFB newsletter *INTERLOCK* around the same time, Shannon declared her plan more baldly:

> Women constitute more than half the population of Canada. That they are so underrepresented in creative roles in this public institution is a travesty of the NFB mandate to interpret Canadians to Canadians and [to] the rest of the world. A priority, then, must be nothing less than to integrate women, in full numbers, into every aspect of NFB production and distribution. It remains not to establish whether, but how soon and by what means. This is the challenge we bring to the Film Board, substantially, to English Production.[22]

As part of her plan to reach women across Canada, Shannon had persuaded the NFB to create *INTERLOCK* as a way "to establish a network of communication among film women in Canada." As publisher, Shannon was in an unprecedented position to create a resource network for women and announced her intention to do so through the newsletter. By pooling research and sources of information, *INTERLOCK* would publish technical articles to keep women abreast of developments in the film industry; it would also compile the names of women involved in the industry, and list upcoming conferences, festivals and workshops. The first edition addressed itself to a Canadian readership, understanding its audience as part of an international women's film community:

> In order to bring this about we need your help: we need information, articles, feedback and ideas … We can use articles about and from women who are involved in the history of Canadian film and reports by women who are setting up their own production units. And it has been suggested that news of the work of women's units in other countries would be useful too.[23]

Shannon envisioned an all-woman studio, decreeing that women within what was eventually named Studio D would receive in-depth on-the-job training as camera operators, editors, directors and producers. Eventually, as trained professionals, they, in turn, would be in a position to host training sessions and teach skills to other women across Canada who wanted to try their hand at making films but had little or no access to equipment. In reality, Studio D would not reach the status of an all-woman studio until 1985. Instead, it was launched midway through 1974 with a modest staff of three, located in the basement of the Montreal headquarters with "a paltry budget of $100,000: [and just] enough to run some training and apprenticeship programs, plan a few films and conduct audience research,"[24] to the satisfaction of a victorious new executive producer, Kathleen Shannon.

A CLIMATE OF CHANGE — A RENAISSANCE FOR WOMEN

During the 1970s in Canada, rights for women had gradually but decisively risen as a matter of national prominence. Shannon's efforts to establish a feminist film studio followed on the heels of a national struggle that was mounted by activist feminists who wanted to achieve a greater voice for women as citizens by dismantling certain institutional barriers in Canada. It would be inaccurate to attribute Studio D's creation solely to the NFB, since Shannon's feminist awareness and activism was clearly the catalyst, and it is important to recognize key events in the English-speaking Canadian women's movement that helped to foster a climate of change.

In 1967, Laura Sabia, a lawyer from St. Catharines, Ontario, and president of the Canadian Federation of University Women, joined up with the Honourable Judy LaMarsh, Secretary of State, to spearhead a national movement pressuring Prime Minister Lester B. Pearson to instigate a formal study into the circumstances shaping women's lives in Canada.[25] Sabia, who had already established a reputation as a fearless activist, called a national meeting of feminists on May 3, 1966, to explore what might be done to improve the national status of women. It was attended by fifty women representing thirty-two women's organizations from across Canada. Out of this larger body, a small group volunteered to form the Committee on the Equality of Women in Canada (CEW). Their solution was to approach the prime minister and request that he instigate a Royal Commission.[26] When Prime Minister Pearson stalled and wavered, apparently hoping to side-step the entire issue, Sabia threatened that, in the event he refused to call the Royal Commission, she would organize a demonstration on Parliament Hill, calling out a million women. Although Sabia would admit later that she doubted she could have mobilized more than a half a dozen women, Pearson, unwilling to court the risk of a *feminist* uprising reluctantly complied, duly launching the Royal Commission on the Status of Women on February 3, 1967.

It is worth noting that this early feminist movement originated with women involved in established women's organizations. Members from Voice of Women (VOW), the National Council of Women, the YWCA, the University Women's Clubs, the Business and Professional Women's Club and the Fédération Nationale Saint-Jean-Baptiste[27] had previously lobbied governments on behalf of women, often with substantial success. In Quebec, feminists had organized the Fédération des femmes du Québec (FFQ) under the leadership of Thérèse Casgrain. The successful lobbying of these groups encouraged their conviction that the state represented an agent of change. This early sisterhood "put into action an 'old-girls' network'"[28] that was supported by professional women like Sabia, sympathetic MPs and government officials like Grace MacInnis and Thérèse Casgrain, and successful businesswomen like Doris Anderson, editor of *Chatelaine,* Canada's most widely read women's magazine. The wish to belong to such a sisterhood also attracted women who had never joined a formal organization but who "felt an affinity with other women [who] worked to further the goals of feminism through personal actions in their homes and workplaces, and through friendships with other women."[29]

The Royal Commission was itself a catalytic instrument in exposing many feminist concerns; as it travelled across Canada, it raised questions and collected information, leaving eddies of evolving feminist thought in its wake that very likely engendered a climate for change. Gradually, it became clear that feminists from all over the political map had become a force to be reckoned with or, perhaps from a more cynical governmental point of view, a force to be "managed." Monique Bégin, secretary to the Royal Commission, notes that during this period feminist resolve was strengthened in many women's groups across the nation, including Quebec. In her words:

> It is impossible to guess what would have happened if the government had not moved on the demand for a royal commission ... The more radical women's movement was at the door, and feminism was becoming a worldwide phenomenon as important for civilization as decolonization.[30]

Recognizing the strength of national support for the findings of the Royal Commission on the Status of Women, the federal government made a commitment in 1972 to contribute to the United Nations' International Women's Year, set for 1975. In Shannon's mind, this represented a perfect opportunity. Fuelled by her own feminist conversion, Shannon recognized this as the moment to confront the profoundly masculine culture within the Film Board. A women's film unit, she reasoned, would be devoted to films exploring women's situations and the films produced by women. As Shannon pointed out in her formal proposal for a "Women's Program" early in 1974:

> In its report to the UN last year, the NFB managed to dredge up 12 women to mention out of its entire history. If it were to list all the men who have made a significant contribution to the organization it would have to start limiting the list, for reasons of space, to outstanding contributions only. A cursory glance at the NFB catalogue for 73/74 reveals that out of 288 directors and producers evidenced, only 25 are women.[31]

Recognizing the growing public awareness around women's issues, Shannon seized the moment and redoubled her efforts, urging the NFB to create a new studio for women in keeping with the UN's International Women's Year initiative. In a proposal to the English Language Division, dated July 23, 1974, Shannon wrote:

> The fact that a few women are beginning to make films in other units

concurrently is a complementary fact, as is the one woman now employed in the sound department, and one woman working as a first assistant for the English Camera Department (though only on short-term contracts for specific productions). Until a balance is more nearly achieved, it will be appropriate for the new studio to emphasize the recruitment and training of women, though there will not be a policy of necessarily excluding men … The short-term goal is the presence of women in all areas of the organization; the long-range goal is the presence of women proportionate to the percentage of those Canadians we are "interpreting to other Canadians and the rest of the world" that are female.[32]

By the time the Royal Commission tabled its report in 1970 along with 167 recommendations for change, feminist demands for more equitable conditions as Canadian citizens had gained a surprising degree of public support. Roberta Hamilton notes that the hearings of the Royal Commission and the publicity it attracted led to "something of a sea change in Canadian life."[33] Angela Burke Kerrigan, the commission's public relations director who had witnessed the change first hand, commented that "... although initially the Royal Commission was regarded with a certain public scorn — attitudes changed like night and day over a two-year period." The changes occurred, in Kerrigan's view, because "consciousness-raising was going on everywhere for men as well as women." [34] Signe Johansson, a core member and long-time producer in Studio D, remembered how a growing social awareness of women's issues shaped her own personal consciousness, which was responsible in part for setting the stage for a shared feminist appreciation within Studio D:

The Betty Friedan book [*The Feminine Mystique*] had come out and I was actually then reading articles in popular women's magazines, making consciousness connections … [so] in a way, a part of the success of Studio D had to do with that fact that all of us were connected with the women in the audience who were also experiencing shared experiences.[35]

Studio D filmmaker Dorothy Todd Hénaut, likewise, credited her feminist consciousness to the pro-feminist climate within her family and, later, through her work as an activist:

My mother sent me a shortened version of *The Feminine Mystique*. I was brought up a feminist. I think I was raised a feminist by my father. He taught me that there was nothing I could not do … I saw barriers but I had enough confidence to break them down. I belonged to the Voice of Women in the early sixties … The support I got from these women was incredibly important.[36]

Indeed, this climate was marked by a newly awakened sense of awareness that flourished over the next two decades and that witnessed the establishment of many organizations for women. One of the most significant outcomes of the Royal Commission was the establishment of the National Action Committee on the Status of Women (NAC), founded by activist feminists in 1971 and consisting of 289 women's groups. NAC would receive federal funding and become "a national watchdog group" ensuring the implementation of sweeping social reforms for women recommended by the Royal Commission, from "equal pay to a national child care program."[37] Though in recent years NAC has been decimated by punishing budget cuts engineered by the shrinking fiduciary support of the federal government, it continues as "a unified voice with the strength of numbers"[38] and continues to focus national attention on women's issues.

By the late 1970s, "feminism" was becoming a recognizable, if somewhat "specialized" component of national cultural life at the local level. Throughout the early 1970s women's bookstores sprouted up in most major Canadian cities, closely followed by the establishment of women's studies classes in universities as sites for the development and study of feminist thought. Canada's first feminist press, Women's Press, was set up in 1973. Further, many communities across Canada established a network of services for women, including shelters for battered women, rape crisis centres and self-defence courses. Feminist culture asserted itself increasingly in the arts and in popular culture. Women entered the workforce in unprecedented numbers, transforming professions that formerly had been exclusive preserves of male privilege and power. While these changes reflected geographic and regional diversities as well as cultural, economic and political specificities, there was little doubt that feminists in Canada had orchestrated fundamental change.

It is within this era that Studio D began to develop conversations with a wide range of feminist groups. Filmmaker Gerry Rogers points out that Studio D, as a player in the broader Canadian feminist community, was able to focus on issues that were just beginning to be understood by the public in general:

> Studio D made films about subjects that the majority of people didn't realize existed. Today, we have a much more sophisticated knowledge about [issues] — sexual harassment, incest, violence and rape [thanks to it].

> Then, most people didn't know how to think, talk about women's issues. We hadn't even coined terms that are now familiar.[39]

Indeed, an unflagging determination to celebrate and promote a women-centred culture remained central to Studio D. This resolution remained undiluted at the heart of Studio D's mission for its twenty-two year history, as wording from a promotional brochure published in the early 1990s demonstrates:

> From its inception, Studio D's filmmaking approach has been grounded in women's culture, politics and values. Our two chief objectives, clearly envisioned since the unit's earliest days, are to bring women's perspectives to the films we produce and to provide opportunities for Canadian women to move into motion picture occupations traditionally dominated by men. We have responded to this dual mandate with a body of women-centred, issue-oriented work — some of the NFB's most challenging yet popular documentaries. Winning awards and respect around the globe, Studio D productions embrace diverse concerns but share common goals. Designed to engage audiences, spark discussion and raise consciousness, they are conceived as tools for social change and empowerment.[40]

New attitudes engendered by feminist organizing, at both formal and grassroots levels, raised consciousness, leading the way to a host of improvements for women. To speculate on any link between Studio D documentaries and concrete improvements for women goes beyond the scope of this book, yet it seems reasonable to suggest that the films played a certain role in shaping public attitudes, at least, in certain quarters. The social and political changes that did ensue bear testimony to a changing climate more receptive to notions of equality. According to filmmaker Terre Nash, Studio D took part in transforming social attitudes during this period. One way it did so was by circulating documentaries revealing the stark details of inequality in women's experiences. As Nash recalled:

> I worked distributing films for quite a while — a year or two. I'd take them out to women's groups and schools and get feedback and put that back into the programming process and that sort of thing.[41]

As far as Dorothy Todd Hénaut is concerned, Studio D contributed to the defining of national values with respect to women's issues, daring to show women a better way:

> It was a time of great social change. In *Challenge for Change* we wanted to give a voice to the voiceless, the idea behind Studio D ... Studio D had the money to make films that needed to be made and we took them out

> to audiences and audiences used them. Studio D films really helped women to live their lives better and more fully. This gave them the courage to continue with the struggle. It gave them [women in Canada] the courage to speak out about things that they didn't dare. Gail Singer's *Loved, Honoured and Bruised* (1980) [for instance] helped women to identify issues around violence committed against women and their children.[42]

Another organization that became vital to securing rights for women was the Women's Legal Education and Action Fund (LEAF), established in 1985. At that time, Prime Minister Trudeau was repatriating the Canadian constitution, in which was included a new Charter of Rights and Freedoms. Canadian feminists were once again galvanized into action, organizing a vigorous and successful grassroots movement to protest the inclusion of language on equal rights that had been taken from the old Canadian Bill of Rights — language that would only perpetuate many laws discriminating against women. Feminists appealed to the government, demanding that section 28 of the Canadian constitution, which guaranteed women's rights to equality, be included.[43] In 1986, Bill C-62 was passed and guaranteed affirmative action for women, visible minorities (Indigenous Canadians and other Canadians from diverse ethnic backgrounds) and the disabled. Their success in challenging the constitution, encouraged the core group of the movement to found LEAF, a legal organization created to challenge constitutional law on behalf of Canadian women, and which is still active today.

*

Shannon's vision for an all-woman studio made a profound contribution to developing political and cultural ideas about women and film in this period. Given its sense of itself as a voice of women's culture, how might we understand Studio D, a state-instigated and state-funded studio, as a cultural instrument for Canadian women? This is but one of the questions I explore in the next chapter.

CHAPTER 2

STUDIO D, THE STATE AND THE NFB: DIVERGING AGENDAS

Somewhere every culture has an imaginary zone for what it excludes, and it is that zone we must try to remember today.

— HÉLÈNE CIXOUS AND CATHERINE CLÉMENT, *THE NEWLY BORN WOMAN*

Although women in liberal democracies are now citizens, formal Citizenship has been won within a structure of patriarchal power in which women's qualities and tasks are still devalued.

— CHANTAL MOUFFE, "FEMINISM, CITIZENSHIP AND RADICAL DEMOCRATIC POLITICS"

There are a lot of double binds in running a maverick minority division within an institution that, in many ways, represents the status quo you are trying to change.

— KATHLEEN SHANNON, "'D' IS FOR DILEMMA," *HERIZONS*

FEMINIST ACTIVISM DURING THE 1960S AND 1970S WAS DIRECTLY RESPONsible for the creation of many feminist ventures. The creation of Studio D in 1974, however, is commonly regarded as a particular federal response to feminist political pressure exerted following the tabling of the Royal Commission on the Status of Women, which included 167 recommendations for reforming women's status in Canadian society and increasing the number of women's organizations. It was not created as an independent institution but became a part of the NFB. As the producer of national culture, the NFB shifted to make a "space" for feminism, without having any clear understanding of feminist work or its implications. Further, when the United Nations set out a series of goals to improve conditions in women's lives, naming 1975 as International Women's Year, the Canadian government committed itself to these goals, implicating the NFB. The commitment was important on the national stage because it gave women working within federal institutions the "moral ammunition"[1] to lobby for improved status for women as both citizens and as employees. Indeed, this development provided the context for Kathleen Shannon's call for the creation of a studio for women within the NFB. As Dorothy Todd Hénaut remembers:

> The Film Board was a pretty "sclerozed" (ironclad) place in 1974 but it was supposed to be International Women's Year in 1975 so the Film Board said "maybe we can do this for International Women's Year." But, it was really Kathleen fighting. It wasn't Ottawa having an idea or the Film Board having an idea, it was about Kathleen fighting to get a women's studio off the ground.[2]

Although Kathleen Shannon's vision was that Studio D be a proponent of "women's culture" that would function independently, from the outset Studio D had a relationship to the state through the NFB. In fact, the state, aware that "'the nation' is constructed through its stories,"[3] was the instigator of a national culture that it fostered through the establishment of such mechanisms as a national film board.

In filmmaker Beverly Shaffer's opinion, both the state and the film board regarded Studio D as a means of keeping up with the times without making any genuine shift in attitude: "The male establishment thought, 'Oh wow, there are some women [here] and, gee, maybe they could make films and bring in an audience. We've never thought of *this* before.'"[4] Shaffer's own experience of submitting a proposal to do a series of films on Canadian children based on *Zoom,* a highly popular children's series she was working on for WGBH television in Boston, demonstrates how she was slotted into a traditional gendered position when her project was deemed "acceptable" women's material:

> I wrote up the proposal and submitted it to the Film Board, then came up for a visit and Colin Low said that I could come in and speak to him

> ... At that time, it was International Women's Year and the Film Board, as you know, had made a gesture to create a little, very little women's studio that would make films "for and by" women. So he read my proposal and he saw some merit in it and ... thought "Oh, children, children and women," and so he submitted it to Kathleen Shannon who was setting up a studio at that time and looking for women with any kind of filmmaking experience ... I never asked how she reacted to it but I can imagine that precisely because it *was* about children and that a man was giving it to her because *he* thought that *that* was a woman's interest — when the subject really wasn't her chief interest. She wanted to make feminist films. She wanted to break that whole patriarchal stereotype that "women and children go together."[5]

The ability of the state to "manage" its citizens through such institutional creations has been amply documented by media theorists.[6] If the primary responsibility or motivation of the state is to construct a sense of identity in its citizen-subjects, cultural policy "becomes a site at which the subject is produced."[7] Commenting on this, Jan Jindy Pettman reminds us that the state holds a masculinist role that replicates perfectly the politics of patriarchy whereby the state is "gendered male and the nation gendered female." [8] Culture, in this formation, functions as a practice of representation that creates its own domain as a system of values and beliefs that reflect state ideology; culture is thus understood as "a historically specific set of institutionally embedded relations of government in which the forms of thought and conduct of extended populations are targeted for transformation — in part via the extension through the social body of norms, techniques, and regimens of aesthetic and intellectual culture."[9]

The government, then, through the process of culture, becomes a force "manufacturing identity as a subject of a nation and identity as a citizen of a polity, while also organizing persons in terms of their certification and aestheticization."[10] The process, itself, yields "well-tempered, manageable cultural subjects formed and governed through institutions and discourses."[11] The evolution of the *idealized*, time-honoured notion of citizenship, however, has, until recently, excluded women[12] and has left little room for women as citizen-subjects:

> Modern democracy is consequently centered around "the narcissistic ego" and not "the other." It is founded on faulty extrapolations by men from their own misrecognition of themselves, their needs, and their history, in a way that denies that anyone is outside the discourse of citizenship. This

> acts to prevent any arousal of the preconditions necessary for encouraging active participation in the affairs of state.[13]

Nonetheless, the Royal Commission on the Status of Women recognized women as political subjects in the public sphere and thus opened up some public space for them.

While these are important concepts for understanding how the Canadian state was positioned to shape and control "women's culture" and "feminist culture" when Studio D was formed, its story echoes one of Beverly Thiele's six vanishing acts that work to divest women of power as legitimate subjects *and* citizens.[14] This problematic exclusion of women in a traditional framework, then, accounts, in part, for a deepening of tensions for feminist filmmaking between Studio D and the NFB that clearly began from the time of its inception.

NATIONALISM AND THE CANADIANIZATION OF CULTURE

Political theorist Sylvia Bashevkin claims that the Canadian state, since the time of Confederation, has consistently converted nationalist ideas into federal policies. Nationalism, in this instance, is "grounded in the distinction between members of an in-group and their loyalty to a preferably sovereign or self-determining political unit which is representative of that in-group"[15] from members of an out-group, loyal to other sovereign or dependent units. The outcome is a pan-Canadian nationalism organized around the overlapping concerns of culture, trade and investment that favours an English-speaking, central Canadian perspective that equates "a powerful interventionist federal state with the defence of in-group interests."[16] Thus, as Bashevkin points out, a sense of identity and a loyalty to this identity is crucial to the development of nationalist sentiments:

> Following the lines of this approach, the basic "glue" that holds together nationalist ideas and movements is in-group loyalty. Identification with other members of the in-group — whether because of pride in this present shared membership, faith in the future of the unit or memory of past experiences — and a concomitant distancing from the out-group are essential components of nationalist ideology. On the crucial level of political action, the establishment of a clear and assertive in-group category usually produces demands for national independence, self-determination and state sovereignty.[17]

The state, then, generates a form of national identity politics through a variety of mechanisms, deploying it in conjunction with economic (nationalism) policies that include tariffs to protect Canadian interests and legislation, as well as film production and distribution.

According to historian J.L. Granatstein, the Canadian state was embodied by a group of "Ottawa men" who believed that power should be concentrated in the hands of the government and its civil servants as possessors of the appropriate (androcentric) vision and skills to make Canada the kind of country it could and should be. [18] Part of this vision included the promotion of culture, organized through cultural policy, regarded as a legitimate jurisdiction of state governance.[19] The state, long concerned with promoting the attitudes and values of national culture, organized its policies around two axioms that either subsumed women in the category of citizen or ignored them altogether:

> … first that the wholesale consumption of foreign cultural products is a national cultural disaster; and second, that national identity is a function of the production and consumption of Canadian cultural products … Culture is the bond that holds the nation together.[20]

The proclamation of a new Canadian flag on January 28, 1967, and the opening of Canada's door to the world with Expo 67 (Man and His World) are two such examples of government initiatives intended to create a vigorous sense of national identity with Canadian culture at its heart.

In the 1950s, an inundation of American culture through mass media caused consternation on the part of those concerned with the question of Canadian identity. The Canadian economy was heavily reliant on American capital and goods, its media industry "perhaps the clearest example of dependent development in the sphere of cultural production."[21] The Massey Report (the Royal Commission on National Development in the Arts, Letters and Sciences, 1951), determined to protect Canadian arts and letters, looked to the state as the appropriate body to underwrite Canadian culture. Equating culture to "an enlightened state of personal and national development,"[22] the commission recommended that funding to the NFB be increased to enhance the production and distribution of Canadian "culture."

The NFB became the site of state-sponsored film production, functioning as a cultural "glue" in the service of "national interest."[23] The "complex and enigmatic"[24] John Grierson, widely acknowledged as its chief "founder" and architect, shaped it to function as a tool to deliver a "new system of education by which people will be made aware of the needs of the state and of their duties as citizens."[25] Grierson regarded the state as "a large corporation with a board of directors looking after policy and management and a group of skilled and trained experts or professionals [clearly, the NFB] actually handling operations."[26] His thinking emphasized the role of the state as a "centralized planning agency"[27] organized in a kind of top-down paternalism, the precise ideological approach he used to shape the NFB.

Under his guidance, the NFB would ensure the development of a more informed and democratic Canadian public. Horrified at how "new forms of mass media pandered to the lowest common denominator," Grierson considered documentary filmmaking as a form of education that would "re-establish the bonds of citizenship."[28] Grierson intended that NFB productions would be tools of "manufactured consent"[29] through which people would respond to the state's expectations of them. Here, the state is generally understood as the "machinery by which the best interests of the people are secured,"[30] and the NFB as the key feature of this technology. The Film Board's central role was to produce "the pictures in our heads"[31] that projected a state-generated version of national identity. These images and the films themselves are endowed, through their origins, with an undisputed legitimacy that documentary theorist Bill Nichols calls "discourses of sobriety," which are capable of effecting action, entailing consequences and perhaps altering the world itself,[32] an idea Studio D would take up.

THE QUESTION OF GENDER AND FEMINIST NATIONALISM

A series of Royal Commissions and state-originated studies, driven by recurring themes of hegemonic nationalism, anti-commercialism and anti-Americanism,[33] not only reinforced these notions of nationalism but also saw the NFB as an important instrument in creating culture. The Massey-Lévesque Commission (1949–1951), for instance, "endorsed the National Film Board's educational function of documentary film production as promoting Canadianism,"[34] although it assigned the production of feature films to market forces and the American film industry. The Fowler Commission (1956–1957) argued more generally that "broadcasting remain a national service governed by the state,"[35] aligning the interest of the nation-state (unity and identity) with the interests of ordinary Canadians. While it must be noted that the state and the Film Board rarely acted in tandem,[36] both institutions held high stakes in the business of nation-building: the state through the business of creating and implementing policy and the NFB through engendering the aesthetic. Arthur Irvin, NFB commissioner in 1950, articulated its mandate as follows:

> The Board is established to initiate and promote the production and distribution of films in the national interest and in particular to produce and distribute and to promote the production and distribution of films designed to interpret Canada to Canadian and to other nations.[37]

Here, the project of engendering concepts of "nation" undertaken by both the state and the NFB is drawn up along humanist lines of political and national geography. Within this framework, women blended into an amorphous whole. The distinctive agenda for each group was to mark out territory for ways of being that initiated subjectivity. Within the dominant male-centred discourse, this amounted to maintaining a cultural, political and social status quo that secured the stability of the white middle-class male, keeping the traditional subject of Western culture firmly in the centre.

However, as Diane Burgess points out, official accounts of cultural identity and nationalism consciously "leave gender aside."[38] Until recently, gender has been an unruly category of analysis in the official record, one scarcely fitting "the traditional definition of the 'national' in terms of gender and cultural hegemonies."[39] Of course, the danger of "leaving gender aside" is that women's concerns can be altogether removed. To make her point, Burgess refers to three respected critical studies of Canadian media — Ted Magder's *Canada's Hollywood,* Manjunath Pendakur's *Canadian Dreams and American Control* and Michael Dorland's *So Close to the State/s* — all of which exclude any discussion of gender. The surface impression that is consequently created is that national film issues revolve around legislation, regulation and business concerns, which disregard any question of gender and agency for women, particularly in the area of decision-making (about anything), as "difficulties arise from the extent to which they both conceal and maintain 'silences around gender.'"[40] This failure to consider gender as a category functions as a form of power politics that muffles or completely silences women's voices — even when they *are* recognized players.

In fact, Burgess's point encourages me to argue that Studio D's version of national cinema turns on a fresh approach, one that is woman-centred and that conflates the notion of "nation and women" so that "nation" is defined as a global community thereby erasing political boundaries or borders. Such an ideological shift, of course, places Studio D and its project at cultural and political odds with both the state and the NFB. Studio D's story, then, becomes a history of "crisis and conflict, of resistance and negotiation."[41]

The Studio's woman-centred stance, while grounded within ideological territory occupied by both the government and the NFB, created a rare instance where women's propositions for radical change were entertained, distributed (nationally and internationally) and "performed." Indeed, Studio D used its documentary films to explore and set out ideas about identity, subjectivity and "nation," making "women" its core subject, whereas the state and the NFB understood this project as one belonging to political nationalism that preserved power relations of the traditional status quo.

Mounting a woman-centred culture at this time, however, entailed carving out fresh territory, resisting the status quo and asserting a new subjectivity for women — a central project for feminist thought in the second half of the twentieth century. In the early phase of Studio D, the task was taken up by middle-class white women (mainly) — a condition imposed, in part, by lack of training in film for most women. This reality, however, shifted and expanded more fully in the final years of Studio D (the late 1980s until its closure in 1996) as women from diverse backgrounds became associated with the Studio and articulated new forms of subjectivity. (Even so, the stories emerging from Studio D make me appreciate that, from the beginning, Studio D contemplated a much more complex understanding of "woman" as a category, a subject to which I shall return.)

To understand Studio D's approach to national cinema as an instance of feminist "national fiction," using Graeme Turner's notion that such fictions construct our sense of who we are, is to acknowledge its power to make authoritative, if sometimes contested, statements on feminist issues through feminist documentaries within the nation's film board. Studio D's body of documentaries produced over a twenty-two year period constitute a series of texts that articulate its own version of feminist cultural narrative:

> As the culture [Studio D] produces its texts it prefers certain meanings, thematic structures and formal strategies. Within these preferred forms and meanings we find the ideology of the culture: the way it makes sense of itself and infers meaning into its institutions and practices.[42]

How, indeed, did Studio D make sense of itself, then, as an instrument of Canadian culture *and* of feminist culture? How did it understand its institutional location and its practices? What possible dislocations or ruptures existed between the public perception of Studio D and its own sense of "location" within the NFB? What disjunctures might have become evident as Studio D undertook to "explore, question and construct" a national feminist narrative?

As a creation of the state, Studio D was immediately invested with national significance and seeming power, but the state continued to hold the dominant position and the Studio was held in a place of *perpetual* dependency. Thus, this "voice for women," which was invested with tantalizing promise that proposed change and launched initiatives, operated in a vexed location — one rewarded with undeniable privilege that, at the same time, masked a debilitating and protracted internal struggle for survival. As we will see, prolonged budgetary constraints kept Studio D firmly under the institutional thumb, undermining its feminist zeal and eventually dividing it against itself.

Thus, although the federal government "gave" the NFB the power to create Studio D, women's concerns did not enjoy a primary rank on the federal agenda. Examining the reality of governance in the context of the "late capitalist era" as one embracing both economic and state concerns, feminist political theorist Jill Vickers argues that the interests of women are bound to take a back seat in a climate where democracy develops only as "top dressing."[43] Women's interests are more usually dealt with in a series of compromises that Vickers calls "élite accommodation."[44] She contends that élite accommodation, a central feature of federal politics during the Liberal era in Canada, entails nothing more than a rhetorical flourish with respect to "participatory democracy." While the state occupies itself serving competitive and individualist market interests, women are largely excluded from the central process of political and economic policymaking. In fact, feminists have long pointed to a structure "based on and sustained by fundamental inequalities … [with] different ramifications for women" when the state is generally accepted as "having the legitimacy to organize social and political relations."[45] For Dorothy Todd Hénaut, "inequity" has another name: "Studio D was born out of oppression. It was born out of women *not* being given a voice to make their own films. It was born out of the energy that comes from seeing the injustice of the 'said' situation."[46]

When Studio D was founded in 1974, the climate within the state and the NFB, as a number of Studio D filmmakers noted, was nationalistic and profoundly male dominated, exhibiting "tightly unified, homogenous models [marked] with rigid exclusions, hierarchies, and binaries."[47] Studio D brought to this landscape the promise of a feminist challenge by creating a place where women's stories would be aired and celebrated. According to filmmaker Gerry Rogers, "In many instances, our work was ahead of its time. We made films about subjects that the majority of people didn't realize even existed or that were not yet out there on the public agenda."[48]

Speaking about women's experiences at the NFB during the war years or for women's films of the past more generally, film critic Barbara Halpern Martineau pointed to "a pressing need for rediscovery and description" when she addressed participants at the 1976 Conference on Canadian Film in its Historical Context held in Ottawa:

> To speak of women in the dominant film culture is to speak of absence, gaps, discontinuities, of appropriation and distortion ... This is held by feminist critics to be a reflection of the filmmaking situation in a world of power, which is, in fact, male-dominated. Although women have made considerable contributions to cinema throughout its history their work has been obscured and underrated, their voices and visions suppressed.[49]

Martineau considered the question of whether there is such a thing as "a distinct women's film culture" as somewhat of a "red herring." She was more interested in remembering women's names and elaborating their accomplishments — women like Evelyn Spice Cherry, former co-head of the NFB agricultural film unit; Gudrun Bjerring Parker, eventual head of the NFB's educational film unit and who sometimes used all-women crews; Margaret Perry, travelling projectionist; directors Laura Bolton and Jane Marsh *(Women Are Warriors, Inside Fighting Canada, Air Cadets* in the *Canada Carries On* series);[50] editors Margaret Ann Adamson, Daphne Lilly, Evelyn Lambart and Alma Duncan in charge of graphics; and

Marge McKay, Grierson's chief administrator and early NFB historian.[51]

However, despite their "vital and central roles," women were gradually but systematically removed from important levels of production and administration following the war, with the result that over the next two decades Film Board production became heavily male-dominated with "almost no participation by women except at menial levels."[52] Ironically, but not surprisingly, Studio D came into being precisely at a time when internal studies at the NFB revealed that women made up a very small percentage of its filmmakers.

When a well-qualified Terre Nash first approached the NFB looking for a position, she was met with what could only be described as a classic case of institutional disinterest in feminist film. Nash, in the process of completing doctoral studies at McGill University in Montreal, arrived at the NFB with an animated short she had made in art school, hoping to "launch" a career. Guided to the office handling prospective filmmakers, Nash was advised by the male administrator that she should seek out Kathleen Shannon. "While *he* handled new, cutting-edge filmmakers, *she* [Shannon] would be looking after all the women … [in] a new women's studio called Studio D."[53] The studio's location signalled its level of prestige within the Film Board's head office, as Nash tells it:

> The first hint I got that this new studio for women was not taken very seriously by the Film Board was when I found out that it was located in what had previously been a janitor's storeroom. I was told that in order to find it, I would have to push the last button on the elevator, marked B for basement. Then I'd have to walk along a maze of dark, deserted corridors with exposed pipes instead of ceilings. According to the directions I was given, once I'd passed a large trap door that said, in big red letters: DANGER, PCBs STORED HERE, I'd know that Studio D was just around the next corner. Sure enough, I turned the corner, and walked into a rather large and dishevelled room with several desks, lots of books, a Steenbeck and a trim bin for film. But it was really the three mops and a pail in the corner that gave me the certainty that I was in the right place. As I was surveying the cleaning supplies, I heard a voice behind me saying: "If you look closer, you'll realize that those mops are leading edge."[54]

The voice, of course, belonged to Kathleen Shannon.

The gendered politics around the development of new filmmakers Nash encountered coupled with the humble location of the Studio invite the conclusion that the implementation of this "women's studio" was merely a political expedient. Indeed, as Nash points out, since the NFB received special funding to celebrate International Women's Year, a studio for women was both "a politically astute gesture and a way of getting Kathleen off their case."[55]

FEMINIST CHANGE AND SOCIAL CHANGE

From the beginning, Shannon's ambition for Studio D was to use it to propose change. The idea that women might occupy a space of their own to pursue subjects they deemed worthy to film was an irresistible proposition. Time and time again, Shannon referred back to the notion that women made up over half the Canadian population and that Studio D would speak on their behalf, leading some to identify the somewhat "separationist" stance the women's studio seemed to be claiming:

> Studio D's philosophy focused on the concept of difference by stressing the "otherness" of the female voice; this means that the cinematic voice that addressed audiences stressed the idea that "we" were the women and "they" were the men.[56]

It might be argued that Shannon embraced Grierson's concept of film as an instrument much more suited to "mind-bending"[57] than any other of the arts. Certainly, the fighting spirit apparent in Grierson's pronouncement about art matched her own stance, one that encouraged a certain animosity within the Film Board against Studio D. "Art is not a mirror but a hammer," Grierson said. "It is a weapon in our hands to see and say what is right and good and beautiful, and hammer it out as the mold and pattern of actions."[58] Certainly, Shannon envisioned the work of Studio D as integral to the work of feminist activism. As she noted with pride, "many of our films did not just report on existing social movements but were part of their impetus."[59]

Nonetheless, Shannon's very ability to build a feminist film unit was often frustrated by rigid Film Board policy. Gerry Rogers remembers, "We were called 'too middle-class, too white' but when Kathleen wanted to hire more broadly, Film Board policies wouldn't let her."[60] Kathleen Shannon remembers, specific instances where her vision was blunted by the rigidity of the institution:

> I know what my vision was and how far we fell short … so I have a lot of … frustration and pain, too, because so much energy had to go into

> just *survival*. There were a lot of compromises that had to be made ... The staff for the Film Board had been frozen some time before Studio D started. So I was only able to put *one* person on staff in all the years I headed the studio and that was a secretary.[61]

Sue Findlay, employed within the federal state bureaucracy as director of the Women's Program Department of the Secretary of State throughout the 1970s, contends that the state is quite adept in responding to *and* controlling women's demands for social change. In describing how the state functions, Findlay's instrumentalist definition, drawn from Marxist theorist Nicos Poulantzas, usefully intepretes the Studio's situation:

> A more convincing definition of the state that reflects the struggles that characterize the policy-making process describes the state as the organizer of hegemony rather than the object of it. While the interests of capitalism and patriarchy might dominate at the societal level, the internal conflicts and competition within and among these forces make it impossible for them to impose a unified position on the state, or to defend their interests against opposing interests in the political sphere. The role of the state, then, is to organize a unity of interests among the dominant groups and disorganize potential challenges to this unity ... It is through this process that the hegemony of the dominant groups is organized and reorganized to control and incorporate the challenges of subordinate groups such as women.[62]

The outcome, Findlay notes, demonstrates "the success of the state in constructing this representation [of women's interests] in a way that controlled women's demands and limited reforms."[63]

Accounts of Studio D's creation certainly suggest a state-sanctioned accommodation of feminist demands for change rooted in political expediency rather than any genuine wish on the part of government for radicalized gender equality. And yet, as Findlay points out, "when the state is more vulnerable to women's demands, feminists can play a more active role ... to promote women's equality ... by taking advantage of the state's need for legitimation."[64] Thus, the creation of Studio D can be understood as a political card played with some skill by Kathleen Shannon. However, her move to ensure that a women's studio would hold a permanent place in the business of state-funded filmmaking was a move that would eventually dissolve it.

While the inception of Studio D by the NFB illustrates a lukewarm accommodation of women's demands, the Studio's successes throughout the 1980s raised the profile of the NFB as a whole. In fact, as Shannon noted, whenever the government threatened to cut funding to the Film Board, the NFB was quick to illustrate its relevancy by pointing to Studio D. When the 1982 *Federal Culture Policy Review* (Applebaum-Hébert Report) recommended that "the National Film Board be abolished and used instead as a centre for training and film research,"[65] Shannon was quick to defend the Board and the women of Studio D as creators of culture — their own. In a presentation to the review committee, Shannon attacked the report for neglecting the most important aspect of documentary film, "those made to inspire, challenge, provide vision and catalyse dialogue about important social issues that affect us all."[66]

Shannon challenged the committee to broaden its scope to include women — "our half of the Canadian people" — in appropriate numbers in positions of decision-making and authority. She insisted "that women participate in the whole range of functions in the art and industry of the media."[67] Further, in a letter calling for support for Studio D, Shannon defended the NFB as the "only entity in the country with a woman-run, women's film program," charging that the report "reflected almost no acknowledgement of the position and concerns of women at all, particularly when it comes to film."[68]

This case of "leaving gender behind" was not lost on cultural critic and independent filmmaker Kay Armatage. In response to the Applebaum-Hébert's *Summary of Briefs and Hearings*, Armatage noted that while fifteen women's organizations and over 150 individual women submitted briefs, the summary barely mentioned women, *despite* its admission that at "almost every one of the public hearings, we heard from individuals and groups about the even more difficult position of women artists, and the loss to Canadian cultural life that this situation creates."[69] Citing a sobering list of inequities, Armatage pointed out:

> Women are denied insights into their own symbolic systems, and the society in general is deprived of the rich variance of possible discourses. And contrary to Pollyanna media distortions, the condition of inequality is growing annually, rather than dissipating.[70]

At the same time Armatage expressed shock at reading Studio D's demand for "the government to offer extra funding to the women's programme *to correspond to its own increased priority for the promotion of women*"[71] given the impoverished state of women in every aspect of Canadian cultural production, particularly outside the NFB. Referring to the broader context of cultural spending, Armatage noted that women's chances for funding anywhere in the arts were woefully slim:

> Over the last ten years, women have fared poorly in all grant programmes (at the Canada Council) and in most disciplines; they have been consistently awarded less than 50 per cent of awards in any discipline; and there is a marked tendency for women to fare even worse as the prestige of the grant category increases.[72]

Whether Armatage was taking issue with Studio D's seeming naiveté or calling attention to a hypocritical official stance shirking its rhetorical (and politically expedient) claims of creating benefits for women artists, her frustration over the lack of funding for feminist initiatives share common ground with Studio D. Armatage emphasizes the bitter irony in what she calls "the most startling figures" to come from International Women's Year:

> In that year, special grant money was made available to finance women's projects in an effort to correct previous imbalances. The apparent result of the special allocations was that fewer women received less money overall than the average for the ten year period! In the film programme, only 15 per cent of the money distributed in grants went to women.[73]

When Studio D was created in 1974, the public prominence of issues of inequality and discrimination across North America generally and in Canada in particular made it impossible for the state to ignore women's demands for change. If the state needed to find "solutions that would demonstrate the commitment of liberal democracies to equality without compromising their reliance on capitalism,"[74] creating a women's studio within a national institutional structure must have seemed the perfect answer. In retrospect, it seems clear that both the state and the NFB "responded" to women's demands, without intending to instigate any *fundamental* change in institutional policy at all.

Indeed, the NFB had already acknowledged its shortcomings with respect to women and employment as revealed in its Equal Opportunity Report generated during the period following the tabling of the Royal Commission on the Status of Women, yet it demonstrated scant interest in addressing this fault. When it became clear that the government was insisting that the Film Board accommodate women's concerns in some way, the NFB cobbled together a women's film unit from existing NFB employees (a willing Shannon and two others). The ad hoc manoeuvre was handled with such little prior consideration that it overlooked a major grant, one that would have guaranteed the fledgling feminist studio a much more auspicious beginning. Officially, Studio D was given the nod without any thought to its potential. Ironically, the implementation of the public policy initiative that only secondarily promoted "feminism" created the impression that the Studio commanded its own fate when, in reality, the NFB held the reins of power, as we shall see.

Thus, the case of Studio D serves as an example of how the voicing of women's concerns was encouraged but managed by the "dominant force" (the state and its network of cultural institutions). Certainly within the corridors of the NFB, voices from Studio D were variously recognized, endorsed, muffled or completely silenced, according to Film Board prerogatives which arguably reflect the fate of women's voices in the broader political arena (then and now):

> Despite rhetoric about "participatory democracy," women were excluded from the central process of political and economic policy making. Only within women's movement organizations were women "in charge" and only there were women-centred policies and processes the main order of business.[75]

Indeed, the newly created Studio D envisioned itself as a self-described collective, "a base for women filmmakers and ... a response to Canadian women's need to see films that address our own realities and our desire for change, bringing Canadian women filmmakers and users together for *reflection and communication.*"[76]

By articulating its purpose through the language of consciousness-raising, Studio D resisted definition purely as a *feature* of state technology. I find it much more accurate, instead, to understand Studio D simultaneously as an instrument of feminist thought and practice *as well as* a feature of state technology. In fact, Studio D might be construed as a self-styled pressure group that emerged with the express purpose of attempting to reorient the ideas and policies of the Canadian state with respect to its treatment of women both "at home" and abroad, women whom the Studio understood as a global "nation."

WOMEN AS NATION

Writing at the time Studio D came into being, Canadian historian Ramsay Cook advanced a popularly received and highly androcentric proposition on the "nation question." Cook suggests that the Fathers of Confederation were unconsciously committed to a view of Canada as a nation-state where "cultural collectivities" might co-exist under that same state:

> The nation-state serves the practical purpose of organizing groups of people into manageable units and providing them with services which they need and which they can share ... The nation-state is the organization within which the individual can realize himself in relation to his historic cultural community and, in an age of the multi-national corporation and burgeoning bureaucracy, maintain at least a modicum of control over his own affairs.[77]

While Cook refers to such national institutions as our medicare program and publicly owned broadcasting system, it is easy to see how the women in Studio D might turn this approach to nation-building to their particular advantage. If the state demonstrates its value "by meeting the needs of its people, and providing a framework within which citizens satisfy their own needs,"[78] Studio D understood implicitly that it was encouraged *as an instrument of the state* to make films for women. Its production of feminist films would "empower women by showing them they do have a history and a culture ... that can validate women's experience in their own eyes."[79]

Taking the lead, manoeuvring within the NFB mandate and its own commitment "to make films by and for women," Studio D sought to influence state policies in ways it believed best represented women's "national" interests, which sometimes coincided with the federal narrative but which often extended beyond local concerns. As Kathleen Shannon noted, "[We tried to] include women's culture in what's called *culture* — which it *not* a neutral term."[80] As a result, she surmised Studio D was commonly perceived within the NFB as a thorn in its side because it consistently overstepped its boundaries.

The Studio's complicated location and determined feminist stance placed it in contested space at a significant moment of political, economic and cultural transition when global politics became marked by a profound shift to the right. In a countermove, Studio D promoted its films as educational material welcomed by instructors of women's studies and gender studies courses across Canada (whose numbers increased substantially during the Studio D years), as women dared to imagine that they might exercise control over their own bodies, careers, expect fair wages, achieve more autonomous positions in religious and political discourse, to name a few. Meanwhile, the state was implicated implicitly in many Studio D documentaries as the appropriate instrument to arbitrate and address inequities affecting women. The reforms contemplated by Studio D sometimes challenged the liberal conception of society and state, moving the issues and players into new territory, territory into which the state, of course, had no intention of moving.

While Studio D's intellectual and aesthetic approach — described by Chris Scherbarth as a "separationist response"[81] — empowered it to make feminist films in a separate space that encouraged and celebrated women's perspectives with audiences generally, it placed the women's studio at odds with both the NFB and the state. Its stance, however, encouraged it to understand "woman as a global nation," uniting women ideologically in a sweeping international community. Their view relinquished the narrow concept of nation as a geographic political entity and replaced it with a richer, more resonant and infinitely varied notion uniting women through common concerns and agendas. Studio D's projection of women as a global community, articulated through so many of its films, then, projects a hopeful, forward-looking if not entirely unproblematic message.

The concept and applicability of national identity in the hands of the state and the concept of identity advanced by Studio D from its feminist perspective was, I suggest, constructed on radically different ground. In the larger NFB institution, the state's version of "nation" was located firmly within the geographical boundaries of Canada. The feminist film unit, on the other hand, imagined its boundaries extending globally to embrace *all* women. In Studio D's mind, "community" trumped "place." Indeed, charged by the state with the task of "building identity," Studio D clearly defined its mandate as one rooted in building feminist culture. As far as Shannon was concerned, the challenge of straddling conflicting territory held a great deal of excitement:

> The fact that I saw, and did things differently from my male colleagues didn't mean my inferiority, or inadequacy. It meant there was a legitimate

difference. That difference was demonstrated daily in Studio D, and contributed to the mandate we evolved, which included a commitment to employment and training opportunities for women, creating a compatible environment for women's creativity, making films that met the needs of women audiences, and bringing the perspectives of women to all social issues through the medium of film.[82]

While her many struggles only underscored the subordination of Studio D within the NFB (mirroring women's subordination at large in society), Shannon was clearly engaged in a battle she relished, that of contributing to the redefinition of the social and cultural location for women in terms of power, agency and citizenship.

Filmmaker and theorist Brenda Longfellow asks, "What are we to make of national identity in the latter part of the twentieth century?" In doing so, she opens up a possibility for reconciling the divergent ideas of Studio D (and feminism in general), the NFB and the Canadian state:

> Perhaps the hope for Canada is that its sense of national belonging could evolve (thanks to the native rights movements) into an idea of political citizenship and respect for difference. Perhaps too, in the face of that irrefutable diversity lies the possibility of recasting national identity as a place in between Old and New Worlds, a place of transnational, transsexual and transcultural movement, a negotiation between spaces of difference.[83]

Longfellow's recasting of nation contrasts the initial emphasis on the quest for sameness that constituted the imagined community of women united by oppressions so prevalent in 1960s and 1970s feminist thought and depicted in many of Studio D documentaries. This recasting of national identity, however, opens up a space for a diverse yet inclusive Canadian feminist identity. Such a formation, of course, links "women as nation" to citizenship, whose aim, according to Chantal Mouffe, "is to construct a 'we' as radical democratic citizens." If this implies the encouraging of a variety of voices to challenge the status quo, fostering a recognition of a variety of struggles, I am interested in teasing out the role Studio D played in such a "a feminist democratic project … [advancing?], indeed, the very condition of its possibility."[84]

CHAPTER 3

BUILDING A NATIONAL FEMINIST CULTURE: LOOKING INSIDE THE NFB

When it comes to portraying women [in] government-sponsored films, more fish than females are filmed.
— STUDIO D INTEROFFICE MEMO, 1974

There were doors all round the hall, but they were all locked …
— LEWIS CARROLL, *ALICE IN WONDERLAND*

My hands were tied in many ways.
— KATHLEEN SHANNON, PERSONAL INTERVIEW

STUDIO D CAME INTO BEING ALONG WITH CANADIAN FEMINISM[1] AND, IN many ways, developed along with it, mirroring its "unfolding drama"[2] by producing documentaries that explored the same territory debated by feminists. Its identity as the *only* state-funded feminist film studio in the world made it unique. Constance Backhouse's description of women who came to Canadian feminism in the 1970s with a certain euphoria, which was tempered as time went on with the sobering wisdom of reflection, also applies to Studio D:

> We had the luxury, however misguided, of thinking that we worked on a fresh slate, that we stood exhilaratingly as the first feminists of this current wave … [who] now find our knowledge, our process, and our

> structures to be confusing and, at times, intimidating and silencing … documenting our sense of victories, challenges, and defeats.[3]

Any attempt to understand Studio D's nature and contribution to feminism, then, must take into account that its experiences, concerns and philosophy shifted in response to those debates, successes and tensions arising from a movement which has often been characterized as straddling territory that shifted back and forth between feminist activism and scholarly contemplation. Indeed, two competing perceptions of Studio D arise in existing literature. One account deems it a "women's room,"[4] a brave (and radical) pioneer into the world of film "by and for women"; the other judges it "a kind of ghetto for women at the NFB,"[5] a white middle-class operation promoting a "liberal feminist discourse" needing "to come to terms with [its] race and class bias."[6] The stories told by members of Studio D admit to both versions.

While there is no doubt that Studio D regarded itself as a significant cultural shaper, it faced a series of contradictions as it sought to fulfill its mandate to confront the inherent ideological complexities of something called "women's culture." Indeed, the very phrase "women's culture" attracted substantial theoretical scrutiny, which evolved throughout Studio D's lifetime, yielding valuable insights, identifying short-comings in feminist thinking and, consequently, creating fresh and more inclusive categories recognizing meaningful differences. The phrase shifted from its initial unproblematized connotation to one suggesting more questions than answers — whose culture? What do women have in common, after all? Who can speak for "me"? Thanks to feminist insights arising from the late 1980s post-colonial analyses, queer theory and feminist philosophy, questions of diversity and difference among women have become significant areas of critical focus. Newly imagined feminist communities emerging from such frameworks may be understood as co-existing, perhaps uneasily, with this persistent belief that women *do* in fact have something in common — that women may collectively imagine a new culture together. This tension played itself out in many arenas within the larger feminist community, and it also marked Studio D's experience, especially in its relationship to the women it hoped to reach.

Many feminists in the wider community saw Studio D as functioning within a liberal feminist framework,[7] identifying it as an organization "working from within an organization" rather than "for" the external community, particularly those who did not identify as liberal feminists. In part, Studio D derived its negative association with liberal feminism from feminists who considered those who turned to the state as the "rightful" mechanism for procuring more equitable status as lacking in radical vision. This was, of course, very contrary to Kathleen Shannon's vision of creating a studio based on a genuinely radical vision. It is important to realize that Studio D attempted to function as an independent feminist entity within an organization governed by liberal ideologies. An important question arises, then: How could a feminist politics and praxis be installed successfully in such a traditional institutional setting?

To put the question more broadly, What conditions need to exist for a feminist venture to be established and to flourish? Studio D encountered a series of stumbling blocks within an institutional structure unfamiliar with feminism and unwilling to cede it an equal place in the business of national filmmaking. This institutional stance misrecognized Studio D's undertaking and its needs, measuring them by humanist standards that favoured the subject as male, middle-class, Anglo-Saxon and heterosexual, emphasizing *his* status, importance, powers, achievements, interests and authority.[8] Resulting tensions forced the Studio from the outset into a series of conflicts and contradictions hampering its ability to produce the kinds of feminist documentaries it envisioned. These operational wrangles (which often played themselves out over issues of budget, ideology or questions over filmic "objectivity"), combined with Studio D's contradictory philosophical constructions of "nation," often placed it at odds with its institutional community.

Consequently, Studio D received a confusing mixture of praise and resistance; disrespect from colleagues was often coupled with incredulity over its documentary "successes." Feminists on the outside perceived Studio D as a privileged liberal feminist collective. Those on the inside of NFB, saw Studio D as too radical and activist and insufficiently committed to an artistic approach to film. Straddling such territory forced Studio D into an irreconcilable position. It had to comply with rigid institutional constraints and, within these bounds, produce films that spoke to a diverse audience of women, many of whom would not consider themselves liberal feminists (although it might be said the Studio did not see itself in those terms, either).

Whether blessed or burdened with its institutional mantle, Studio D was positioned to make authoritative statements with respect to feminist issues, but found itself criticized from time to time by independent feminist filmmakers who did not share entirely its approach to documentaries or its philosophic stance. In fact, the Studio's privileged location made it a lightning rod for criticism among the ranks of many independent feminist filmmakers whose own requests for funding were often refused by funding bodies or inadequately fulfilled. Remaining within the parameters of Griersonian-style documentaries geared to "educate" the nation earned Studio D a reputation for making often pedestrian and problematic films from others favouring a more avant-garde approach. Further, Studio D was criticized for inviting only those feminist filmmakers who shared its vision into its ranks or for insisting on imposing its vision on filmmakers who might be invited in.

As the Studio began to produce documentaries that explored women's struggles and that spoke to the broader feminist community, it also fought for respect and sometimes survival within the NFB. Studio D's inward-looking struggle to survive revolved around budget uncertainties making it difficult for the Studio to investigate and foster effective widespread collaborative relationships with other members of the feminist community. (In one notable example, Studio D sent out a call for film proposals based on a five-year funding model which the Film Board subsequently reduced to one, forcing the Studio to reject proposals it received from hopeful feminist filmmakers in the wider community.) These influences enforced an inward-looking mindset on members of the feminist studio that, admittedly, attracted certain negative perceptions from without which deserve closer scrutiny to better understand the position of Studio D overall.

SETTING UP THE STUDIO

Studio D, closeted within the NFB's head office in suburban Montreal, was organized as a feminist film studio, sharing numerous ideological connections with the Canadian women's movement. The institutional context in which it found itself was both hierarchical in nature and dominated by men. Initially, the *Film Act* of 1939 that created the NFB required that a minister and a Privy Council member sit on the NFB board of governors. However, to emphasize the arm's-length nature of the relationship, the *National Film Act* of 1950 placed the NFB board under the responsibility of a single government minister who was, in turn, responsible to Parliament for NFB control and direction. By the time Studio D was created, the NFB board consisted of five representatives drawn from the main geographical areas of Canada and three government figures representing the civil and defence services. According to the *National Film Act,* the NFB commissioner was (and continues today as) both chair of the Board and chief executive officer. This structure left the NFB free to operate as an independent agency of the state, as a site of knowledge-production and nation-building,[9] with politicians situated a comfortable distance from any contentious issue that NFB filmmakers might take on.

Studio D's mandate to make films "by and for" the women of Canada was designed to fall within the spirit of the NFB's broader mandate to "interpret Canada to Canadians and to the world in the national interest."[10] The overall institutional perspective regarded women unproblematically as citizens without taking gender or the complications of race, age or ability into any serious consideration. However, when she was appointed as the first executive producer in 1974, Kathleen Shannon envisioned a revolutionary approach that stood "on the border between traditional thinking and feminist change."[11] In an untitled internal memo she released on August 6, 1974, she hinted at the complexity of setting up a new "women's unit":

> Interim report from a pumpkin: though we may have wheels by the time you receive this there are many things of varying complexity to be sorted out in the launching of a new unit, so I have not been able to respond to questions with definite answers. As I will be away from Montreal until September this seems a good time to send out some words to those who have been in touch with us.[12]

Those "words," in fact, expressed Shannon's radical vision for a "women's room" at the NFB, a "rare opportunity afforded women."[13] She clearly imagined Studio D as a creative hub for filmmaking by women. Indeed, her memo noted that, while the "new Unit D" was not expressly a "woman's unit," it would be managed by women and its priority would be "the hiring and training of women." The memo also encouraged potential members to apply to other areas in the NFB if their qualifications and experience were appropriate. Presumably Shannon had sent out a notice of the NFB's intention to establish a women's unit through its marketing channels since her memo notes that 120 women from outside and within the Film Board had responded, wishing to join. Obviously, even in this early stage, Shannon's strategy was directed at changing the entire Film Board. Her memo further directed:

> An important thing is for women to be represented in all areas of the Film Board. There should be women employed in all production units, and more women in positions of responsibility and authority in Distribution, Administration, Technical Services. There are still no women in animation camera, no women projectionists, no women sound mixers or transfer operators, no women employed full time in the camera department.[14]

Shannon planned to draw on the combined force of four main groups from with the 120: individuals outside the NFB wishing to work in film but lacking professional training or experience; those working within the NFB who wanted to transfer into the new unit; independent women filmmakers outside the NFB; and women who had worked without pay, borrowing equipment to make films in order to "get" experience and who wanted their unofficial investment to be officially recognized.

Shannon was recruiting professional women, women who had attained a certain level of education and training and who were oppressed by gender in the workplace or in the classroom. Her wording identified the oppression specifically — "women taking courses in film who complain that the men students always get the equipment, and women who have been caring for the next generation and only now have the time to develop themselves."[15] Initially, "Unit D (English)" would be comprised of a small permanent core group: executive producer, technical producer, production co-ordinator and secretary. In time, the Unit would hire a training co-ordinator, liaison person and a Unit administrator. Producers, directors, editors, sound editors, researchers and writers would be attached to the Unit for the duration of their film projects. Shannon emphasized that the new Unit would be flexible: "We want a responsive structure to evolve in terms of creative realities rather than to model ourselves blindly on other structures that have been instituted in other circumstances at other times."[16] Training, with an emphasis on practical applications of equipment, would be an important part of the Unit's activity as Shannon's memo detailed:

> A very significant part of the program of Unit D must be training. Women have usually not had access to camera and sound equipment, whether as employees of the NFB or students attending film courses. In private industry, too many occupations have been perceived exclusively as "masculine" or "feminine" (you don't hear of men script girls). Training will include the following areas:
>
> • editing, sound editing and finishing, explanations of lab, titles, and optical processes
>
> • on-the-job training, apprenticeship with crews on regular NFB productions
>
> • production of short, simple, low-budget films on useful-information topics
>
> • "advanced" training — opportunities for established women filmmakers to expand their experience beyond the specific skills by which they earn their living at present.[17]

Shannon's vision of a bold transformative project — creating gender parity within the NFB — comes through loud and clear. As women gained experience and professional credibility, she reasoned, they could be hired as regular NFB employees in other units:

> The short-term goal is the presence of women in all areas of the organization; the long-range goal is the presence of women proportionate to the percentage of those Canadians we are "interpreting to other Canadians and the rest of the world" that are female.[18]

Yet she was fully aware of the Studio's tenuous position and the privilege that state-legitimacy had given her: "It was the only place in the world where women could make films not under the direct [influence] of men, not having to please men at every stage of the way. So in that way, it was a tremendous privilege, but it wasn't exactly handed to us."[19]

Despite a rather patchwork beginning, the scope of Shannon's radical vision was substantial:

> If the creation of the women's studio was intended as little more than a token gesture, Kathleen Shannon was determined to seize the opportunity, however grudgingly it had been offered. She … saw the studio faced with three major demands: to train women as filmmakers; to make the films needed by the studio's female audience; and to achieve a level of professionalism that would establish Studio D's producers' credibility as filmmakers.[20]

The sweeping promise of Shannon's vision, of course, was sharply undercut by reality. The "women's room" was opened with little fanfare and no new positions to accommodate it. The initiating members – Kathleen Shannon, Yuki Yoshida and Margaret Pettigrew — were all NFB employees reassigned from other units. Since there were almost no female filmmakers at the NFB, Shannon urged the management to hire women to fill the new positions that might open up in other units as a direct result of the new studio's formation. In the meantime, Studio D would have to rely heavily on freelance filmmakers.

However, when Film Board employees requested reassignment, they were met with incredulity and resistance from the NFB's organizational structure. Both Ginny Stikeman and Signe Johansson had to insist that NFB bureaucracy allow them to be formally associated with Studio D. As Stikeman recalls:

> By the time Studio D was formed, I was part of some of the meetings that went on among women inside and outside the Film Board who were pressuring for change and for having some programs for women. Kathleen had done her successful *Working Mothers* series that had been so well received and she was the senior filmmaker among us so she convened a lot of the meetings. To make a long story short, an astute manager finally said "yes" in the middle of the year, in August: "Here's some money and this sounds like a good idea. Let's have a place for women." I joined officially in 1975 and became the staff editor for Studio D. I remember telling the person in change, "I'm moving to Studio D." And she said, "Well, it's only on paper. You know, you can be moved back at any time." I said, "Excuse me. I'm *joining* Studio D." To me this was more than a paper transfer even though I continued to edit films in other areas because *Challenge for Change* was still ongoing in another form. So that's how I came to be one of the people in Studio D.[21]

As Johansson grew more aware of women's issues, through personal consciousness-raising, she decided to work full time in the women's studio:

> For a couple of years, I did both [worked as a unit administrator for *Challenge for Change* studios as well as for Studio D] — Kathleen decided that I should start producing because the way Studio D operated was that we were all included in the process and as time went on she became convinced that I should have a try at this. I started producing this abortion film while I was a full-time unit administrator. It was an enormous workload. There were battles all the time to move me *firmly* back into being

only a UA even though I was doing both jobs perfectly adequately. It was the male managers and the financial officer who were insistent that I not even spend a half day in another office, that I be in my office doing the administrative work. Kathleen just fought and fought and fought and, so, fifteen years ago I started producing full time.[22]

Similarly, Ginny Stikeman's work experience at the Film Board aroused her awareness of feminist issues and her desire to join the feminist "struggle." What Johansson and Stikeman shared was an express desire to work for feminism and to be considered full members of Studio D:

> A job came open in the *Challenge for Change* program in 1968 and I tried out for it and I got it. Dorothy Hénaut, a filmmaker who eventually worked in Studio D, also tried out for it and she went into another aspect, marketing. So both of us met up at the same time. I had been working at *Time Magazine* as a researcher, doing print research. I'd had *nothing* to do with film, although I'd come once as a researcher to review a film here at the Film Board so I'd been into the screening theatre at the NFB but what did I know about film? *Nothing.* In those days when I graduated from McGill, I don't think there was any place to study film in the country except maybe Ryerson in Toronto. I was into languages and art — no film. So I came in as a researcher — that was my skill — into the *Challenge for Change* program and I assisted the executive producer. I hired researchers matching them up with filmmakers. A number of really great films got made.[23]

Assisting the executive producer of Studio D, Stikeman went on location and obtained a greater understanding of the process involved in making documentary films. Like many women working in the film industry at that time, she had the opportunity of learning the necessary skills "on the job":

> Then I went on location once and I began to understand what making film was — documentary, that is. We made some very good films that still stand up, by the way, in the *Challenge for Change* tradition. Then, about 1970, the head of *Challenge for Change* asked me if I wanted to be an editor. So I was given a little film to edit. It was about ten minutes long, called *A Crowded Wilderness*. It featured Jean Chrétien as head of Indian and Northern Affairs and some environmentalists … I worked with a male director and a good producer, so I learned the rudiments of the job well.[24]

DOCUMENTING FEMINISM

Once established, Studio D was free to begin operating as a feminist studio, patterned predictably according to Shannon's vision. Its documentaries would make history using "female rather than male experience to focus and comment on social life,"[25] accomplishing what few other NFB studios had ever achieved. Here again, Shannon had a radical vision. She argued that Studio D must be prepared to represent women across the different regions in Canada, envisioning a series of in-house staff development workshops for women wanting to work in film that could be designed and mounted within the Job Creation Branch of the Department of Manpower. Once again, Shannon's ambitious plan fell on deaf ears within the larger institutional structure.

Shannon's insistence on "self-consciously feminist films" was only one of a series of "differences" that began to emerge, signalling a gradual separation of Studio D from others in the Film Board. Studio D films "came out of the same ethos as the consciousness-raising groups and had the same goals."[26] As Shannon noted: "The fact that I saw, and did things differently from my male colleagues didn't mean [there was] inferiority or inadequacy. It meant there was a legitimate difference."[27] Likewise, Shannon rejected the notion that a women's studio might suffer the fate of a women's ghetto: "Ghettos are where others put you, in their minds. Studio D is where we wanted to be, it wasn't a ghetto but a refuge. Besides, no one ever calls all-men situations a ghetto."[28]

Shannon, herself, stands as a classic example of the reluctant recognition of women's concerns within the ranks of the NFB. Hired away from Crawley Films in Ottawa, where she had worked since leaving high school, Shannon gained an exemplary record at the Film Board, training a number of men who were subsequently promoted through the ranks:

> I was already wanting to change all our lives with the *Working Mothers* films and the reading I was doing then suddenly illuminated why there had been these puzzles in the past. Like the puzzle where nine men I'd trained all made more money than I did. And when I asked the director of production about that, he said "You must have trained them *really* well." Around that time I realized that if I'd never left sound editing I'd be earning more than I was then because I'd had to take a cut to become a picture editor till I proved myself. I never got a reinstating raise until

> Studio D had been going a number of years. There was one point where I realized that I was almost at the bottom of all of the executive producers even though I had more experience, more tenure, more this, more that on every level.[29]

Personal experience, then, coupled with a certain growing political awareness, was responsible for Shannon's own consciousness-raising. In fact, Shannon credited her work on the *Challenge for Change* series as a vital initial catalyst. Over time, Shannon would learn that "working on the border" never meant a smooth ride:

> As a woman heading a feminist enterprise within a larger non-feminist bureaucracy, it was sometimes easy to feel hard done by and misunderstood — by management colleagues to whom the Studio's goals seemed downright traitorous; by women in the Studio who didn't get their way; by women outside the Studio who sometimes seemed bent on destroying it rather than building what they needed *in addition to* Studio D; and by critics who treated our films as though they were made for festivals rather than as tools for women changing the world.[30]

Her experiences as head of the women's studio strengthened Shannon's convictions that women had only a tenuous hold on any measure of institutional respect. The following anecdote of a private and public memory at odds with itself suggests that within the larger organizational structure, senior officials gave Studio D low priority status, although it was celebrated in official accounts of Film Board history. Shannon recalls seeking out Sydney Newman (then NFB commissioner) to determine his reasoning for agreeing to open a women's studio:

> The Film Board knew it had to acknowledge women's issues. The Royal Commission had focused a lot of attention but it wasn't the direct cause [of NFB action]. The Board had had to do some "Gee, we've got to get something [for women] together here." They assigned a guy to do a report on what women had done so a lot was made of a few people and a kind of ignoring of all the women who were frustrated — the women who'd not got ahead in the positions they were in. [My own report] was put into slightly more positive terms, as I remember, than I'd originally written it. I think I'd written it in a more sarcastic tone of voice. Later, I was in England and went to the guy who had been the [NFB] commissioner at the time, Sydney Newman, to ask him "What do you remember? Why did you say Studio D should start? Was it you? What happened from your perspective?" He told me that, frankly, he remembered nothing. That year he had been totally overwhelmed with French production … [he

> being] a unilingual anglophone, and he didn't remember a *thing* about Studio D.[31]

Later, on the public record, Newman spoke with pride of his role in encouraging the formation of Studio D;[32] his restored memory apparently eliminating previous "amnesia," raising a cool skepticism on Shannon's part:

> Two years later, the BBC made a film about the NFB on its fiftieth anniversary. There was Sydney in the film saying that there were a lot of talented women in the place and that, as I was the most articulate (a funny job qualification for filmmaking), he would put me in charge of starting this new studio for women — when two years earlier he'd remembered *nothing* about it.[33]

Admittedly, at the time Newman gave the go-ahead for Studio D, he was deeply immersed in "national" politics of a different nature. Not only was he struggling with the fall-out from the 1969 October Crisis, an event that had cleaved the Film Board along French-English national loyalties, Newman was also battling the Canadian Broadcasting Corporation over its adoption of commercial messages, which forced the Film Board to restrict length of films so that they fit into broadcast slots. Further, the federal government complained that the NFB needed a major overhaul since too many films were being produced over budget. Externally, Newman was resisting federal pressures to compete with private industry for sponsored-film companies. Internally, the NFB was beset by union problems over employment policies with respect to freelance filmmakers. However, in Shannon's view, Newman's "amnesia" was a barometer of his level of interest in women's issues.

Thus, while Studio D enjoyed a protected position *as* an NFB studio, it clearly lacked internal clout. The Studio was often hampered by wrangles over budget allocation and by the criticism of some colleagues in other studios who lamented that Studio D relinquished artistic considerations in favour of feminist arguments. Its films were viewed with disdain, judged unbalanced, doctrinaire or otherwise problematic.[34] As Shannon points out, "We were sometimes dismissed by our male colleagues as having a 'special interest,' instead of being 'objective' in the detached way they considered themselves to be."[35] Internal struggles taxed the creative resources of Studio D, eating up valuable time and creative energy, and contradictions around competing ideological notions of "nation" and the "imagined community" distanced it as much as its "collective" philosophy in conducting daily business and film production. Unbeknownst to those on the outside, Studio D's unswerving feminist direction, broadly deviating from the "official line," placed it at awkward variance from the NFB as a whole.

One of the chief points of divergence was Studio D's conceptualization of "women as an international or global nation." If the NFB understood its mandate to be presenting Canadians to one another and thus presenting Canada to the world, Studio D "imagined" its audience and the subjects of its documentaries to be women everywhere. While producing its films ostensibly for Canadian women, Studio D drew its material from international sources when the subject demanded. In envisioning women as a broad, international community, Studio D aligned itself with English-Canadian radical liberalism, espousing an implicit belief in "the ordinary political process, tolerance of ideological diversity, encouragement of dialogue, and a commitment to service."[36] Ironically, while Studio D viewed women generally as an intergenerational and international community, understanding and accommodating differences in its working relations with Canadian women was much easier to maintain "across class lines and between generations ... than across the lines of linguistic, racial, and ethnic differences."[37]

WOMEN AS "IMAGINED COMMUNITY"

Indeed, it might be argued that Studio D's conceiving of women as a nation, an all-encompassing global community unified by gender and a discourse of oppression and liberation, illustrates an example of Benedict Anderson's ubiquitous "imagined communities."[38] Communities, Anderson contends, are distinguished "not by their falsity/genuiness, but by the style in which they are imagined."[39] Studio D, I argue, understood women as an international nation configuring them as an imagined political entity, *imagined* although they might never know the majority of their numbers, as belonging to a common group. Thus, despite "the actual inequality and exploitation that may prevail in each, the nation [women] is always conceived as a deep, horizontal comradeship"[40] joined by personal and cultural gendered "oppressions." Studio D, as a result of this *imagining* of community, embraced filmmaking for women as a vocation that allowed it "to see and recognize the different parts and histories of [women], to construct those points of identification, those positionalities we call 'a cultural identity.'"[41] The scope of a number of its films, in fact, reflects this philosophical position.

Shannon drew on this concept to defend Studio D's position as a unique instrument of Canadian culture — women's culture — in response to the Applebaum-Hébert Commission in 1981:

> You speak of the Massey-Levesque Commission's broad thrust to improve the capacity of Canadians to be the creators of their own culture. We believe that women have the capacity, but we need the opportunities to be the Creators and transmitters of our own culture … In the area of film alone, our experience tells us that a broad range of films made by and for women … that speak the language of women, would go a long way to maintaining, and indeed creating, new lines of internal communication within [Canada] … The commonalities in the experience of women are far greater than the differences that divide people, whether those differences be regional, linguistic, national, racial. We know from our own experience the deeper level of trust and communication that is possible when a female crew interviews women … The seemingly unbridgeable divisions between an industrialized country like Canada and a developing country like Nicaragua, have not been unbridgeable when women communicate with each other.[42]

Many of Studio D's documentaries "imagine" women as a community, a global company united more or less unproblematically by oppressions related to the politics of gender. Films such as *Abortion: Stories from North and South* (1984), *Behind the Veil: Nuns* (1984), *Speaking of Nairobi* (1986) and *Goddess Remembered* (1989) document evidence from women around the world.[43] As NFB historian Gary Evans notes, these documentaries were organized around the credo of "integrative feminism" that emphasized "the 'otherness' of the voices [in the films] that spoke to the audience: 'we' were the women and 'they' were the men,"[44] a split that further reinforced the idea of women as a global nation joined by its struggles against patriarchal forces, however differently formulated.

Critics of Studio D, however, pointed out that Studio D's dependence on popular American feminists as voices of authority narrowed its otherwise laudable ideological engagement with important feminist issues. Brenda Longfellow, for one, identifies a (likely unintended) reductive argument at the heart of such films as *Behind the Veil: Nuns* (1984),

Speaking Our Peace (1985), *Goddess Remembered* (1989) and *The Burning Times* (1990):

> The repeated presence of Susan Griffin in a number of [Studio D] films allows a definition of this ideology [essentialism]. Griffin is an American author of such works as *Women and Nature: The Roaring Inside Her* and *Silence: Culture's Revenge Against Nature,* key texts of what is popularly called "eco-feminism" or "cultural feminism." This particular vision of history is grounded in the grand recurring narrative of an originating matriarchy, presided over by a variety of sister goddesses destroyed by institutional Christianity ... Although this grand narrative of the oppression of women is a rhetoric powerful for its force and its attraction, the reduction of the identity of "woman" to a phenomenon in which her form is perpetuated across history and in all cultures is a phenomenon of "essentialism" ... the problem with these totalizing narratives is that they fail to take account of other histories, those of non-Christian women, Muslim women, for instance.[45]

Indeed, Longfellow points to the narrowly drawn ideological boundaries within these films that contradict Studio D's conception of women as an international community. Differences are subsumed into a Eurocentric world view when these experts speak. The Studio's philosophy fell into line with a liberal feminist perspective, described by Diane Burgess as "unity in difference that exerted a reductive pressure on the shifting definitions of feminism,"[46] whether Studio D realized it or not.

If Studio D could be typified as liberal and feminist, it was also, to some degree, attracted to a particular formulation of popular radical feminism that had migrated to Canada with American feminists.[47] This feminism, in turn, was combined with Canadian versions already influenced by the writings of Simone de Beauvoir (France), Kate Millett (American), Shulamith Firestone (Canadian) and Germaine Greer (Australian).[48] Given its struggles for agency within the Fim Board, the attraction of this brand of feminism must have held undeniable appeal to the members of Studio D. As director Margaret Westcott pointed out, Montreal's cultural ideology was closer to New York's than it was to Toronto's, not to mention its geographic proximity, explaining the frequent exchanges between American feminists and the women in Studio D.[49] Radical feminists (if not united in approach) saw themselves as striking out on a profoundly new course. Envisioning a new world view with no corresponding new world on the horizon, these women could fashion "a fragment of a new world" by creating small feminist communities, a perspective Studio D certainly embraced in defining itself. The radical feminist analysis of women's conditions grounded in "a discourse of oppression and liberation"[50] dovetailed neatly with Studio D's own view, likely accounting for the appearance of many American feminists (Mary Daly, Starhawk, Jean Bolen and others) in a number of Studio D films, in particular *Goddess Remembered* (1989) and *The Burning Times* (1990). For Studio D, the sense of being oppressed by large institutions and the men who ran them (a frustration expressed by American radical feminists) influenced its own brand of radical liberalism (a particularly Canadian feminist position rooted in the belief "that change is possible and that state action is an acceptable way of achieving change").[51] As a consequence, its vision of women was one of a global "sisterhood ... oppressed *because of their sex.*"[52]

This hybrid ideological stance, as Roberta Hamilton suggests, reveals a progressive feminist politics that *would* reasonably "read" women as an international community:

> Feminists seek to demonstrate that what passes for knowledge is historically specific and enmeshed in discernible ways with existing relations of power ... [and] that men of the élites have had privileged access to creating knowledge — that is, to developing the descriptions and interpretations *about the world* that are deemed important for educated people to know.[53]

Studio D's opportunity was unique. As the only state-funded feminist film studio in the world, it was poised to consider the problems of its "sisters" *and* to address them globally. Studio D, then, elected to imagine itself as a spokeswoman both as a studio within the Film Board and as a member of the global woman's community seeking betterment for its members, although it must be noted that improvements were grounded in Studio D's own particular vision. Thus, Studio D's philosophy exhibited a form of feminist cultural nationalism embracing *all* women as nation.

Another point of divergence from other units in the NFB was Studio D's adoption of practices associated with North American second-wave feminism. A conviction that "the personal is political," an important rallying point for 1970s feminism, was foundational to much of Studio D's documentary work. This was coupled with the idea that feminist change could be effected through spectator consciousness-raising. In fact, spectators attending Studio D screenings in venues as diverse as church basements and mainstream cinemas were often invited to discuss a film's contents in "break-out groups" following the screening. Hitching "the personal is political" to "consciousness-raising" created an important feminist juncture that linked "the individual experiences of each woman's life to the wider political context, thus making sense of them."[54]

INTERNAL DYNAMICS

It may well have been Studio D's insistence on a unique approach in operating a studio that helped to further distance it from other studios at the Film Board. Although Shannon was the undisputed head of the Studio, its meetings and day-to-day operations followed a non-hierarchical structure and process, patterned after a feminist collective, setting Studio D apart from the traditional hierarchical organizational structures employed by other NFB studios. Meetings were conducted with all members in attendance and, at least in theory, all voices were given the opportunity to be heard.

Bonnie Sherr Klein, long-time filmmaker at Studio D, recalls this striking difference in approach. Her comments also hint at tensions with other units within the NFB:

> On the one hand, Kathleen was responsible to the hierarchical management ... On the other hand, the pull from feminism and her personal inclination was to be a collective, to operate on a consensus basis. Not just for some theoretical reason, but basically because we were all learning everything. In those days of feminism everything was new. We were making it up. We were creating feminist theory as we went to the extent, you know, where you decide not to accept the "givens" and then everything is up for grabs. So what I'm saying is that it was not as if she had the answer but she thought she should be democratic [and feminist]. It was a common search and struggle. It was wonderful. It was just a fantastic — intellectually and emotionally — stimulating time. It [also] created enormous pressure and difficulty for Kathleen personally.[55]

Studio D extended this collective approach to its research into women's interests through an intricate system of "audience research." This meant contacting academics teaching women's studies in universities, members of women's groups and women who were involved in the film industry to find out what subjects needed to be addressed. In developing subject matter, Studio D engaged in a collective process of consciousness-raising, eliciting information from outside groups invited in for consultative draft screenings. Ginny Stikeman remembers it as a "would-be collective":

> Everybody had different salaries, different job responsibilities. We weren't a true collective that you would meet outside your work hours. The thing that Kathleen would say is that we were a "forum." We would get together; we had meetings about film subjects and audiences; we had strategy meetings about how to get more women into the Film Board. We'd look at every film that came out each week and critique it in terms of who was behind the camera — noting every single craft where there were women as well as how women fared as subjects.[56]

Stikeman's memories reveal that this "would-be collective" approach became the studio's usual way of conducting its business:

> We pressured the Program Committee to have a balance in numbers of women ... We participated in official studies at the Film Board about the representation of women. We [the independent contractors and staff members] got together and discussed ideas. When an independent filmmaker was coming to town, she would be invited to a meeting at the Studio. We'd go to all the women's conferences to have our films shown; we participated in everything we could related to women and the media.[57]

Moreover, an early list of proposed film projects for Studio D was broadly inclusive, belying the criticism that the Studio was a preserve for self-interested middle-class white feminists. The subjects included, among others, immigrant women; maternity and abortion; women in the workplace; childhood identities in Canada; teenagers; women and religion; divorce; child abuse; and the autonomous lives of Indigenous women before the advent of European patriarchy. A list of film proposals from Studio D archives demonstrates a wide range of interests. *The Psychiatrists* intended to question the assumptions embedded in traditional psychotherapy with respect to women; *C.O.F.I.* chronicled the friendship developing between three women — a refugee from Allende's Chile, an anti-communist from East Europe and an Arab woman — attending a government-sponsored language class; and *Melodrama*, a "silent" movie, detailed the misogynous underside of the *Dowry Act* (where the right of the eldest legitimate son to succeed his father's freehold land prevailed over the wife's) entrenched in the legal system in the province of Alberta. The Studio even envisioned animation films: *The Diet* (plasticine figures); *The Dress* (line drawings and fabric); *The Object — Woman* (drawings and magazine cutouts); and *Murality Squad* (work of young artists painting murals in hospitals).

In 1976, after two years into its tenure, Shannon released a report detailing Studio D's accomplishments. Noting that although it had been "handicapped by lack of funds (Studio D had received a minuscule portion of the NFB allotment that year) and a small ratio of women to men on staff,"[58] the Studio had had a busy year. Studio D released *Great Grand Mother* and *Maud Lewis*, completed three films in the *Working Mothers* series under the umbrella of the *Challenge for Change* initiative (*The Spring and Fall of Nina Polanski*, *"... And They Lived Happily Ever After"* and *Our Dear Sisters*). These early documentaries began to map out the ideological territory that Studio D occupied for the balance of its existence. In addition, director Beverly Shaffer finished two films, *My Name Is Susan Yee* and *My Friends Call Me Tony.* These documentaries of children's lives were destined to become part of the NFB's multicultural program.

Studio D's report detailed two significant areas of endeavour for the women's studio: its strategies for identifying audience needs and for communicating with the women's film community in Canada:

> The needs of our audience are discovered by contacting them directly. Studio D was the first to hire its own distribution co-ordinator — who keeps in constant touch with women's groups across the country. Meetings with teachers of women's studies and representatives of various groups were arranged so we could determine what audiences need.[59]

One of the first things Studio D did when it was formed was to implement *INTERLOCK*,[60] an information newsletter designed to link together women interested or working in film. The fact that its call for short dramatic scripts had elicited responses from over 700 women demonstrates that its imagining of itself as a national centre point for women and film was justified.

It was at this early stage that problems began to emerge with respect to the Studio's relationship with the wider National Film Board. In part, it was Studio D's strong feminist position. Bonnie Sherr Klein remembers simply that Studio D conceived of its main commitment as one of bettering women's life conditions, a commitment bound to distance it from other NFB studios. As she points out: "We did feel our primary obligation and commitment was to women, not to the institution. We had, I think, and this may sound very arrogant, a sense of mission [to women] that most other filmmakers at the Film Board did not have."[61] She remembers that Shannon was so angry about "patriarchal power" that she alienated many, explaining why Studio D's determined stance was often misunderstood, unappreciated or regarded as downright hostile within the NFB. Indeed, a kind of self-fulfilling prophecy about women and oppression seemed to be at work, as Studio D was forced to mount a rear-guard action merely to survive, constantly plagued by budgetary uncertainities and battles for legitimacy, and at the same time deeply and vigorously involved with the women's movement engaged in the heady business of "trying to change the world."[62]

One of the early casualties of this uncertain funding was *INTERLOCK*. In its first edition early in 1975, Shannon had proudly announced its national scope but cautioned that because it was more than an in-house Film Board publication, it would need at least partial funding elsewhere. Mid-way through 1976, Shannon made the following announcement:

> This will be the last issue of *INTERLOCK* in this format. The original hope was that it would find its own funding and become an entity separate from Studio D. As this didn't happen, we're faced with the crunch: Should we be putting increasing amounts of money into a publication at the expense of films?[63]

INTERLOCK would continue in a more modest format and would be sent free of charge, Shannon promised, appealing to its readership to continue submitting material, although *INTERLOCK* would no longer be able to pay for contributions.

Tensions of this sort clearly taxed the energy of Studio D, placing individual pressure on members and associates alike. Studio D director Beverley Shaffer remembers how uncertainties and funding crises contributed to divisiveness within Studio D's "would-be collective":

> One thing you have to bear in mind is that during the whole era of Studio D it was a small studio with a small budget and there were a lot of filmmakers vying for that budget to make a film they really wanted to make. In any environment with a small amount of money, you find mean-spiritedness and competitiveness. It's only when there's more money and more opportunity for everyone that an individual doesn't feel threatened by the next person that there *can* be (any kind of) largesse. So that was the environment: a little bit of money and *I* want to make *my* film. *You* want

to make *your* film. *She* wants to make *her* film and the most feminist content wins.[64]

Pressures of this nature, of course, raise some interesting problems. Who is the most "feminist"? What are the *real* issues? This rather counter-productive atmosphere also forced members to divide their attentions between producing feminist documentaries and merely staying afloat. In an angry memo to NFB commissioner André Lamy in late 1975, Shannon points out that a significant source of potential funding had been lost through inattention:

> Though no one at the NFB has yet officially informed me, I learned casually some time ago that the NFB's request to Treasury Board for extra funds, for programs connected with International Women's Year, had been turned down. This is one of those times when it's not very satisfying to say "I told you so"; but the three NFB women who attended the inter-departmental information meeting about International Women's Year in February were all convinced that there was money in Ottawa for related activities, but it should be requested *separately from other projects*, and requested *as soon as possible.* The programs that made their application during the spring got the money they requested (i.e. Women's Program of Secretary of State). Those that waited until August, didn't ... So, here we have a new unit [Studio D] in English Production, with interest high across the country and less money than any other unit to operate (less even than the as-yet-non-operational Winnipeg office). Having created units to be managed by women, then not funding them, leaves the NFB open to justified charges of tokenism.[65]

Even after she had retired from Studio D, memories of underfunding still frustrated Shannon, a condition she credits with hampering the ability of the Studio to fulfill its rich potential in every aspect of its operation: "Funding was always a problem. It meant that we could *never* undertake a fraction of the good ideas that we had coming in. We could *never* employ more than a fraction of the people coming to us. We could *never* do the kind of outreach we wanted to do." In her view, Studio D always straddled a series of contradictions. In spite of being hobbled within, it enjoyed, nonetheless, enthusiastic support from many outside quarters:

> ... when there was a lot of pressure to amalgamate Studio D with another studio one of the *other* times it was threatened, the response from outside was so immediate, so powerful that they [the NFB] couldn't do it. But it took a lot of energy and a lot of vigilance and it would have been wonderful to have been able to put that energy into developing what was

> going on in the Studio rather than trying to do that *as well* as keeping it *existing*.[66]

Indeed, Shannon spent much of her time waging battles with the NFB to the detriment of her own work as a filmmaker. Filmmaker Gerry Rogers, contracted by Shannon in 1986 through the Federal Women's Film Programme, remembers that Shannon "fought and fought for the Studio and gave up her own filmmaking career,"[67] a sentiment echoed by filmmaker Terre Nash:

> She really fought. I think she wore herself right out. She fought the cuts and went to government hearings and fought and fought and fought and fought for the Studio. It was quite underappreciated in terms of what she did to keep it alive for other people. She, in a sense, gave up her own filmmaking to do it, to create a space for filmmaking for others.[68]

BUDGET TENSIONS

Budget uncertainties would plague Studio D throughout its existence. By 1976–1977 its budget had reached $600,000, and by 1977–1978, it inched up to $853,000. The funds, however, had to cover all of the Studio's resources, including staff, services and overhead. In reality, a "budget" was comprised of actual cash dollars and "in kind" services, obscuring fiduciary circumstances to all but insiders at the NFB. A more telling budgetary story emerges if we examine the phenomenon of "free money" within the bureaucratic structure of the NFB.

Resources were divided between two branches — English and French. The English Branch had its headquarters in Montreal with five regional sites, and was divided into ten studios. Its headquarters was home to five studios, including Studio D. Thus, Studio D was one of ten nationally and one of five locally. Free money was allocated to the branches, which distributed the wealth between headquarters and the regions. Headquarters distributed the money within its studios. Shannon argued that as one of ten national studios, Studio D ought to have received at least 10 per cent (a level Studio D achieved only once), and as a studio representing 51 per cent of the national population, its allocation ought to have been much higher, an opinion that clearly fell on deaf ears. Shannon's account of her approach demonstrates an admirable skill and invention. If ordered planning was impossible, Studio D became finely attuned to the possibilities of the moment:

> We started out really without any money but we started with a piece of structure. The way the Film Board worked was there was money allocated at the beginning of the year and some of it was allocated to, say, technical services. You know, you pay the staff, pay for the chemicals and all that kind of thing. And then the services were a kind of inside cost. It wasn't cash money, but it was a kind of money. So then we were in the sort of situation where we could afford to have a certain amount of film stock developed because that was a technical service *but* we might not have the money to buy the film stock. What we started out with was $10,000 of money and a chunk of (dollar figures don't have any meaning here) technical services. So we had monopoly money to buy services from the lab, from the sound department and pay our share of the overhead and all that kind of thing. So we started out with very little cash but we did have technical services allocated to us. We were able to finish the film *Great Grandmother* because that needed technical services …
>
> I was the only woman executive producer [at the NFB], which meant that I was the only woman at those management meetings. Well, because we were a studio and part of the structure we got part of the resources. But, we often got a very small part of the resources. The maximum I ever got was 10 per cent of the money of the English Production Branch … So for us to have one-tenth of the money, if we were all regional studios equivalent to each other, that would be fair but when men had had 100 per cent for fifty years, it didn't seem appropriate …[69]

Roadblocks like slim budgets and lukewarm support were synonymous with feminist endeavours more generally in the mind of Studio D director and producer Dorothy Todd Hénaut. While Shannon's plan was clearly visionary, her victory was "qualified" at best. Although the women's studio was, indeed, a unique venture, won through dogged persistence and eagerly anticipated in many quarters, the newly appointed head would receive only a shoestring budget and skeleton staff:

> They ended up giving her absolute peanuts. Anne Claire Poirier in French Production refused to set up a studio under those circumstances. She said there's just not enough money to do it. But Kathleen, frugal, said, "All right, we'll do a series called *Just-A-Minute* and we'll make a whole bunch of one-minute films because we have to develop a whole bunch of women filmmakers." She [Kathleen] developed a lot of new filmmakers … she'd help somebody here and somebody there. There was hardly any money and she was stuck in the basement [at the NFB]. It was *inglorious.*[70]

If Shannon's model enjoyed a certain success, her strategy of making short films on relatively low budgets may well have dictated the years of slim budget allotments that Studio D would receive. Beverly Shaffer remembers Shannon saying, "You know, it reminded me of the poor housewife who has a little bit of money and she has to make it go just so far."[71]

In reality, many of the women in Studio D associated their budget troubles to lack of respect for their projects, suggesting that Studio D was tolerated rather than celebrated. Bonnie Sherr Klein, remembering how staff at the inception of the women's studio had been cobbled together from existing Film Board employees, considered budget uncertainties as further evidence that Studio D was not taken seriously:

> Kathleen had to use the resources that were on hand and they were very thin. She selected a few women who were in clerical positions. Yuki had been in a lab, I think, and Margaret Pettigrew had been a clerk. Basically they were her producers. Basically, in the making of feminist films, Kathleen didn't have respect. There weren't other women producers ... so staff was reassigned from within the Film Board. Kathleen had worked for the Film Board in every position going ... So that was it for staff. Everyone else [was] freelance. Gloria Demers was a clerk in the Program Division. She was a secretary to the head of programming and happened to be a brilliant writer. She wrote great minutes. You could tell when you read the minutes what a brilliant writer she was. So Kathleen — I [think] — nurtured Gloria through sound editing. Then she became a sound editor ... And Margaret Wescott, I can't remember what she was doing — she may have worked as an assistant editor before coming to Studio D.[72]

Long-time Studio D producer Signe Johansson's memories of a sparse economic start-up echo Klein's. Her reminiscence attests to the reality that this problem would become endemic to Studio D, plaguing subsequent executive producers and hampering the flexibility, though not the success, of the women's film unit:

> [Kathleen] started with two other women and it [Studio D] evolved from an office space in the basement with half a unit administrator — that was me — to offices on the main floor and a full-time administrator with very, very little money. That was consistent throughout everybody's term as executive producer. As Kathleen said, with few resources we made significant films and got a lot done.

Despite long-standing budget uncertainties, feminist innovation led, nonetheless, to a series of successful initiatives within the Studio. Johansson adds:

> One year we had so little money, that we decided to make a whole series of short films rather than to use all of the money for a single film — remember, we wanted to allow as many women to have a voice as possible

> — so everyone agreed to program something that we called "the quilt," a patchwork of issues and ideas filmed by women. This meant that everyone could be working on something that could eventually be stitched together, metaphorically speaking.[73]

By adopting creative approaches, like those employed for the quilt and the one-minute films, Studio D earned a reputation for innovative tactics and a willingness to experiment. It became known as a place "where you could try things and get [them] launched."[74] Demonstrating her ability to work creatively with materials at hand, Shannon crafted inventive means to advance a feminist agenda by engaging in a variety of filmmaking ventures that created unprecedented opportunities for women to make their own films and to find their own "voices" through this medium. If means were scarce, she would stretch them to their fullest.

Over the years, planning was always ad hoc and the Studio was ready for anything and everything, small and large projects alike. Persistent funding problems, in addition to draining valuable staff time and energy, also frustrated the Studio's ability to establish a coherent programming schedule. Ginny Stikeman points out the futility of mounting long-range programming in a shifting, downsizing climate experienced by Rina Fraticelli, Shannon's successor in 1989. In one instance, Fraticelli, encouraged by the Film Board, developed an imaginative initiative only to discover that funding was already allocated to ongoing projects before her program could be implemented:

> Rina [Fraticelli] and Sylvia [Hamilton] developed the NIF (New Initiatives in Film) Program as a five-year program in 1989. It went into its pilot year in 1990. With the federal film programming we had been getting three-year funding so I know Rina, in looking around and thinking of this kind of thing as a program, felt confident to get multi-year funding. By the time 1990 hit, we couldn't get any more [funding] and all of a sudden funding shrank to one year only. All of a sudden there was a big change. We tried a lot of places, a lot of agencies, a lot of departments in the Film Board and we didn't get anything. Finally, funds for NIF came to Studio D from inside the Film Board, but the years of multiple funding were over.[75]

HIRING STAFF

Intransigent bureaucratic structures meant that the women's studio faced additional stumbling blocks. Hiring practices at the Film Board prevented Studio D from building a more diverse group of filmmakers. By the time Studio D devised a more inclusive method of producing documentaries by women filmmakers from across Canada, the Board had frozen its funding. Shannon remembers being cornered into an intractable position early on in negotiating the salary for a new Studio D hire:

> When the Film Board had to take on several women who'd been freelancing on staff, a couple of them were coming into Studio D so I was the person negotiating the salary they would come in at. The director of personnel and the director of production at the time were two extraordinary misogynists and they were bringing in a guy who'd gone to Stanford University at such and such a salary. They were also bringing in Bonnie Klein who had also gone to a prestigious university and who also had a lot of Film Board experience, having worked for *Challenge for Change.* They were suggesting a much lower salary for her. So I was saying "No, no, no — I think she should be making the same salary [as they were offering the Stanford man]." So then they compared her salary to all these women already on staff, [arguing] "How would it make them feel if Bonnie was brought in at a much higher salary?" They were comparing her to other women's salaries rather than to an equivalent salary [based on her education and experience]. The struggle I had with them was extraordinary.[76]

On another occasion, frustrated by constant political battles for funding and for autonomy within the NFB, even in the face of substantial public acclaim, Kathleen Shannon commissioned a cartoon that she subsequently hung in the lunchroom frequented by Studio D staff:

> The more positive attention we got from outside the Film Board, the more awards or the more publicity or the more whatever, the more *the squeeze* went on back there. I got someone to do a cartoon once that we put up on the wall. It was a bunch of guys sitting around having coffee and one of them saying, "It's just not fair, those girls are getting all the publicity. And they're winning too many prizes, too." And somebody else says, "We'll cut their budget."[77]

Sadly, the cartoon resonated with the reality of Studio life. During the 1980s, Studio D gained more recognition and certain critical success. In Dorothy Todd Hénaut's view, this public attention fuelled a sense of competition and a condescending attitude towards feminist filmmaking, isolating the women's studio even further: "The guys in the cafeteria were saying, 'It's no fair. They get all the good subjects.' The *same* subjects they would have never allowed us to do had they been making the decisions."[78]

The "them and us," "male versus female" attitude in evidence in so many Studio D documentaries may well have reflected, then, not only a philosophical belief that gender differences between men and women were the most compelling raison d'être of feminism but also the everyday experiences of the women's studio on its home turf. As Kathleen Shannon recalls:

> I think in a way the Film Board always wanted to get rid of Studio D … Any answer I surmise can easily be denied by a lot of the men around … but there was a great sense of threat — among men. Our films upset them. One told me years and years afterward that he had been really personally hurt by *Not a Love Story* because he was a man.[79]

Studio D, then, existed at the behest of the larger institution, ignored, threatened or celebrated depending on the circumstances of the day. In the process of cleaning out her papers, at the time of her retirement from the Film Board, Signe Johansson remembered how Studio D was always a weather vane to the political needs of the larger institution:

> There were several attempts to disband it, close it, merge it with another studio. In the process of cleaning out my office, I was looking through one of my files and, once again, we're making an argument — this is years ago — not to be combined with another studio, not to be closed down. The contradiction was that when the institution was in trouble, Studio D would always be trotted out and, you know, *displayed* — anything to keep the Film Board open …[80]

Ginny Stikeman, the executive producer who faced the NFB decision to cut its feminist studio, sums up the difficulties that the Studio laboured under throughout its twenty-two years:

> I'm angry and upset at the syndrome — the curse of the executive producer — *each* executive producer. We should have been able to do "stuff." We had the right ideas; we were ahead of our time but enabling it to happen was difficult with all of the changes on the outside. Gradually

> we were not supported, even though we were given lip service. Looking back, even though we had loyal support from some areas in the NFB, I can see it was not on the books ... If I were giving advice, I would say, "If you're going to do this in any institution, you've got to get the institution to give you autonomy. You've got to find a place where you can trust — a safe place." I don't think we ever had that with Studio D with all of its variations.[81]

From the beginning, Shannon's intention and ambition for Studio D was to propose change for women. Certainly, through its documentaries and in its daily operations, Studio D advocated equality of opportunity and equal rights. This testimony from Studio D filmmakers reveals a firm belief that their films would act as an advocate on the part of women, educating and lobbying through the positions advanced by the documentaries, allowing women to achieve new social and political powers, regardless of the Studio's own tenuous position.

INSIDER/OUTSIDER CRITICISMS

While Studio D was embattled within the NFB, to the outside eye, it enjoyed a highly advantageous position — assured funding, an official location, state-of-the-art equipment and an efficient and international distribution network always at hand. However, this "favoured" location, as well as Studio D's approach to the politics and aesthetics of the documentary form, left the Studio vulnerable to criticism. It was labelled as too mainstream, too pedestrian in terms of content and form and too remote. As cultural historian Chris Scherbarth points out:

> Women freelancers, who either honestly or cynically looked to Studio D as their best bet for equal opportunity at the Film Board, became discouraged and critical of the privilege held by the Studio's dozen permanent employees. Others knocked the Studio's apparent predilection for documentary, and equated its limited film inventory to limited imagination.[82]

Shannon, herself well aware of criticism levelled against the Studio, held steadfast in her project to "demonstrate" the social: "A lot of feminist theorists are very scornful of Studio D films [but] I think the really important thing was to provide a means for women's perspectives to be applied to major social issues."[83]

Notably, Studio D spearheaded a unique collaboration with government agencies to produce films about women. Actively encouraged by the

Minister of State for the Status of Women, Judy Erola, Studio D initiated discussions with women's bureaus and programs in federal government departments. The result was a proposal for the Federal Women's Film Program (FWFP) administered by Studio D. Studio D would supply filmmaking and training expertise while the content of the films would be based on department priorities identified by the Interdepartmental Committee (IC).[84] Program costs would be equally shared. Studio D's sweeping and unapologetic plan for social change was embedded in the program's principles:

> … to address the Status of Women issues perceived as priorities … in a coordinated manner; to provide information to women across the country, empowering them to better understand the society in which they live, and make the needed changes both in that society and in themselves; to provide feedback from the community of [Canadian] women to the federal program; to increase communication among both majority and minority groups of women, enabling them to collaborate to take action on issues that affect the quality of their lives and to contribute to public education on broad social issues.[85]

As early as 1983, in collaboration with a government education agency, it produced a series of films dealing with women in non-traditional occupations through the Federal Women's Film Program (FWFP). This collaboration was attractive in that much-needed funding was supplied by the government agency itself, thus protecting Studio D's own financial resources. Budgets also included positions for inexperienced women who were able to get on-the-job training in the art of filmmaking.

Further, Studio D generated a number of direct training programs. It sponsored apprenticeship programs, craft and writing workshops, a film production workshop and even held a contest for drama script writing.[86] Freelance filmmaker Terre Nash, in fact, attributes her initial contact with Studio D to one such script-writing contest in the early 1980s:

> I really didn't have a background in film. I'd done a little bit of animation and had done film workshops at the university for fun. There were no credit courses or degrees or anything in film but I was interested and because I had done some animation and the NFB was big on animation, somebody said "go there." I ran into someone in the hall and he said, "Oh, Kathleen Shannon is just about to open a [women's] studio. Go talk to her." So I went down to the basement and found her … She said, "We're having this competition for scripts so send yours in." I went home,

> thrilled, and [the work I] sent them was chosen. There were something like twenty women [selected] from across the country.[87]

Also, in collaboration with the International Youth Year Secretariat in 1986, Studio D offered in-house training and mentoring to twenty-six novice filmmakers, one-third of whom were women of colour and Indigenous women.[88]

Nonetheless in 1984–1985, Studio D was the only studio in the English Production Branch to receive less money than in the previous year. As Shannon points out in a memo dated February 20, 1986, "that means we were the only one of ten studios to have the dollar-amount of discretionary funds actually cut." Indeed, between the fiscal year 1983–1984 and 1985–1986, Studio D's share of discretionary funding from the English Language Branch had shrunk from 10 to 6 per cent. Shannon goes on to boldly express her suspicions about the NFB's 1986 five-year plan as she urged the Film Board to fund the Studio appropriately:

> In fact, there are increasingly visible and seemingly coordinated attempts to whittle away Studio D's base within the N.F.B. ... This means that the money taken away from Studio D has been supplemented with additional money and redistributed to the regions to be administered by men for "women's projects." Meanwhile, because of our cut, we in Studio D can no longer support the work of women in other regions of the country.[89]

Thus, despite its successes — Studio D received the Woman of the Year award in 1982 from Salon des femmes for *Not a Love Story* (1981); a number of its films won a series of national and international awards, including two Academy Awards for *I'll Find a Way* (1977) and *If You Love This Planet* (1982) — and being designated a "national treasure" by the Canadian Institute of Women's Culture, Studio D remained in embattled territory. By 1986 Shannon, who had just received an Honorary Doctor of Letters from Queen's University "for her contribution in founding the Studio and developing it into a place of creative excellence,"[90] was ready to resign. For one, she was drained from battling the sweeping recommendations of the 1982 Federal Culture Policy Review Committee that proposed the closure of the NFB. A second initiative that was blunted at the proposal stage was Shannon's request for a separate Women's Production/Distribution Branch; an initiative she believed was a reasonable solution to the overwhelming response from women across Canada wanting to become involved in filmmaking.

Painfully aware that Studio D was forced to refuse assistance to the many requests it received from women interested in making films across the country, Shannon conceived of a plan for the proposed new Women's Branch. Once established, it would relieve the impossible burden placed on an individual studio, precisely by making sufficient financial resources available. As Shannon points out in her plan:

> We have the responsibility of a branch — now everyone sends us the women who apply to them. We receive countless letters from women all over the continent asking [for] information. There is no other area of the NFB that has this information — not Distribution, not Public Relations. We receive requests to visit from women in Europe, Australia, from the US all the time. We receive requests from departments in Ottawa for information on Women and Film — there is no other centre. The load is far too great for a studio, particularly a studio restrained by branch realities, prevented from hiring necessary staff because "the Branch" has too high an overload. Studio D is already a focused program, ready to do far more, but crippled by the policies and priorities of the larger English Language Branch ...[91]

Shannon's proposal was extensive, requiring a five-year implementation period. The new branch would encompass eleven units: English- and French-language components, a regional production unit, continuing liaison with the Federal Women's Film Program, marketing, training, women's drama development (an environment for women "to tell their own stories in their own way"), a unit for research and policy development with respect to status of women at the NFB and a children's service. Her proposal was simply ignored.

Meanwhile, the NFB, attempting to combat the Applebaum-Hébert recommendation that the entire Film Board be dismantled, tabled its own five-year plan and appointed Joan Pennefather as vice-commissioner, director of planning and of corporate affairs to study its internal operations. On top of these duties, Pennefather was charged with launching the Employment Equity Programme to guarantee women equal access at all levels within the NFB.[92] Studio D, stung that it had not been consulted, lost no time calling a meeting with Pennefather and her assistants Francine Fournier and Bonnie Diamond. Clearly, the embattled Film Board felt it needed to mount an overall defence against the report and to establish itself as an equitable employer; Shannon was convinced that Studio D was best positioned to present an effective argument for protecting national film production for the women of Canada and, by doing so, could illustrate the need for a women's national film agency. Studio D, in Shannon's mind, would offer a model for the "new" mandate on women.

On January 15, 1986, Shannon introduced Pennefather to the twenty members of Studio D gathered in the NFB boardroom. Shannon noted that although the Studio had called repeatedly for a meeting with the film commissioner, the two parties had not met since February 1985. Further, she pointed out, no one had consulted Studio D regarding the NFB's "mandate for women,"[93] including Pennefather. When Bonnie Klein questioned how Studio D's exclusion was to be interpreted, she was advised that an independent study needed to be conducted *within* the Film Board since Studio D's success (falsely) exempted the remaining NFB studios from supporting the Federal Contractors' Programme. Minutes of the meeting record that Pennefather defended her decision to avoid consulting the women's studio since its ascendancy skewed results across the Film Board as a whole: "The success of Studio D is ironical in that it obscures the picture. Studio D has done wonderful things which make women think their situation is much better in the film industry than it is."[94]

When Pennefather admitted that a recently received operational plan called for the establishment of a training program for women at the NFB and mused that such a plan would usefully promote an affirmative action strategy, Klein's response mirrored the anger and disbelief experienced by the rest of the Studio:

> The greatest area of expertise on training women filmmakers is in Studio D. We've been doing that for years. And we have not been consulted [by the report]. Studio D is the best model and example of where women are in film and it's dying … its resources, morale and energy are being drained away. We are getting no support within the NFB.[95]

Substantially disheartened and fearing that dissolution was imminent, Studio D lost no time in reaching out to women's groups for help. The result was the establishment of a high-powered Advisory Group, numbering among its members such public figures as Doris Anderson, Marion Dewar, Chaviva Hosek, Michele Landsberg, Kay Macpherson and Denise Rochon. Agreeing that Studio D had been "slowly suffocating within the NFB, with neither resources nor autonomy to do the job which we are mandated to do," these high-powered women recommended that Studio D launch a public relations campaign in the press and in other media. They drew up a list of politicians and NFB board members and volunteered to contact them to lobby on behalf of the women's studio. The organizations represented by the Advisory Group would "use their networks and newsletters to organize the letter-writing campaign."[96]

Two months later, Sheila Finestone questioned NFB commissioner François Macerola at a meeting of the parliamentary Standing Committee on Culture and Communications, which was reviewing the financial situation at the NFB. Finestone asked Macerola, "Could you give me some idea of what is happening with Studio D and the dollars that are applied in the Studio D women's concerns?"[97] Tellingly, in his opening remarks, Macerola promised to present "what may perhaps be a new perspective on the Film Board and its activities." His direct response to Finestone's question reveals a certain lack of sympathy for the feminist philosophy of his women's studio:

> First of all, I think Studio D is very important. Nevertheless, it is presenting only one point of view. What I am planning to do is really to open the place to women at the NFB. I want to have more and more films produced by women for women. [What] I mean by that [is] that I will not give all the financial resources to Studio D.[98]

Justifying his budgetary request, Macerola went on to point out that the NFB was already spending money on films made by women across the country, films that were not produced by Studio D, naming a sum of $1 million for the Federal Women's Film Program and $350,000 for a women's training program:

> So the overall expenditure would be close to $4.5 million at the NFB on films made by women. But not only in Studio D: because I want some other point of view to be expressed by women at the NFB. I do not want women, at a certain point, to have to adhere to a certain point of view or a certain philosophy in order to have access to their own financial and technical resources.[99]

Taken aback by what she perceived as a direct attack, a furious Kathleen Shannon accused Macerola of implying "that the deficiency had been on the part of Studio D! And that by providing funds that circumvent Studio D, women will be better served!" Shannon lost no time in reminding the film commissioner of Studio D's battle for more funding for the precise purpose of funding women filmmakers outside of the NFB: "It would be naïve to assume that Studio D has *decided to deny* funding to all those women filmmakers we were always *unable to fund*, as long as our resources remained below 10% of the English language allocation."[100]

Shannon pressed Macerola on the charge that Studio D represented only one point of view, "If sincerely meant, this reveals a remarkable lack of familiarity with the women's movement in Canada and Studio D's place within it," at the same time skewering an omission in his testimony:

> I am surprised that you imply that other sections of the NFB deserve credit for the Federal Women's Film Program and the International Youth Year Training Project, and that both these programs represent "another point of view" from Studio D's. The FWFP has always been administered through Studio D, precisely because the collaborating departments want the Studio D perspective and experience reflected through the program. And, of course, there would not have been an IYY Training Project if a member of Studio D hadn't written the proposal that raised the money for it.[101]

Shannon concluded her remarks, regretting the "great distance [that] has come between our perceptions," hoping it could be attributed to "lack of communication."[102] Macerola's response was both pompous and evasive, "I hope that, as an institution, we will always have the wisdom, foresight and awareness to be able to pinpoint what ['the opposite position'] is and who holds it."[103]

Meanwhile, a swell of support for the embattled Studio began to rise from women across the country. Shannon's contribution to cultural life and feminism was recognized with her appointment as a Member of the Order of Canada. The National Action Committee on the Status of Women voted unanimously to support Studio D and its initiatives at its Annual General Meeting in June 1986. On July 10, the president of the National Council of Women sent a strongly worded letter to François Macerola (copying federal ministers Flora MacDonald, communications, and Barbara McDougall, Status of Women) informing him of their adoption of an emergency resolution urging the NFB to increase Studio D's budget to enable it to carry out its mandate. Citing the Studio's "strong and positive contribution to the advancement of the status of women … a contribution which must not be diminished but rather strengthened," president Margaret MacGee reminded the commissioner that Studio D was valued at home and abroad:

> Fourteen NCW Canada delegates recently attended the Triennial conference of the International Council of Women in London, England. The need for better communication and better information access to all areas of the media was discussed by the international delegates. We from Canada were aware of how fortunate we are in Canada to have Studio D. However, the National Council of Women of Canada recognizes the need to ensure that the positive work begun during the decade for women does not now slacken. There is a growing need for the services provided by Studio D both nationally and internationally.[104]

Members of the press entered the fray. The *Globe and Mail* published a feature on Studio D, detailing the three years of budgets cuts and the crippling financial crisis, repeating Shannon's baleful assessment: "The first year, I was told it [the budget cut] was a mistake but it wasn't fixed the next year, or the next. So I can't believe it's a mistake any more."[105] The article quoted Studio officials who predicted that no new productions would be started that year and that some work in progress might have to be frozen.

By October 1986 an exhausted and embittered Shannon resigned as executive producer, taking a year's sabbatical leave, believing that Studio D would benefit from her absence. But Barbara Janes, acting executive producer, continued to meet with Studio D's Advisory Group and predicted that Studio D's position would become desperate in the following year. By early November 1986, Ginny Stikeman succeeded Janes and on November 3, Peter Katadotis, director of English-language programming, announced that Rina Fraticelli would become the next executive producer of Studio D as of April 13, 1987.

The lobbying of various Advisory Group members had met with some success. In her *Globe and Mail* column of September 1986, Michele Landsberg celebrated Studio D as a "rare source of images from Canadian culture"[106] at the same time revealing Macerola's reluctance to give it adequate funding. Months earlier, Doris Anderson had made a similar attack:

> Studio D gets only a measly 2.2 per cent of the total film board budget of $69 million, but one of its films has sold more prints than any film ever made by the board. In terms of impact-per-cost-per-film, Studio D is a capitalist's dream and should have our Tory government in Ottawa in ecstasy.[107]

When the Caplan-Sauvageau Report[108] was issued in October, it lauded the effects of both Studio D and the NFB. That same month, Chaviva Hosek met with the film commissioner and managed to extract a promise of short-term funding of $200,000 from him,[109] although a draft of an action plan drawn up by Joan Pennefather in the previous year names this figure as money already designated to assist Studio D's 1987 program.[110] To the delight of the Studio, Flora MacDonald informed Anne Usher of the Advisory Group of "her admiration of and support for Studio D."[111] While it seemed that Studio D had won a reprieve of sorts, Dorothy Todd Hénaut's memo on Studio D's financial picture was fairly dim. The new executive producer would be faced with a daunting challenge:

> When our 84/85 share of the free money dropped to 6.2% we never recovered from this reduction in funding. Our momentum was broken. The result is that we had to carry a certain portion of each year's work into the following fiscal year. The cumulative effect this year was that more than $300,000's work from last year had to be paid for out of this year's budget. And the net result is that there was virtually no budget left for this year, and we were out of money by July. We have had to stop work on most productions. If we do not get the required new funds, we will start off the next year in the same position ...[112]

Barbara Janes summed up the situation as she prepared to hand over the reins: "Studio D is definitely in the worst position it's ever been in."[113]

A NEW DIRECTION

Known for her personal dynamism and organizational skills, Rina Fraticelli, an anglophone originally from Montreal, had come to the NFB from Toronto where she had established her estimable feminist credentials as an activist, publisher and theatre arts administrator. Although she had no formal background in film, she was author of "The Status of Women in Canadian Theatre" submitted to the Applebaum-Hébert Commission and was seasoned in feminist artistic production and feminist political issues. Further, Fraticelli's involvement with feminism through the respected periodical *Fireweed* and as creator of Fem Cab — an original theatre idea that showcased feminist artists, comedians and political figures — meant that she was very close to feminist debates and struggles "on the ground." Given her background, Fraticelli was aware of the challenges feminists faced from many quarters: charges of racism within the women's movement had erupted between feminist women of colour and white women at the Toronto IWD (International Women's Day) celebrations in 1986, forcing a festering problem into the open and threatening to split feminists into two camps. In retrospect, this moment is now recognized as an important rupture, revealing how white hegemony had (unwittingly) distorted or obliterated the experiences and oppressions of non-white women, particularly in intersecting issues of race, class and sex. This moment, although turbulent, was responsible for unleashing productive new directions in feminist theory and social practice.[114] Speaking publicly at the time of her appointment, Fraticelli pointed out that Studio D's work was more crucial than ever before as a unifying force given that the women's movement was under siege, referring to the fact that women were becoming scapegoats for economic woes by critics of equity, a time we recognize now as the beginning of a new wave of social conservatism in Canada. (Remember, this was the era of pay equity and employment equity, which had just been enshrined in the 1985 Charter of Rights and Freedoms.)

Likewise, the public debate over abortion rights made Studio D a target for conservative factions like R.E.A.L. Women.[115] Staunchly defending the right of women to legal safe abortions, Fraticelli warned, "The forces against choice are vigilant in their campaign to restrict the right of women to choose in the major decision of their lives."[116] Under Fraticelli's watch, Studio D would be attacked repeatedly by R.E.A.L. Women, who were also seeking federal funding and who viewed such films as *Behind the Veil* and *Abortion: Stories from North and South* (1984) as attacks on religion and morality. Why, they asked, should Studio D and other feminists (NAC) be "milking the taxpayer to promote their views"? Once again, as we shall see, Studio D found itself embroiled in these very feminist confrontations. However, budgetary concerns remained uppermost for Studio D. As newspaper columnist Ina Warren pointed out, Fraticelli would have to find a solution if Studio D were to move ahead:

> Until she can lobby the federal government for more money, Fraticelli will have to work miracles on a paltry budget. Studio D has been repeatedly cut in the last four years, so that this year's budget of about $2 million is already largely earmarked for finishing last year's projects.[117]

Aware that she had stepped into a shifting climate in the Film Board, Fraticelli prepared a press release in which she invited Studio members to join her in sharing the "sprawling" new mandate (exchanging resources and ideas with a variety of women: Josée Beaudet and the filmmakers of her French women's unit, women creating films through the regional offices, the members of the newly formed women's media network and Suzanne Chevigny's employment equity program), which would be achievable *if* Studio D was given the dollar funds to carry out its work. In defending Studio D's approach to feminist filmmaking, Fraticelli pointed out its relevancy to the classic traditions of the NFB:

> As a newcomer, I sometimes see Studio D as Grierson's perfect, albeit unexpected and sometimes troublesome, heir; not the heir he might ever [have] imagined, certainly, but nonetheless the legitimate offspring of his philosophy of making films of frank advocacy, films which grapple with and reveal the implications and contradictions hidden within the vital issues of our day, films which shed a new light on these events and suggest committed or challenging new interpretations.[118]

While it certainly could be argued that Fraticelli extended Grierson's legacy through her film initiatives, the years of reduced government spending and Macerola's "belt-tightening regime"[119] eventually crippled operations inside the Studio.

In 1989, responding to internal pressure to make Studio D more accountable and to broaden its film scope to new voices, Fraticelli announced a reorganization plan. As of April 1, the Studio's six permanent filmmakers would be absorbed into other Film Board units. Studio D would continue to be known as a "women's unit" but its $795,000 production budget would now be destined for freelancers. A primary goal of the reorganization Fraticelli said was to increase the participation of Native women, new Canadians, women with disabilities and other minorities in the Studio: "We have a tradition of working with freelancers, but as budgets have got tighter and tighter in the last few years, there's been a conflict between fully employing staff film-makers and the need to extend our accessibility in the women's community."[120] Expressing her intent in an NFB newsletter, Fraticelli noted that instead of working to maintain and protect the privilege of a few, Studio D had attempted and would continue to attempt to expand the rights of all.[121] Kathleen Shannon, who had returned from her sabbatical, weighed in on discussions in an unpublished memo, to which she added a handwritten gloss, "Hope this is useful – K.":

> … moving in the direction of equity in the headquarters studio, recalls the initial vision of Studio D … to provide a base of core staff — producers and administrators — to whom a large number of women (both freelancers and NFB staff from other studios) could bring their individual film projects … Change can be alarming, but experience has shown that it is often also healthy. It is understandable that some of the directors may feel some qualms about moving into a situation of being outnumbered, after working in an all-woman environment. But it is important that the opportunities that they have had over many years be shared with a larger number of women.[122]

While some members of the feminist film community considered shifting the Studio from a staff-based to a freelance-based unit a refreshing innovation, others (not surprisingly, a number of Studio D's in-house directors) regarded the move as foolhardy and wholly hostile. "We were turfed out," was the way one of them described the move, speaking anonymously, contradicting Fraticelli's claim that the decision to dispense with staff positions was unanimous.

Indeed, the shift constituted a major turning point for Studio D, gutting the "collective" and altering its identity radically, thus setting the stage for its dissolution six years later. Certainly, Fraticelli's manoeuvre represented an effective and sensitive response to the growing number of burgeoning feminist filmmakers across Canada, an acknowledgement that new stories deserved to be heard in an era of shrinking funding. Nonetheless, the plan's implementation would be "one of the first steps towards the demise of Studio D."[123] I am reminded here of Shannon's warning about the consequences for feminists proposing organizational change generally: "I learned that if you open doors, you can be held responsible for everyone who hasn't passed through those doors as well as those who have."[124]

Although Fraticelli's move effectively dissolved the Studio's community, she deserves credit for two major initiatives. First, she reactivated the Federal Women's Film Program, a collaborative move that would save the Studio roughly half the cost of producing films; secondly, she organized and launched the New Initiatives in Film (NIF), which was designed to address "the under-representation of Women of Colour and Native Women in Canadian film."[125] This initiative outlined a program that would provide training for these women and allow them to tell their own stories in their own voices, creating an ideological link between NIF and Studio's

D insistence on the promise of social change through empowerment of specific communities. To conceptualize its development, Fraticelli hired Sylvia Hamilton, a Black filmmaker and advisor on race relations to the Secretary of State in Nova Scotia.[126] Further, Fraticelli brought to the attention of Studio D a group of Toronto-based independent feminist filmmakers, who included Kay Armatage, Patricia Gruben, Brenda Longfellow and Midi Onodera. This group rejected "the didacticism of earlier feminist film forms"[127] and were experimenting with form as a way to question the politics of representation. Taking inspiration from Shannon's *Just-A-Minute* strategy, Fraticelli launched *Five Feminist Minutes* to celebrate Studio D's fifteenth anniversary in 1989, "an innovative project designed to increase the participation of independent filmmakers, across Canada and within Studio D."[128] When the film was released in 1990, it featured fifteen films created from "interviews" lasting no more than five minutes each. One of these is the well-known feminist rap-style performance piece "We're Talking Vulva" by Shawna Dempsey and Lorri Millan. But by March 1990, a disenchanted Fraticelli had left Studio D, replaced on April 2 by Ginny Stikeman, who would remain executive producer until the Studio's closure in 1996.

As well as providing training for diverse communities through its program, NIF furthered feminist filmmaking by developing a computerized list of women in film across Canada, conducting intensive summer workshops on specific areas of filmmaking and running an internship program offering annual one-year internships at the NFB. Documentary production within Studio D during this period (1991–1996) began to reflect the concerns of feminists questioning the politics of race, sexuality and identity. Increasingly, filmmakers associated with Studio D, still faithful to its original mission to "produce women-centred, issue-oriented work," came from increasingly diverse racial and cultural backgrounds.

CHAPTER 4

RAISING PUBLIC CONSCIOUSNESS: DOCUMENTING A SOCIAL MOVEMENT

Consciousness-raising? It definitely conjured up all those old media portrayals of what seemed to be very angry women burning bras, or perhaps some amateur approach to encounter therapy.

— ANNE CROCKER, *EQUAL TIMES* (OCTOBER 1975)

I remember when we first articulated that we were feminists. I was seventeen and you were eighteen years old … I asked you [Mutriba Din] if you were a feminist and you very matter of factly said, "Yes, of course I am." I mumbled and fumbled thinking, "Well – if you are, so am I."

— RAVIDA DIN, "SISTERS IN THE MOVEMENT," *FIREWEED* (SPRING 1990)

On consciousness-raising: Quite simply, we intend … to tell a young audience what we know … We will be funny, poignant, enraged, hilarious, tragic, tender, farcical, betrayed, compassionate …

— STUDIO D FILM PROPOSAL FOR "THE QUILT PROJECT" (1976)

THE DOCUMENTARIES PRODUCED BY STUDIO D FILMMAKERS CONSTITUTE a distinct and important body of material history that traces the development of major issues and debates which emerged in feminist thinking as women sought to understand how they were being oppressed through gender categories and various social arrangements. It is important to signal that this documentary production occupied a singular position of authority derived from Studio D's identity as a studio within the National Film Board for over two decades. Hence, Studio D, a voice of feminism *and* an instrument of national communication, played a dynamic and variable role in both adopting and contributing to feminist theorizing as a component of the Canadian women's movement. Although Studio D did not enjoy an inordinate degree of power within its institutional setting, it did command a certain power to make authoritative (if sometimes contested) pronouncements on feminist concerns as the maker of feminist documentaries. Michel Foucault has pointed out that the production and circulation of ideas can have as their consequence certain results in the realm of power, although results are never uniform or consistent:

> In a given society there is no general type of equilibrium between finalized activities, systems of communication, and power relations. Rather, there are diverse forms, diverse places, diverse circumstances or occasions in which these interrelationships establish themselves according to a specific model. But there are also "blocks" in which the adjustment of abilities, the resources of communication, and power relations constitute regulated and concerted systems.[1]

Studio D was such a "block," capable of putting into operation its technical capacities, the game of communication (through its development and dissemination of documentaries via the NFB distribution system, a highly efficacious national and international network that continues to circulate Studio D films) in a thematics of power. Power of this nature is, then, not "fundamental" but rather a relationship or series of relationships that can be grasped "in the diversity of their logical sequence, their abilities, and their interrelationships."[2]

Jill Dolan identifies the ideological stance of a feminist artist as beginning "with a keen awareness of exclusion from male cultural, social, sexual, political, and intellectual discourse."[3] This defines the stance assumed by Studio D. Its documentary film practice embodied the feminist slogan "the personal is political" and was organized around the process of change instigated through consciousness-raising. By embracing feminist cultural production as a means to encourage the development of a feminist awareness, "enabling women to recognize and analyse the multiple sites of oppression that affect their lives as its chief undertaking,"[4] Studio D made a unique and valuable contribution to the women's movement in Canada, while illustrating some of the problems of engaging in a politics of change. What we need to understand is the work of Studio D in moments of tension — tension within the women's movement and within feminist film theory, with particular emphasis on feminist documentary film which contributed to that politics of change.

Pointing to the complexity of this territory, theorist Teresa de Lauretis notes: "women's cinema refers to and includes not just a set of films or practices of cinema, but also a number of film-critical discourses and broadly-cast networks of cinema-related practices that are directly connected with the history of feminism and the development of a feminist socio-political and aesthetic consciousness."[5] One of the issues for feminism as a powerful social movement was to develop an understanding of cinema, generally as "a cultural practice representing myths about women and femininity, as well as about men and masculinity."[6] Early forays into film criticism addressed issues of representation and spectatorship, with criticism levelled mostly at Hollywood.[7] Critics called attention to the power of cinema as a form of popular culture presenting "fixed and endlessly repeated images of women"[8] as problematic distortions that offered stereotypes as *normal* and *natural* depictions.

Certainly, Studio D intended to challenge and counteract the Hollywood constructions of women through consciousness-raising documentaries that explored the lives of everyday women. Indeed, cultural critic Kass Banning notes that the documentary form offered itself as a vital feminist instrument for change:

> Feminists assimilated the strategies of earlier social movements, made them their own, and took up the documentary form as a tool for consciousness raising: to elaborate, in filmic terms, the modalities of female experience — in all its corporeal, psychic and political/social registers.[9]

Filmmaker Terre Nash was struck by Kathleen Shannon's sense of vision in producing feminist documentaries that explored women in social settings, focusing on their needs and making their voices central to the story at a time when the public perception of women as legitimate "subjects" was just beginning to be politicized:

> Kathleen had her own particular commitment to feminism. There wasn't much done on women at all but the stuff that had been done before at the Film Board had been made by men. As Kathleen mentions in Gerry's film [*Kathleen Shannon: On Film, Feminism & Other Dreams*] we were talked about as "they" all the time — we were "good mothers" or the "figure" at

> the window, looking out, waiting ... Our experiences weren't generally included or respected or understood.[10]

The contributions of Studio D and other feminist documentary filmmakers were instrumental in airing and changing attitudes about women. Indeed, Tania Modleski remembers this as a heady time for feminists in universities where such documentaries served as dynamic teaching vehicles for new "women's studies" courses then being devised:

> For our part we were delighted to play the role of barbarians at the gates. In my courses on women in literature, I taught novels, supplemented with films, explicitly as consciousness-raising devices, and indeed, saw no difference at the time between teaching and consciousness-raising. At times I would go into the community and take films with titles like *Growing Up Female* to various women's groups so we could compare our lives with those depicted on the screen, and so I could (woman of the world as I was at twenty-three) educate them about their status as an oppressed group.[11]

The questions underlying my discussion in this chapter, then, are as follows: What models of feminism did Studio D project/celebrate through its films? What did the ideological position(s) of the films suggest in terms of representation of women's lives in Canada? How does this question of representation differ in other feminist documentary visions produced by independent feminist filmmakers?

CONSCIOUSNESS-RAISING AND REALIST DOCUMENTARIES

When Studio D came into being, the feminist documentary film as a genre was just emerging. It is during this time that feminists engaged in revising, revisioning and rewriting their stories as a way to give "voice" to their stories and thus find and assert their identities. The revision of aesthetic forms — women's literature, for instance — yields ample evidence of this undertaking. The structure of the traditional documentary — "the creative treatment of actuality"[12] — lent itself, equally, to a feminist revision, revealing as a consequence, a series of previously hidden truths about women's lives. The male narrative voice (the authoritative knowledge producer) was replaced with a woman's voice. Lightweight cameras available at a relatively low cost allowed women to shoot footage in locations of their choosing. Using *cinema verité* techniques, featuring female "talking heads" and an interview format intercut with documentary footage supporting and/or illustrating the points women were raising, allowed women to speak for themselves and to narrate their own stories, which exemplified the feminist slogan "the personal is political."

In the 1970s, feminist film theory and criticism was in its early years, framed within the context of the women's movement. In 1972, the short-lived American journal *Women and Film* (Canada had no such critical counterpart) published an editorial charging that women were oppressed within the film industry in at least three areas. It pointed out that women seeking work in the film industry were most likely to be hired to junior positions as receptionists, secretaries or prop girls. Film images, the editorial complained, projected stereotypic images. Further, film theory revolved predominantly around male projects. If burgeoning feminist film criticism grew from "a pressing political impulse,"[13] the same can be said of the documentary practice of Studio D. Feminist filmmakers, certainly those in Studio D, were drawn to the traditional "realist" documentary structure "because they saw making these films as an urgent public act."[14] Indeed, they were mandated specifically to create them.

Feminism's engagement with film began as "an urgent political act."[15] In these early days, the women's movement was enmeshed in a politics of representation, leading to the making of "an unprecedented deluge of feminist films, the majority of which were documentaries."[16] Such feminists as Simone de Beauvoir argued that myths embedded in cultural production shaped the ways men and women interpreted and experienced their material existences, maintaining that "though representation ... is the work of men: they describe it from their own point of view, which they confuse with absolute truth, women, too, must inevitably see themselves through these representations."[17] Building on de Beauvoir's critique, Shulamith Firestone complained that culture was so saturated with male bias that women almost never had a chance to see themselves culturally through their own eyes,[18] a view corroborated by Julia Lesage who noted that the "iconography of everyday women [was] completely absent from mainstream media."[19]

Critics like Mary Ann Doane, Patricia Mellencamp and Linda Williams analyzed how stereotypic representations of women in Hollywood cinema projected "real social attitudes, opinions, cultural values and patriarchal myths"[20] that reduced women to three main categories: the glamour goddess, the *femme fatale* and the self-sacrificing mother. Arguing that movies are "one of the clearest and most accessible of looking glasses into the past, being both cultural artefacts and mirrors,"[21] Molly Haskell fingered entertainment cinema for its ingenuity in holding up (frustratingly) irresistible *and* reductive models for women to be judged by or to emulate. While there is little evidence to indicate that Shannon had consulted these works, caught in the bureaucratic flurry of organizing a women's film studio or subsequent budgetary struggles, there is no doubt that she, too, had these repressive stereotypes in her sights. As Julia Lesage notes, significant and sometimes powerful revisions resulted when feminists turned their imaginations to this task:

> Many of the first feminist documentaries used a simple format to present to audiences (presumably composed primarily of women) a picture of the ordinary details of women's lives, their thoughts — told directly by the protagonists to the camera — and their frustrated but sometimes successful attempts to enter and deal with the public world of work and power.[22]

Shannon would foreground this technique, making it one of Studio D's defining marks.

Feminist film theorists like Eileen McGarry began to express doubts about the transparency of direct cinema or *cinema verité* — her classic essay "Documentary, Realism and Women's Cinema" remains as "one of the few feminist works of that period to actually confront and engage with the tradition of documentary studies."[23] Nonetheless, Studio D aligned itself resolutely with "realist cinema" and activist feminism throughout its existence, holding a certain skepticism for "theoretical feminism." Indeed, a brochure promoting one of the last films that Studio D would produce outlines an approach that is still formulated in the language of the early second-wave struggle:

> Perhaps more than any other studio at the National Film Board, Studio D was conceived with a clear and simple mandate: to make films by, for, and about women. These films were timely and brave, popular and critically acclaimed, exploding with subjects and issues that were at the vanguard of social change ... born out of the wider social and feminist movements of the early '70s ... [I]ts legacy survives in its films and in the hundreds of women filmmakers across the country who struggle on with the same spirit of those who bravely led the way.[24]

Given that women had been excluded from filmmaking, the filmmakers of Studio D were now placed in a unique position of privilege.

Certainly, as Kay Armatage contends, while these women still needed "ingenuity, determination, charisma, creativity, and stamina to overcome the barriers thrown in their way,"[25] their institutional location created an unprecedented advantage:

> Despite the contradictions inherent in the working conditions for women at the NFB, its unique situation as the principal source of pre-television films in much of the country gave those films and filmmakers an opportunity to make a profound mark on the culture ... To a certain extent, such women filmmakers were able to generate their own projects and they enjoyed the luxury of production budgets that were consistently higher than any independent women in the private sector could ever dream of.[26]

During the 1970s, women entered documentary filmmaking from two directions: "The first group were women already working within the film industry, as independents, as artists, or as editors, who were stimulated by the greater opportunities now being offered and who chose to explore their own [feminist] consciousness on film." The second group came from within the women's movement and viewed film as "a tool for raising consciousness and for implementing social change."[27] These were women who had themselves engaged in various forms of consciousness-raising and were committed to illuminating subjects of importance to women that male filmmakers had so far ignored.

In terms of documentary history, Kathleen Shannon, of course, fit into the first category, and Studio D, having drawn on the insight and vision of Canadian feminists, would draw from both categories. In fact, Shannon had no formal training in filmmaking. She began her career in the film industry in 1952, with a summer job as a background music cataloguer at Crawley Films in Ottawa. Rather than finishing high school, Shannon was determined to seek practical training, learning all she could about sound and music editing. Four years later, at age twenty-one, she was hired by the NFB.[28] Later, she would become a pronounced champion of the social realist documentary as a powerful feminist tool. Through Shannon's influence, the ability of Studio D films to instigate consciousness-raising among its audience members remained a consistent aim throughout its twenty-two-year history, culminating in what Shannon hoped would be improved attitudes and practices towards women. Within the institutional context of the NFB, Shannon the zealous activist was perfectly positioned to promote her view as a feminist visionary:

> My intention back when I was working on the *Working Mother* films was to make a difference ... I had juggled for years feeling guilty, inadequate and feeling that I was probably going to fail totally tomorrow and I wanted to let other women know that it was *not* their own inadequacy, that it was impossible circumstances that made [them] feel like that. So, in a way, it was letting people [women] see themselves on screen and seeing that "it wasn't all my fault."[29]

Illustrating what Jill Vickers calls the "intergenerational nature of Canadian feminism,"[30] Shannon credited her own encounter and subsequent embracing of a feminist consciousness to an earlier generation of feminist thought. She recalled picking up a book on "women" in a train station for what she thought would be some light "travel" reading. Shannon noted that while the book's language seemed rather antiquated, its discussions of women's issues were entirely contemporary. Checking the book's date of publication, she realized with a certain shock that she had been reading a reprint of feminist struggles written a century earlier. She describes this as the dawning of her "feminist conversion":

> What was a [further] revelation to me was a collection called *Voices for Women's Liberation.* I bought it just to be broad minded because I had the attitude, you know, it's hard enough, everything's hard enough, without women making fools of themselves burning brassieres. By the time I had finished that book, *long before* I had finished it, my life had changed. Revelation upon revelation — and then for a while I just read, read, read, read. I don't even remember all that I read.[31]

Dorothy Todd Hénaut, both a director and producer in Studio D and likewise involved in the *Challenge for Change* series, remembers how Shannon's determination to film the circumstances of women's lives at the time was inspired by their stories which further galvanized her desire to create a site where films about and for women could be made. Evidence suggests that Shannon was, herself, committed to the notion of "many voices, many lives, many stories," a tradition that would mark Studio D's documentary production:

> Kathleen, who was an editor at the time, directed a series called *Working Mothers.* At the time it was supposed to be one film about working mothers and she interviewed some promising subjects. She felt that it would be better to make a series of short films — eight-minute films, ten-minute films and twelve-minutes films that were portraits of single, different

> kinds of working mothers. *Challenge for Change* had a theory that it was just as important to use the films to talk to people, in other words, to show them [the films] as it was to make them and put a lot of money into the distribution. So Kathleen took the films across the country and she did workshops in every major place from one end of Canada to the other ... That was in 1973. The women were so hungry for images, truthful images of themselves, images done from a woman's point of view and not a man looking to see how elegant she was or how sexy she was ... it was women being themselves and talking to each other.[32]

Gender consciousness as well as considerations of class and race, despite criticisms to the contary, were encouraged through Studio D's feminist documentaries. In this regard, Shannon's *Working Mothers* series made a substantial contribution, reflecting a range of theoretical and political approaches with respect to the issues they documented. *Working Mothers,* originating in the *Challenge for Change* series, placed women's lives and their governing conditions under scrutiny. Working from a model established by Colin Low[33] in the late 1960s, Shannon directed eleven documentaries that ranged from six to fifteen minutes in length. They explored the new socio-economic order that still depended on women in the home to ensure reproduction but increasingly required their massive and prolonged employment in the world of waged labour.

This collection of short documentaries was underscored by the notion that a "whole new area of social relationships needed in depth exploration from a female perspective."[34] Later skeptics of Studio D's focus on women as a (global) nation and its statist orientation that seemed to imply a uniform disregard for differences of race or class, might have been surprised that Len Chatwin, executive producer for *Challenge for Change*, had chosen Shannon precisely for her political insights with respect to the interlocking issues of race and class evident in her later work on the controversial and award-winning NFB documentary *You Are on Indian Land* (1969). According to Ginny Stikeman, this served as a defining moment, one that would be carried over to Studio D:

> [Kathleen] also worked before becoming a director as an editor on *You Are on Indian Land*, a fabulous film. She and I both worked outside the Film Board as well as in the Film Board with some of the Aboriginal film training crew people and, with struggles in newspapers around Aboriginal issues. Thanks to this experience a penny dropped for us in terms of the political imbalance of different cultures.[35]

As editor for *You Are on Indian Land* (1969), Shannon had cut the material — which captured a potentially inflammatory scuffle between the Mohawks of the St. Regis reserve and an overly zealous newly appointed Canada Customs officer — from six hours down to two. Accompanying an NFB distribution officer back to the reserve where the film was screened for the protestors, Shannon witnessed how the resolve and confidence of the Mohawks was galvanized as they witnessed themselves confronting authorities with conviction and reason on film.[36] This sharing of rough cuts with film subjects would become Shannon's signature model for developing film material in Studio D documentaries.

Shannon had also distinguished herself for her philosophical stance as a filmmaker and team member of *Challenge for Change* as one who "thought the idea of giving oneself over to the community and forgetting one's ego was critical"[37] if the message of the films was to be received successfully by the viewing public. In fact, Shannon was so intent on the potential of consciousness-raising facilitated by short films screened for small groups depicting material conditions shaping women's lives that she experienced scant disappointment when her films were not aired on television as was the feminist series *En tant que femmes.*[38] Instead, the Film Board in its distribution strategy targeted teachers in universities and community colleges and "hard-to-reach" people such as those "mothers working either exclusively outside of their homes or those working exclusively at home." Creating an innovative approach to distribution, Shannon made sure that a package of supportive material accompanied each film so that viewers could "take off on their own," discussing the film informally or using the films in a more structured workshop-type setting.[39]

Shannon, who made no secret of her antipathy for the more theoretical strands of feminist film criticism beginning to emerge, was clearly bent on creating a transformative cultural statement that centred on women:

> We're hoping that people can move beyond seeing a particular film and wanting to know "what's happening to her now," to seeing how that particular person, captured in the film at a particular time and in a particular place, provides something to learn from, a place to start identifying one's problems as the first step towards a solution.[40]

Espousing this more personal approach, Shannon preferred that films be shown to small groups where interactive discussions could take place to stimulate feminist or political awareness for both audience members and, when they were included, with the team of filmmakers (a signature of the Studio D style I take up more fully shortly). In fact, NFB commissioner Sidney Newman later credited this innovation for according the NFB new credibility as it struggled to redefine itself in the years following his tenure.[41]

By using her own life experience as a measure, Shannon demonstrated her implicit commitment to the idea that life experience imparts valuable self-knowledge. All ten of the short films in the *Working Mothers* series are characteristic of the 1970s feminist documentary. They are organized, as Julia Lesage says of the traditional realist documentary film, along the lines of "biography, simplicity, trust between woman filmmaker and woman subject, a linear narrative structure, [and] little self-consciousness about the flexibility of the cinematic medium."[42] In viewing the *Working Mothers* series as a whole recently, I was struck by their inclusivity and relevance; a relevance described by the NFB's online description of the series as "offering audiences a point from which to assess the gains made by women over the last two decades, and emphasizing the ongoing need for social and political change."[43]

While the interview format is consistent throughout nine of the ten films (the exception is an animation film),[44] the choice of subject, generally, demonstrates Shannon's sensitivity to the politics of difference and to class. For instance, *It's Not Enough* (1974), the first in the series, explores the troubling conditions that women experience in the paid labour force. It criticizes women's low salaries, making useful comparisions with their male counterparts; illuminates the realities of the service sector (boring, ill-paid work and job insecurity); and points out the problems of the "double-day," mothers' guilt and the lack of reliable daycare facilities (daycare is a thematic thread linking the films).

In all the films, footage is shot, for the most part, in classic talking-head mode set in real time, a prototypical example of *cinema verité*, with Shannon's voice as the (mostly invisible) interviewer and narrator, although she appears in some films, shot from the back or in a background profile, thus ensuring that the women "testifying" remain the central focus. The inclusion of a diverse range of women in the *Working Mothers* series refutes the critique that Studio D gave voice mainly to white women. Indeed, the films feature women who range in age from the very young to the very old and who include east and west European, Greek, Asian, Black as well as First Nations women — illustrating Studio D's insistence on recognizing difference in women's voices. In the films, the women discuss their circumstances, offering opinions and judgements about their own work and personal lives that yield important revelations. The significance of these films can be understood through Julia Lesage's insistance on the urgency of naming women's experiences:

> Conversations in films [like these] are not merely examples of female introspection; ... rather, the women's very redefining of experience is intended to challenge all the previously accepted indices of "male superiority" and of women's supposedly "natural" roles. Women's personal explorations establish a structure for social and psychological change and are filmed specifically to combat patriarchy.[45]

Revelations about women's expectations and sometimes sharply contrasting realities of their everyday experiences are the common thread throughout these ten short films. *Mothers Are People* (1974), for instance, makes a clear case of the needs of a working mother. In the film, an African-Canadian research biologist, who is a widow and mother of two small children, explains her circumstances and demonstrates the incompatibility of the public perception of dedicated motherhood measured against her necessary "bread-winner" reality. As the cinematographer focuses tightly on her face, the mother speaks directly into the camera lens, recalling that at the time of her job interview she was coerced into saying she would never let her children "come between me and the job." When her children were ill, of course, *she* took a holiday or claimed illness herself, a strategy many working mothers of the time would have related to immediately. This professional woman voices a sharp critique of government policies around childcare: "The notion that 'the future of the nation depends on the youth' pays only lip service. There are no services in place," she says. The lack of reliable, affordable daycare was an important political and personal issue for the large number of women flooding the workplace and, as citizens, they expected the government to address this need.

The documentary practice in the *Working Mothers* series aligns itself with a literary paradigm arising from the same period that has come to be identified as "images of women" literature. In her study *Feminism and Its Fictions,* Lisa Maria Hogeland contends that this body likewise engages in "transacting CR" with its readers and, like documentary films of the period, was "important and influential in introducing feminist ideas to a broader reading public, and particularly in circulating feminist ideas beyond the small-group networks."[46] While both genres come under fire for assuming that meanings about women's lives were transparent and had a "truth" that could be unproblematically communicated to the audience, such works emphasized the value in *expressing* female experience, even though analysis of such experience was largely absent. Another criticism was directed at the practice of privileging the director/author as the person with "the knowledge," which created a troubling hierarchy in which the feminist filmmaker was positioned as "the 'woman who knows' and can reveal the 'truth' to her less aware audience [or film subject]."[47]

An example of this surfaces in a painful juxtaposion of two women's lives represented in sharply contrasting terms in *Tiger on a Tight Leash* (1974) and *Would I Ever Like a Job* (1974). The films are positioned in this order on the compilation video, perhaps for reasons of efficacy in sequencing them rather than a conscious decision by Shannon to place them side by side at the time she was filming them. The subject of *Tiger on a Tight Leash* is an attractive university professor, mother of three young children and head of the linguistics department at Mount St. Vincent University in Halifax, Nova Scotia. As the film opens, Shannon's voice is heard in "observational mode":[48]

> I was somewhat surprised that the head of a university department would face the same mundane problems affecting working mothers. But just being able to afford a live-in housekeeper doesn't solve all those problems. When I met Cathy her housekeeper had just quit with one day's notice leaving all the kids' clothes in the washer.

The documentary then switches into "interactive mode":[49] Shannon as filmmaker interviewing the professor. The interview is staged in Cathy's kitchen, her well-appointed office at the university, on the beach during a family picnic and on board the family sailboat, where the woman crews under her "captain" husband's direction. Cathy's work-related problems revolve around the need for but poorly esteemed domestic work and the lack of fringe benefits for childcare givers and mothers alike, which, in her experience explains the unreliability of live-in housekeepers. As she says, "Our society doesn't accord much prestige to housekeepers and babysitting ... our national interest is not such as to provide these things [reliable day care]." Undeniably, her complaint (a tangential critique of undervalued gendered labour) remains an urgent matter for Canadian working women, but her material conditions are so vastly superior to those of the mother featured in *Would I Ever Like a Job* that I couldn't help but wince at the gulf.

Would I Ever Like a Job profiles the bleak life conditions of a welfare mother of seven children, ranging in age from twelve years to eighteen months. This mother expresses frustration with unaffordable daycare costs at $15 per child per week which effectively chain her to the home. While both women come from the Maritimes and share similar appearances (both are young white women with long brown hair), the welfare mom is considerably more disadvantaged. The film opens in the kitchen with lunch in progress. As the sound track records the clatter of dishes and the mother's command to "Shut up and eat," the camera captures her slapping a child and pushing him to sit straight in his chair. This "welfare mom" goes on to explain how much the children, the noise, the clutter "get on her nerves": "I'm in the house all the time. I don't get out. I live on welfare. It's kind of hard — but we do it." Shannon, more visible in this film as the interviewer, asks the mom whether she would like to work outside the home. Her response, "Would I ever like a job," provided the film with its title.

Describing herself as unsuited for domestic work, the woman tells Shannon, "I could work as a waitress," seemingly unaware of the parallels between that job and the work she performs in her own kitchen. As details emerge about her life experience — married young and pregnant, another baby a year later, an abusive and alcoholic husband, a tubal ligation at age twenty-three — it seemed to me that any consciousness-raising around this film might have taken on the broader socio-political analysis of the impact of poverty and women's inability to control their reproduction. However, this portrait provides an example of the moral dilemma confronting the middle-class filmmaker who films a subject living in less-privileged social circumstances (and an example of what inspired Brian Winston's classic essay "The Tradition of the Victim in Griersonian Documentary").[50] Shannon faces a sticky situation. In order to function as a "propagandist for a better and more just society," arguing for improvements for women trapped in poverty, the film's subject is, by the very dint of her circumstances, construed as a victim while the film itemizes, "almost at random, a wide range of [social] problems"[51] beyond her control. Although Shannon's sensitivity to the woman's plight and her desire to preserve the woman's dignity is evident in her gentle but probing questions, the divide between director and film subject remains. Mediating this uneasy relationship is the knowledge of Studio D's practice of inviting the women it filmed to view their representations and to provide feedback — a practice, one hopes, followed with this film.

However, in *Like the Trees* (1974), the hierarchy between filmmaker and subject, a Métis woman, is blurred. The film through its direct cinema approach, projects another mothering narrative at the same time that it establishes an example of First Nations' identity and subjectivity. Heard uninterrupted throughout the entire film, is the woman's voice, giving testimony that established the legitimicy of the needs of First Nations women whose rights are not properly addressed in Canadian society. A recovered alcoholic, she is now the owner of a successful horse farm in northern Alberta; she speaks with Shannon about how dispossessed she was in a white world: "To survive, you [had] to live up to something that you [were] not … you [had] to speak in a certain way or people look[ed] down on you." She describes being forced to wear "pumps" instead of moccasins to waitress in a restaurant and having to teach her husband to drive a car and speak English — "If you [didn't conform], you didn't get along."

The invisible cinematographer follows the two women in easy conversation as they walk around the horse enclosure on the edge of a wooded expanse, capturing their converstion. Drawn out by Shannon's questions, the woman speaks simply but powerfully of a life where her own identity was systematically denied in white society — a life circumscribed by low wages and hard, menial work ("It was always white bosses we had"), a broken marriage ("We had so many pressures it broke down"), and burdened with childcare and breadwinning. She was eventually so worn down that she contracted tuberculosis. "I was really bitter, I hated everyone. I hated white people … I started drinking and fighting. I just didn't know where to turn." The Métis woman's struggle to fit into a diffcult world is reflected in Shannon's later revelations about her own alcoholism, her power struggles within the NFB and her withdrawl to a Kelowna mountain retreat (set out in Gerry Roger's documentary portrait *Kathleen Shannon: On Film, Feminism & Other Dreams*), foregrounding the "sisterly" cameraderie apparent in the interview, illuminating the bonds women share that override barriers of class and race.

Filming on the Métis woman's land helps the film develop a strong sense of place, of home, and underscores the value of the right to land for First Nations' peoples. The woman explains that her cycle of hopelessness and self-destruction was broken only when she claimed her own culture — tracing it back to the history of her ancestors, the Woodland Cree. "I started to feel better when I got my identity ... to learn about myself and about my people, to know that in our culture we had everything — even medicine." Withdrawing from white society, she created a new life of her own design, making clothes out of hides for her family, building a craft business selling beadwork. Gesturing towards the woods in the concluding moment of the film, she says, "Now, I'm just being myself. Like the trees, we belong here," arresting testimony to personal will, agency and self-determination.

As Canadian feminists became aware of the power of consciousness-raising groups (or CR groups) that were inspired by American feminists, Studio D documentaries became important complements to feminist discussions within lobby groups, women's centres, women's caucuses, women's cultural and business initiatives and among feminists in the academy. Thanks to its status as part of the NFB, the Studio was responsible for opening up a new space for women's demands through "the collective and social act of feminist filmmaking,"[52] bringing a feminist analysis to many women it might otherwise never have reached. It is easy to see how Studio D films could play an instrumental role within CR and other groups in encouraging women to imagine change:

> In the early 1970s hundreds of such groups met weekly in Canada. The groups were small, perhaps eight to fifteen participants, but the atmosphere was often electrifying as women shared experiences and feelings formerly considered too personal, shameful, or guilt provoking to discuss. Women talked about husbands, children, mothers, fathers, sex and sexuality, about double standards of sexuality, sexual harassment, rape, isolation, and full-time motherhood. In some ways CR groups were confessional; but the response was more often anger than guilt, and the answer was not penance but personal exoneration and social change. In other ways, CR groups were similar to group therapy; but while individuals altered their lives, the problems were defined as collective and systemic.[53]

The value of consciousness-raising lies precisely in its ability as a process to allow women to interpret the political and social significance of their personal experiences. Of course, the process emphasizes the value of women's voices, thereby validating their experiences. In the confidentiality of a group, women could speak freely and were invited to make discoveries about themselves that made visible the invisible connections between their lives and the wider world. A 1975 notice posted in a women's centre in Fredericton, New Brunswick, profiles what might typically have been expected:

> Who is in a CR group? — certainly no more than 10, probably about 8 women. The element of trust and confidence is absolutely essential. What is said in CR is never repeated outside CR — It goes without saying that men have no place in your CR group — There are no leaders. Everyone participates on an equal basis — [A] cardinal rule: never interrupt, except to clarify a point you've missed — [Y]ou will discover that your fears, anxieties, problems and crises are the legacy of all women with the opportunity of being taken seriously and of offering support to other women — [Y]ou will become more aware of the political position of women, the power relationships that control your life, and you learn of practical ways to shift the balance of power.[54]

Studio D not only adopted key elements of this process as a model for conducting the internal business of the Studio, it also fashioned its relationship with potential audiences in a similar way. As political procedures, both are, of course, intimately bound up with its adoption of a realist approach to documentary film practice. Studio D's praxis, in fact, illustrates that "many of the political aspirations of the women's movement form an integral part of the very structure of feminist work in and on film."[55]

But there are many ways to arrive at a feminist consciousness, and Studio D filmmakers did not necessarily arrive at the Studio with clearly articulated feminist ideals and pre-formed strategies for working together. Signe Johansson remembers a particular configuration of life experience that led to her association with Studio D, illustrating how she (like many women, myself included) became involved unwittingly with the women's movement through individual circumstances rather than as a result of collective imaginings of feminism:

> I started working [at the NFB] in September 1972, almost twenty-five years ago. I had actually just left a marriage with two small children. My children were one and four and I needed to support them. I had not finished university. I did not have marketable skills and I needed to get work right away. So I actually started out by taking a typing course. The typing school got a call from the Film Board wanting someone to type tapes. I

> said to the director of the school, "It's not really a good week for me to be starting a new job because my sister is coming from England for a week." He looked at me as though I had *lost* my mind. He said, "You know, I think you better go and check this one out." And so, I took his advice. It turned out that they were looking for someone to transcribe location tapes and translate from French to English. My French was just not up to that, neither was my typing, so they found me something else to do. I ended up going from doing odd jobs there, to managing an office, to being unit administrator and eventually when Studio D began, I became Studio D's unit administrator.[56]

Ginny Stikeman came to the Film Board specifically to engage in activism. Her experience working with Kathleen Shannon as assistant director and writer on *You Are on Indian Land* (1969) and *God Help the Man Who Would Part with His Land* (1971), both about Mohawk land rights, forged moments of collective and political consciousness-raising — the learning about and appreciation for First Nations' cultural politics. This sealed Stikeman's interest in "getting more women of different ethnic backgrounds into filmmaking," although, looking back, she admits the institutional vision sometimes fell short:

> Studio D didn't exist at this time but Kathleen was working as an editor with *Challenge for Change* along with Bonnie Klein and Dorothy Hénaut so the four of us had roots working together for social change ... I wanted to encourage different filmmakers with different backgrounds. It was much harder than I had thought and much harder for a lot of reasons ... white women had been getting the track record and having the chances and not everybody wanted to widen the circle.[57]

Not surprisingly, a number of Studio D members do not credit the women's movement *initially* as the prime motivating factor in attracting them to the Studio. Rather, according to their accounts, they were already poised for reassignment as employees and utterly willing to join with other like-minded women as members of a new women's studio. A feminist consciousness would be cultivated as the group coalesced. Dorothy Todd Hénaut remembers a deepening sense of this feminist community in the context of making her film *Firewords*:

> You have to remember that we started in 1974. There was no room for women anywhere. The main problem then, as we saw it, was that *men*, as opposed to *women* held all the power. So we [feminists as a community] were just looking for a space for "women." Louky Bersianuk I had

met at the book launch for another friend. She said she would send me some of her material and some photocopies of newspaper articles on a subject we had been discussing and I thought "what a generous woman." Nicole Brossard and I both worked together at the Youth Pavilion at Expo 67. We've known each other ever since then. Nicole had also worked on *Some American Feminists* at Studio D ... I'd just known her over time. Jovette Marchessault — I think she sent me some material on pornography [when I worked on *Not a Love Story*]. So we all just knew each other and worked collaboratively.[58]

A LITTLE FEMINIST FILM HISTORY[59]

At the time Studio D came into being, the National Film Board was "virtually the only training ground for women in the profession, and the single source of permanent employment for women filmmakers in the country."[60] Toronto's York University offered its first degree program in film studies in 1969, and in universities across Canada, "a generation of women developed Canadian literature courses with gender as a conscious and primary consideration,"[61] mainly within Canadian studies and, later, in women's studies courses. Many of these courses and those taught from a feminist perspective in other disciplines used Studio D documentaries as teaching tools, a practice that continues to some extent.

Studio D's documentary practice shares much with the practice of activist American feminists from the 1960s who used realist feminist documentaries as obvious vehicles of consciousness-raising. The flexibility of new camera technology — hand-held super-8mm and 16mm cameras — gave filmmakers greater mobility in shooting (the ordinary woman could be captured easily in her home), infusing the medium with a vibrant new political potential. Of this phenomenon, Lesage notes:

> In the late 1960s and early 1970s in the United States, women's consciousness-raising groups, reading groups, and task-oriented groups were emerging from and often superseded the organizations of the anti-war New Left. Women who had learned filmmaking in the anti-war movement and preciously "uncommitted" women filmmakers began to make self-consciously feminist films: and other women began to learn filmmaking specifically to contribute to the movement. The films these people made came out of the same ethos as the consciousness-raising groups and had the same goals.[62]

However, at the same time that Studio D was opening its doors, feminist film criticism was moving away from "social realism" as the preferred model. In fact, this period gave rise to two divergent approaches to feminist filmmaking. Significantly, the two critical accounts aligned themselves around a dichotomy developing in the women's movement — "two concerns of political strategizing [activist and theoretical] and two types of film work [realist and formalist],"[63] seemingly at odds with each other. The early film model, labelled the American or sociological approach, reflected the reality of women's lives. The second, originating from a British approach, while maintaining an interest in the "real," emphasized the primacy of the film text itself. The new branch of "British" feminist film criticism was comprised of such figures as Claire Johnston and Pam Cook (mid-1970s to early 1980s). Noting that social realities were, in fact, ideological constructions, these critics turned to theories within European structuralism and semiotics and to Marxist concepts of ideology and psychoanalytic theory to flesh out the sociological approach, claiming that theory ("women had no easy access to her voice in the phallocentrism of semiotics and psychoanalysis")[64] revealed the insidious value system that perpetuated women's second-class cultural location. Primarily, this approach scrutinized film as the bearer of ideology, defined as a representational system that, while appearing "natural" or "universal," was in fact the product of specific power structures that constituted a social system, where the sign "woman" acquired its meaning within sexist or patriarchal ideology.[65] It is worth noting that theorists acknowledged that finding an appropriate form and style for feminist documentary film presented a more acute challenge for documentary filmmakers than for fictional filmmakers. As Claire Johnson argued, "A strategy should be developed which embraces both the notion of film as a political tool and film as entertainment … a revolutionary counter-cinema will interrogate and demystify the 'truth' of women's oppression, not merely reflect it."[66]

This critical "turn" ushered in an era of complex feminist methodologies where theorists "struggled to construct a new theoretical language with which to speak by interrogating the very methods they had appropriated or adopted,"[67] an approach to film criticism that baffled and frustrated some feminists with its impenetrable vocabulary. The advent of continental philosophy — Saussurian structural linguistics/Barthesian semiotics and poststructuralism (Althusser's structural-Marxist work) — and post-1968 *Cahiers du cinéma* film and genre theory provided a rich (if not dizzying) range of theoretical constructs from which to draw.

Midway through the 1980s film critics such as Christine Gledhill and Annette Kuhn turned away from these models, "denouncing them as essentialist," and used instead an approach that combined textual analysis with studies of audience reception (spectatorship), proposing a critical model more sensitive to the "more complex and nuanced relationship between text, spectator and the institution of film."[68] Their insights paved the road to greater interdisciplinarity in feminist film criticism, as critics focused on how postmodernism and theories of race, ethnicity and post-colonialism might now inform feminist film criticism. While this entire period engendered a number of valuable works that represent a fascinating moment in the development of feminist thought on film, its theoretical complexity was nearly impossible for many women to decipher, save those with some connection to feminist intellectual debates within the academy. Of course, Studio D sidestepped these complexities by remaining true to the social realist documentary.

This shift in emphasis effectively created two feminist filmmaking communities. Activist feminists were convinced of the value of realist documentaries to reveal important insights into the circumstances of women's lives. Feminists more interested in theorizing around these experiences embedded in social reality, however, were much more compelled by the need to deconstruct the political territory around questions of representation. The two sites, consequently, generated heated discussions among academic feminists, while activist feminists, often mystified by complex theoretical paradigms, remained detached, favouring the more transparent realist feminist documentary. Tania Modleski remembers that in those "heady days," feminists in literary or film studies generally felt at ease with sociological approaches to the study of both literature and film. However, when she returned to graduate school at Stanford, she found she was "in for a shock":

> Students had taken over the program [Modern Thought and Literature] and were introducing Marxism, feminism, poststructuralism, and deconstruction ... Those of us still stuck in certain older ways of understanding film and literature were summarily dismissed for not understanding the complex workings of language and representation and for our naïve belief that literature and film did or could (insofar as it presented positive role models for women) reflect reality. I recall the moment when I felt the full force of the powerful sea change.[69]

The sociological approach, now considered somewhat naive, still subscribed to the notion that the personal was political and that the filmic representation of women's lives could be organized to transact consciousness-raising with its spectators — that "positive images" of women, for example, were intrinsically linked to change. Kathleen Shannon remained skeptical of the value of the theoretical approach, maintaining that an emphasis on theoretical concerns would undercut the activist project of realist feminist documentaries, dividing feminists into the educated élite and an alienated mass of women who could not attend university graduate programs for whatever reason. Shannon was much more interested simply in finding women whose voices were not being heard:

> I think it's a matter of going to the people whose real lives [have gone unnoticed] rather than weaving some theory then going out to find illustrations [for it]. If you bring those real, genuine people [on screen] then get out of the way of their communicating with the audience — then you're not putting all sorts of cinematic *"value"* in the way, or manipulating them or leaving *your* handprints all over the film so *you* can be lauded by the people writing the reviews. I think I was always very inspired by these genuine human beings who had so much to say and that no one ever listened to.[70]

Years later, Shannon remained resistant to theory and talked about how all of her energy was consumed in the daily practicalities of the "fight" to run Studio D, leaving scant time for theoretical contemplation. I had asked her about the importance of emerging theoretical paradigms for Studio D, specifically Michel Foucault's insights about power. She snorted:

> Who needs Foucault? What Canadian women told me they need is safe, affordable universal daycare. I wanted to document their demands on film. If enough women could get their voices heard — loudly enough — the government would have to listen. What good is élitist theory for *this* project?[71]

Her statement, I realized, demonstrated the utter frustration of the activist feminist driven by a certain sturdy social pragmatism who had made choices about where to expend her energy.

Early Studio D works painted a compelling portrait of the contributions women had made to society, at the same time signalling some of their concerns: *Great Grand Mother* (1975), a tribute to the pioneering women who settled the Prairies at the turn of the twentieth century and fought for and won the right to vote provincially; *Maud Lewis* (1976), a celebration of the Nova Scotia artist, one of Canada's most celebrated primitive painters; *The Spring and Fall of Nina Polanski* (1974), an animated six-minute feminist fable of a woman who, following a fairytale wedding, becomes so trapped in domestic drudgery that she transforms into the very machines she uses until she walks into the woods one day and regains her old self; "*... And They Lived Happily Ever After*" (1975) takes a long, hard look at the fairytale wedding as a commercially driven enterprise in the actual lives of a group of young women; and *Our Dear Sisters* (1976), Shannon's prophetic portrait of the much celebrated Alanis Obomsawin, a member of the Abenaki Nation and a gifted young filmmaker, singer and an adoptive mother whose unique story challenged traditional cultural assumptions. These films are still relevant today because they are grounded in the reality of the every day and continue to yield critical insights about social and personal challenges women confront.

Studio D's *Forbidden Love: The Unashamed Stories of Lesbian Lives* (1992) stands as an exception to its decision to remain resolutely in the camp of feminist realist documentary. Departing from the Studio's oft-criticized "didactic aesthetics," this documentary plays with theoretical constructs, mixing genres and celebrating lesbian reality as it embraces diversity and experience broadly For Diane Burgess, this indicates that "it can be concluded that the potential did exist for shifts in Studio D's philosophy and practices and that the segregation of feminist filmmaking did not necessarily have to result in a limiting pressure on the articulation of diverse views."[72]

Kathleen Shannon, however, never regarded film as an "end product." According to Terre Nash, "it was a stage in a transformative process. Its function was to give women a common frame of reference so that we could talk to one another about our lives."[73] Shannon puts into her own words the power of feminist film: "Women must speak to the issues facing us all, and one of the most important contemporary tools of speech is film — because of its capacity not only to inform and instruct, but to change attitudes."[74] The important theoretical shift here is from "an understanding of cinema as reflecting reality, to a view of cinema as constructing a particular, ideological view of reality."[75]

THE WOULD-BE COLLECTIVE

Although it has often been associated with liberal feminism, Studio D was comprised of members who held widely differing approaches to feminism and filmmaking. Despite their diversity in origins and a mix of viewpoints among its members, a climate of co-operation existed within the Studio, at least for the first decade. Bonnie Sherr Klein, for one, named herself explicitly as a feminist and a political radical. Speaking about the early period of developing feminist awareness, she recalls the radical opportunities afforded by feminist thinking: "In those days of feminism, everything was new. We were making it up. We were creating feminist theory as we went along, to the extent where, you know, you decide not to accept the 'givens.' Everything was up for grabs."[76]

At the opposite end of the spectrum is Beverly Shaffer, Studio D filmmaker whose film *To a Safer Place* (1987) is widely regarded as a critically authoritative feminist documentary. Shaffer would not have identified herself as a "well-versed" voice for feminism:

> The women's studio was a pocket of dynamism. So, in that sense, it was a very good place to be. There were a lot of meetings where the direction of the Studio was discussed. There were a variety of types of women in the Studio. There were some lesbian filmmakers; there was the middle-class feminist. There was Kathleen who was so very focused in what she wanted to accomplish ... Talk about feminist theory — it was really very clear in her head while with everyone else, there was more of a specific perspective and then, there was me, who did not fit into the classic definition of feminist.[77]

Dorothy Todd Hénaut, whose feminist sensibilities were shaped in part through her membership in Voice of Women (VOW), the second-wave feminist peace organization, suggests that this very diversity was encouraged by Shannon who recognized the value of many voices in opening up new sites for debate. In Hénaut's mind the early Studio D quilt project — *Just-A-Minute* (1976) — captures Shannon's intention and leaves important evidence for consideration. Hénaut credits this approach as one that generated a unique feminist intellectual climate, which was dependent on and illuminated by the synergy of the group:

> We had discussions of feminist issues usually within the context of a film project. There were meetings, yes, but they were working meetings. Somebody would come up with a film project and we'd discuss the research that had been done and we'd make suggestions for further research. It was really on a project-by-project basis that we deepened our knowledge of various issues.[78]

Shannon organized the project in such a way as to give as many filmmakers within the Studio as possible the opportunity to contribute their own ideas towards and to be part of the making of the film. The idea of producing a film made up of a collection of short documentaries was Shannon's response to a budget that was only large enough to allow the production of a single regular-length film:

> I'll give you an example of what happened in 1976 when there wasn't enough money for each of us to make a film. We had these big meetings and we thought "let's make a quilt." We called it the "quilt project." Each of us would do a little five-minute segment. I wanted to do something on women aging and so did Margaret Westcott, so we did a little bit of shooting on video, a little bit of research on that. Bonnie [Sherr Klein] started thinking about doing something on pornography, a little five-minute thing within this quilt. I don't remember what everyone else was going to do but it was all going to fit into a quilt. That way we would spread the money around. I thought that was a great idea. Each person or group of two people was autonomous in their idea. They weren't being told what to say by the others. It was going to fit into a context with other things. [W]e had done a fair amount of research and a fair amount of work, but we weren't ready to shoot and all of a sudden a big chunk of money came in. Bonnie was quite close [to shooting] so she got the money to make the whole pornography film [*Not a Love Story*] which I produced.[79]

Clearly, a project such as this not only allowed for a polyvocal enunciation on the part of Studio D members but it also demonstrated a synthesis of feminist knowledge produced by women situated in a specific and emerging moment of social change.[80] Their collective knowledge embedded in these films offered a self-conscious account of the experience as the filmmakers processed feminist ideas and produced them.

Studio D, then, developed around a loosely structured collective, tapping into the strengths and diverse knowledges of its members as well as mobilizing their "sameness." Their promotion of gender-consciousness culminated in the production of a distinctive body of feminist documentaries. Beverly Shaffer discusses how this collaborative approach encouraged an integrative praxis that was instrumental in her directing *To a Safer Place* (1987). This film would go on to win many awards and contribute substantially to a feminist interrogation into the subject of incest, in its genesis at that moment:

> Another filmmaker, Anne Henderson, had been researching women with non-traditional jobs. She was out in Vancouver and she met Shirley Turcotte who had a technical job working with BC Tel and she recognized that this was a remarkable woman and in an interview, I guess, they got to talking and their talk went beyond Shirley's work situation to her personal situation. Anne brought the story back to, I guess, Kathleen and, at that time, Gerry Rogers was a producer at the Studio and Kathleen mentioned to Gerry that Anne had met this women who impressed her very much. So, Gerry went to meet Shirley and came back and decided, yes, we should make a film on incest survivors. Initially, there was no director attached [to the project] and she thought she would put herself in the film. She was really just thinking about an approach and somehow I became involved. They knew they needed a director and Gerry was a producer. I thought this was an interesting subject so I flew out to meet Shirley and I was really impressed by her.

On hearing Turcotte's story, Beverly Shaffer was struck by her affirmative stance. Here was a woman who refused to construe herself as a victim. Instead, she insisted on revisiting her story, illuminating aspects that she could not grasp as a child. Turcotte revised the role she had been consigned by dominant notions of victims and sexual abuse through a radical rewriting of the script. As Shaffer tells it, Turcotte's quest for knowledge proposed a dramatically fresh and value-shifting narrative for the film:

> The way to do this film was just to have Shirley tell her story. I wrote up a proposal and it was accepted and what I got from the Studio [in terms of group discussions] was very helpful since I had no background in [understanding] incest or sexual abuse … The intention was to show this film to victims, to make them feel very safe watching it and, hopefully, they would see themselves as survivors of incest and *not* victims. That was something that was very, very important to me — that was Gerry's idea — you have to make the audience feel safe.
>
> When we invited victims of incest to preview the film, [we ensured] that they wouldn't see what they had been seeing on television. [A]t that time, incest was just beginning to be discussed. How? We'd see on TV women with their heads in black so they wouldn't be identified, telling horrific stories in very feeble voices … portraying them as having experienced the blackest human experience and having to keep it secret. What was so beautiful about Shirley was her attitude: "I'm not going to cover my face. I have nothing to be ashamed of. I did nothing wrong." It was such a wonderful attitude. I hadn't seen anything like that — "I'm an incest survivor and I'm not ashamed." It was a question of the Studio

> working at its best ... Kathleen, Gerry and I having discussions and finally the film getting made: *that* was the Studio working at its best from my perspective.[81]

Turcotte took control of her destiny rather than becoming the woman who succumbed to forces greater than hers. The camera follows the subject as she interviews her mother, her siblings, her neighbours, measuring their recollections against her own, demonstrating how dominant values about family, parental authority and social relations between men and women failed to protect the rights and the person of a small and defenceless child.

At the same time that Studio D members generated their own forms of feminist theorizing and investigations of feminist concerns among themselves, their documentaries provided material for both theoretical and activist debates outside the Studio. Shaffer remembers the international attention *To a Safer Place* received:

> I met a woman once from Minnesota, a social worker who knows the film. This past summer there was a letter from New Hampshire asking for the film. So it's still widely used. In Israel they made a big thing about it. They brought in all the social workers, a lot of lawyers and judges. This was at a time when they hadn't begun "the" discussion yet. [T]here's a Japanese version of that film as well — I'm very proud of that film.[82]

Likewise, other Studio D films — among them *Not a Love Story* (1981), *If You Love This Planet* (1982), *The Burning Times* (1990) and *Forbidden Love* (1992) — generated substantial critical debate and contributed to the development of feminist theorizing outside the Studio.

STUDIO D AND AUDIENCE RELATIONS

While Studio D admittedly sidestepped "the theory question," its methodology for viewing and reviewing films constitutes a unique example of a broader application of consciousness-raising. Studio D's strategy for developing a film subject, in fact, created a dynamic position of agency for the spectator, giving Kathleen Shannon's approach to spectatorship the authority of a process grounded in consciousness-raising with a surprising prescience. If the account of "the male gaze" as a structuring logic in Western visual culture ordinarily leaves "no room for the female spectator nor for a female gaze,"[83] Shannon's approach to screening Studio D documentaries provided a countervailing feminist scrutiny. Her approach afforded women opportunities where they could engage in female (feminist) spectatorship as an exercise in consciousness-raising. The process contained a political urgency and at the same time evoked the centuries-old ritual of women gathering around a kitchen table to talk about their lives.

In developing her *Working Mothers* series, Shannon implemented a highly interactive process to arrive at the final version, a technique that would be used in all of Studio D's films. She first trained a team of filmmakers how to consult with their film's subjects as the film was being shot, a practice employed by other Film Board studios. The women who had been filmed then viewed the results and offered comments. Later, when the film was completed, it would be screened in small informal group settings. Following the screening, the filmmakers would lead discussions using workshops designed to explore the issues presented in the film to access audience reaction and to instigate consciousness-raising. Bonnie Sherr Klein contends that Shannon used this process to create a unique documentary aesthetic:

> What Kathleen really embodied was a relationship with the audience. The films always came from a research base that *was* the audience. It wasn't theoretical — it wasn't [formalized] feminist theory. It happened because you met somebody, you saw something, wherever. Then, while the film was being edited — well, all along the way, in the making and audience testing [of the film] — it was always brought back to the initiating group of women. That was where the validation happened. It was really wonderful, having women see your film and saying "that's me up there."[84]

In her 1989 essay, "Real Issues in a Reel World," Shannon catalogues an impressive variety of techniques she developed for audience interaction: pairing off, taking turns talking and listening; writing responses on paper, jumbling them then reading and responding to someone else's comment ("an effective way of dealing with differing reactions from men and women"). All of her experimentation, of course, was designed to promote the inseparable relationship in her mind between the inquiring spectator and the film:

> One of film's strongest advantages is its ability to bring people together … But it isn't just [its] information that changes our attitudes and opens our minds. The most effective means to change our attitudes is hearing another individual's own experience. Because it communicates emotionally as well as factually, the film is a wonderful medium for transmitting people's own stories and ideas. The person we've just heard on the screen

> can't be engaged in argument or refutation. Her reality just is. The issue is how do we respond to her from our reality?[85]

In fact, Studio D's approach to filmmaking (and consciousness-raising) as feminist praxis dovetails with renowned feminist historian Joan Kelly's theorizing of the instructive value of "experience." According to Kelly, knowledge, based on lived experience, lies at the root of an ongoing process that she names "oppositional consciousness," which is the "spark of feminism ignited in a woman's consciousness at the moment when she senses a discrepancy between the cultural definition of 'woman' and her own experience of herself or of other 'women.'"[86] Whether Shannon would have described her strategy as one designed to engender "oppositional consciousness," the way she managed the feminist studio and its developing body of documentaries encourages me to consider it from this theoretical perspective. Terre Nash credits Shannon with a unique approach to spectatorship:

> I've never met anyone with as much respect for the audience as Kathleen — because, of course, she made no distinction between the filmmaker and the audience. She encouraged us to make films that we ourselves needed to see and talk about.[87]

Nash recalls that Shannon often quoted Gloria Steinem on the power of consciousness-raising:

> A roomful of people can set off a chain of thought that leads us all to a new place — a sudden explosion of understanding, a spontaneous invention. We hear ourselves saying things we had felt but never named. In any one audience, there is enough energy, skill, anger and humour for a revolution.[88]

Studio D fostered new attitudes, often the catalyst behind an intricate and complex web of feminist thought. In large measure, Shannon's methodology was instrumental in creating the "resistant spectator" who would be empowered to analyze her social, cultural location, reading against the grain of stereotypes, social structures and hegemonic thought. As a consequence, "she" would be empowered to resist against forces of manipulation and control.

In fact, in addition to screening completed films for small discussion groups, Shannon liked to invite groups of women to participate in a process of evaluation and deliberation as a film was being developed. Following the screening of a documentary, spectators were encouraged to discuss its subject matter and presentation style using a discussion package prepared by the filmmaking team (usually a series of questions and discussion topics designed specifically to accompany the documentary). The discussion was facilitated by a representative from the Studio. According to media theorist Anita Taylor, this giving of "voice" to women is the first step in a feminist restructuring of society:

> Studio D films have at a minimum participated in a dialogue through which women can learn to seek changes. In so doing, they meet a major Studio goal and contribute to helping women's voices be heard. Most of the films frame issues and evoke viewer responses in ways that lead women to confront views different from their own and to uncover issues previously submerged in their own lives. The shared experience of viewing a film and discussing their reactions with each other has helped many women frame and clarify issues of similarity and difference.[89]

Women would thus be encouraged to frame various feminist responses, based on individual interpretations that the Studio hoped would lead to political activism. Of course, these spectators, urged to "read against the grain," were not being urged to resist the message of Studio D's sisterly struggle itself.[90]

Studio D documentaries also constituted a valuable contribution to feminism in that they bridged a gap between ordinary women's lives and feminist academics' formal study of "women's conditions" and the construction of female subjectivities. As well as providing insight into the historical development of the women's movement from the early days of second-wave feminism to the late 1990s, these documentaries furnish provocative portraits of women's lives and experiences that invite speculation about contemporary feminist concerns, potentially diminishing the gap between the two moments in theorizing feminist film. Along these lines, Terre Nash tells this story about the non-linear research process involved in the creation of her Academy Award-winning *If You Love This Planet* (1982):

> I was at McGill doing my PhD and heard Helen Caldicott and I thought "this just has to be." I wasn't thinking it had to be a great film or anything like that. I thought "what can I do to help spread this message." Here I am, fairly educated and I knew *nothing* about this sort of thing. I had never thought about it. What would happen if the bombs actually went off? I thought "people have to hear this." I thought of her talk in terms of [access] — she's only speaking in the major cities across the country

> — but what about the people up in Prince George, in Nunavuut and all those little places where people don't have access [to her talk]. People need to know this information. I thought if she can't get there, I'll just film it. I went to Kathleen and had a talk. Amazingly, she just totally backed me and I went down to Washington, DC, on a research trip for something else for her. She budgeted for another five days for me to stay there and do research at the National Archives to see what I could find for this film — it hadn't even been proposed yet but the most amazing things happened when I was there.[91]

Nash outlined how her research was shaped by a series of happenstance events: her attendance at a conference where she learned that the U.S. military had been three minutes (out of a total of fifteen) into a nuclear alert caused by a computer chip failure; her encounter with a delegation of Hiroshima survivors; her locating of military medical footage on the aftermath of the Hiroshima bombings; and her chance viewing of a Hollywood war propaganda film featuring none other than former movie star Ronald Reagan, then the president of the United States:

> I also came across this film called *Jap Zero* that Ronald Reagan was in. I didn't even realize it was him at first. Not everybody thought it was funny [to include it], but *I* did … [B]y the time I left I thought, "I have no choice but to make this film. It's all just fallen in my lap." And Kathleen was a total, total support.[92]

With such compelling research it was an easy matter for Nash to construct a cogent and hard-hitting documentary setting out the horrific consequences of nuclear war. The clip from *Jap Zero* is a perfect black-comedy cameo of an impetuous young pilot champing heedlessly at the bit, dying to take a crack at the enemy (a thinly disguised attack on Reagan's enthusiatic support for the euphemistically labelled Star Wars campaign, the U.S. race against the USSR for nuclear armament supremacy mounted during Reagan's presidency). Nash was understandably stupified to learn later that she was expected to include "the opposite point of view," the reason cited by the CBC in refusing to air the film — at least, until *If You Love This Planet* bagged an Academy Award. Indeed, as Nash outlines, before the Academy Award, the film ran into hurdle after hurdle in official channels:

> I shot it in a day and then edited it. Then I showed it to distribution at the Film Board. There was a big distribution meeting at that point at the Board in the early '80s. They had this huge distribution network

internationally and they were all having a meeting. I thought I'll give them a preview of my rough-cut. So I scheduled a screening and the guy who handled American distribution came up to me after the screening and said, "I will not allow that film to be shown in the United States." This was a distribution guy who was supposed to be helping us distribute films, I mean, [a man] who works *for* the Film Board. I thought "who the f—are you?" but didn't say that. I knew that this guy was there to serve the needs of the Film Board ... *not* to censor its films. So I thought "the hell with him" and went on with the film. Then I got the letter from International Distribution asking me to make two versions of the film: one for the United States and one for elsewhere, [saying] that they wanted the Reagan material out. That was outrageous enough. I wrote him back quoting John Grierson and all of that sort of stuff. Kathleen was incensed. It was so great, having someone so high profile on my side. Then the head of *all* distribution said, "Don't make two versions. Make one version without the Reagan material. We won't allow it." Kathleen was *really* incensed. I was just fighting mad and so was she. So that was great. It was like an unbeatable wall. It was beyond belief — I was that furious. So we fought them. [The film] went all the way.[93]

If You Love This Planet illustrates indisputably how Studio D's voice, when representing a woman's point of view on political and military matters, resonated in unshakable contradiction within the structure of Canada's "patriarchal state." Political theorist Roberta Hamilton attests to the difficulty feminists encounter in taking on the state:

> Since Confederation, the vast majority of those with formal power in all aspects of state relations — from Members of Parliament to primary school principals — have been men. The legislation of the state — from family law to criminal law — has been gendered in ways that disadvantage women politically, socially and economically. Not only have those with influence been predominantly male, but they respond to the world in ways that protect the interests of men throughout the society, and ruling-class men in particular.[94]

Indeed, as Nash recounts, her film unleashed unparalleled political and legal controversy on both sides of the Canadian border:

> It took three months of my time to fight [NFB Distribution demands to cut the Reagan clips] ... It went all the way up to the Commissioner of the Board, Jim Domville. He said something like, "Leave one Reagan clip in and take one out." Anyway, we left *both* in. I think I had a third one I was going to take out anyway. So I said, "Look, I'll take *this* one out." (It was already out by that time.) The main thing they said was that it would

> offend the United States to have a Reagan clip in. It wasn't our job to placate people and, at any rate, it wasn't offensive to the American people — *only* to Ronald Reagan and his cohorts. Anyway, it was a real film that the clips were taken from — a film that Reagan was in. My film went out there and caused a huge impact. It was out in Canada for a year before it went to the States. People started screening it in school basements and in churches and everywhere. It had a real grassroots effect. People started peace groups over it. It was incredible.[95]

When her film was nominated for an Academy Award, as Nash explains, the issues it raised ignited a fresh set of complications and more notoriety:

> Three days later, my distribution guy in the States, not the Film Board guy, an independent (you have to hire somebody, an American to distribute it) called me and said, "You're not going to believe it but the film has just been labelled political propaganda. What that means is that it has to have a label on it that says 'political propaganda' and anybody, any group who rents it or buys it has to be reported to the FBI." I was just stunned. But the thing is, it could not be withdrawn ... That's one of the rules ... Once a film has been nominated for an Academy Award it remains. They made this rule mainly because of problems with films from Eastern Europe where governments would get cold feet or something and want to withdraw films. So that was a rule — it couldn't be withdrawn. So that meant everybody who had to vote for the film, the movie stars, had to be reported to the FBI.[96]

Even though the United States Department of Justice issued an order under the provisions of the *Foreign Agents Registration Act* requiring Nash to register as an agent of a foreign government and, in Canada, the Canadian Broadcasting Corporation (CBC) declined to air the documentary on national television, Nash still refused to incise the clip. As a devotee of the Grierson tradition of public-service filmmaking, she used another Grierson tradition (progaganda as education) to defend her film in the face of those, conspicuously an American president and his advisors, who argued "for the proliferation of nuclear weapons in the name of security."[97]

Almost a decade later, *If You Love This Planet* was still influencing Canada–U.S. relations, demonstrating what Nash described as an "amazing life that nobody knows about." In 1990, Nash was invited to appear before a U.S. Congressional Hearing to defend her film afresh, this time in support of a Democratic senator, hoping to have the U.S.

propaganda law repealed. Nash's stance, through all of this, illustrates Studio D's belief in "stressing the 'otherness' of the female voice," reflecting its philosophy of "separatism" alongside a desire for "equity" and a need for social betterment.[98]

STUDIO D AND PUBLIC NOTORIETY

Responding to concerns of the Canadian women's movement (influenced by both North American and European feminist debates), Studio D generated documentaries that contributed to the feminist movement and to feminism as a form of culture. If, as theorists Nancy Adamson, Linda Briskin and Margaret McPhail claim, the Canadian women's movement remains an undisputed social shaper — "one of the most significant and successful [on-going] social movements in Canada"[99] — then Studio D's position is one of prominence.

A number of Studio D documentaries instigated debates in this context, contributing to a more informed social understanding about women's issues over the last four decades, including matters of national and international scope. Most notable among these are Bonnie Sherr Klein's *Not a Love Story* and Terre Nash's *If You Love This Planet*. Speaking in retropect, a retired Shannon would claim "many of our films did not just report on existing social movements but were part of their impetus."[100] Burgess credits *Not a Love Story* for making "an important contribution to the anti-pornography debates,"[101] although not an uncontested one. Both films explore important issues — the sexual exploitation of women and the menace of nuclear weapons — in ways that still offer relevant insights.

Indeed, *Not a Love Story* remains the most high-profile film associated with Studio D. One of the most popular films and most broadly circulated documentaries in NFB history, it was highly controversial and was described in a Studio D press release as "a central work in the burgeoning movement against pornography."[102] It was banned by the Saskatchewan and Ontario Censor Boards but was quickly picked up by commercial distributors across North America. In the first year it was released, even though it could only be screened in educational venues, *Not a Love Story* attracted an audience of more than 40,000 in Ontario alone. Its U.S. premiere in New York on June 8 and 9, 1982, was organized by *Ms.*

Magazine and featured a crowd-attracting post-screening panel discussion moderated by Gloria Steinem, featuring Bonnie Sherr Klein and Linda Lee Tracey in conversation with audience members.[103] Canadian cabinet minister Judy Erola, responsible for the Status of Women portfolio, and Linda Lovelace Marciano, star of the notorious porn film *Deep Throat,* were also in attendance. The event was broadly publicized, and members of the press, no doubt, intrigued by the combination of feminists and sex trade workers, were out in full force. Elizabeth Anderson descibes one publicity shot that was featured in a number of American newspapers following the event:

> In fact, a photo published in numerous newspapers in the U.S. showed Linda Lovelace, Gloria Steinem, Linda Lee Tracey, Bonnie Klein and Judy Erola standing arm in arm in front of the 57th Street Playhouse marquee under a large flag with the title of the film on it. The main caption under one such photo reads: "Imported from the great white north."[104]

It became clear that the film had touched a social nerve when impassioned reviews — both positive and negative — began to surface from Canada, the U.S. and Britain. At home, Sid Adilman, writing for the *Toronto Star,* tabled a largely sympathetic review; several days later, Jay Scott, the influential critic of the *Globe and Mail* (Toronto), labelled it "bourgeois feminist fascism."[105] Reversing positions, Adilman revised his stand in another review, now siding with Scott. A week later in her regular column, feminist journalist Michele Landsberg discussed their responses, debating the masculine and femininst responses to feminism and to women's sexuality. Feminist film critic B. Ruby Rich, writing for *The Village Voice,* raised the paradox of the "feminist" camera deployed to track the exploitation of a nude sex-trade worker, referring to a peep-show sequence shot over a male customer's shoulder as the woman inside the cubicle entertains, "... zooming in for a closeup ... thereby presenting us with an intimate view not even available to the real-life customer."[106] Rich's question drew attention to the ideological minefields feminist filmmakers confronted in dealing with questions of gender and sexuality and was echoed by Susan Barrowclough in London's *Screen.* Barrowclough also speculated on the theoretical question of "otherness, rather than sameness":

> ... the middle-aged man watching younger men, the sexually inactive watching the active, the individual watching the archetypal. It

> may be that his gaze falls, not on the female genitals (which he may be accustomed to seeing elsewhere) but on the male, and that the chief part of this pleasure, which he may disown subsequently, is homoerotic rather than heterosexual. This ambiguity pornography permits.[107]

If the film touched a popular cord as "the biggest commercial success in the Film Board's 43 year history,"[108] it also made a decisive mark on sexuality discussions in various feminist communities. Although Klein insisted that her stance was neither wholly anti-pornography nor in favour of censorship, *Not a Love Story* has been linked to both. The film, uniformly regarded as a significant landmark in feminist filmmaking, provided valuable ammunition for women combatting violence at the same time it was roundly criticized by some respected feminist critics — such as B. Ruby Rich, E. Ann Kaplan and Linda Williams — as a film whose "moral outrage against pornography otherwise leaves little room for thoughtfulness."[109]

However, a year after its Canadian launch, Robert Fulford noted that *Not a Love Story* had "helped launch an international debate on the problem of pornography."[110] Detractors pointed out that clips from actual porn films, used by Klein to drive home her indictment of pornography, merely replicated the pornographic "moment," as Rich had argued, encouraging (in a perverse way) the same kind of voyeurism that porn was designed to elicit. Members of the feminist community split into two camps: anti-pornography vs. anti-censorship. Debates between the two were often acrimonious *and* productive as fresh insights into female sexuality surfaced, resulting, over time, in a rich body of feminist theorizing. From a grassroots perspective, spectators viewing *Not a Love Story* for the first time, still remember leaving the theatre numbed by its powerful impact but awakened to issues they might not have previously contemplated.

The film generated much useful debate in many quarters. Rich, looking for a way to align herself more closely with the New York Institute for the Humanities (through its seminar on Sex, Gender and Consumer Culture, "a testing ground for all the new, more inclusive theories of sexuality and representation that were being developed")[111] and to distance herself from the warring forces of WAP (Women Against Pornography) and FACT (Feminists Against Censorship Taskforce), in fact, welcomed the opportunity to review *Not a Love Story* in order to tackle some of the issues it raised. Within the Film Board, *Not a Love Story* was being referred to as a "phenomenon," but for Studio D, its notoriety and problematic commercial distribution raised alarms. Despite Klein's intention that her film be used to raise feminist consciousness, particularly in women's groups, the Studio discovered that its film was being exploited by some distributors for its pornographic content, a matter Elizabeth Anderson analyses at some length in her doctoral dissertation, "Pirating Feminisms."

Clearly, *Not a Love* Story, controversary aside, stands as one of the originating Canadian voices that launched a protracted and highly fruitful series of discussions about women's sexuality, however contentious and in spite of its oft-cited foibles. Indeed, this documentary and the ensuing debates demonstrate the developmental process embedded in feminist theorizing. As insights are gained, feminists must, of necessity, rethink old territory, identifying and naming landmarks that until recently had been invisible yet powerful shapers of ideology and social practice. These landmarks, in retrospect, seem only too obvious.

Not a Love Story received huge notoriety because of its subject matter, unleashing widespread discussions, which led to useful insights about the issues of pornography and censorship that were considered separately and in relation to each other — for instance, the recognition of sexual pleasure in diversity, and of women's varieties of sexual identity and expression. However, it is useful to remember that feminist achievement is gained through a process of reconsideration and revision only when the instigators are able to assess the status quo and their own particular locations within it critically. This was an era that would witness a variety of new ways of thinking about women's issues — sexuality, social organization and gender roles — which led to radical questioning about social and political locations of citizens "that is still spinning itself out."[112] Undeniably, *Not a Love Story* put Studio D on the map and created a substantial appetite for further feminist documentary production, a remarkable achievement for the small Studio.

Behind the Veil: Nuns (1984) and *Kathleen Shannon: On Film, Feminism, & Other Dreams* (1997) model the kind of vision Shannon held for the power of film made by women, tempered organically by "a type of 'separatism' alongside a desire for equity."[113] Both films celebrate communities of women living harmoniously in a cultural space of their own, each featuring a well-spoken woman, an articulate avatar of a woman's world. Both construct their arguments through history, exploring "how lives intersect with history, that field of feminist investigation where the private and the public intersect."[114] The question of Studio D's separatist politics aside, the appeal of women engaged in women-centred pursuits formed the cornerstone of Shannon's world view, as she argued repeatedly, "we (the 'we' being women) perceive things differently." Women filmmakers, of course, embodied this different way of seeing:

> Studio D's purpose [is] to provide an opportunity for women to develop and express their creativity in film ... to bring the perspective of women to bear on all social issues ... to provide an environment where women can work together in an atmosphere of female support and collectivity ... to develop in women confidence in themselves and in other women and a sense of their own value and importance as human beings.[115]

The value of mining the past in these two films reworks Shannon's early admonition, "If we can have no appreciation of the role of women in ... history, then we misunderstand the nature of our roots. And to be alienated from our roots dulls our understanding of our cultural present and future."[116]

The temptation to examine the parallels between a group of women within a religious order and the women in Studio D (both toiling in the service of a better world) is irresistible to some degree. What drew Margaret Westcott to the story of nuns was the appeal of the cloister, a space exclusive to women. Westcott recalled a comment by her partner Gloria Demers that the cloister was a religious haven for nuns in the way that women-centred communities were for lesbians. The film became an exploration of the politically personal. While *Behind the Veil* grew out of "our love for each other," Westcott contends, she was also seeking a way to celebrate women's spirituality as a means of recovering from her own traumatic educational experiences at the hands of "punitive nuns." The film, an act of collaboration, was a perfect choice for the two women joined in a commitment "to alleviating the constraints on women."[117] Alluding to a 1959 papal declaration that the Church open its windows "so that we can see out and let the people see in,"[118] Westcott proposed the film to Studio D, noting that the "once-closed doors of convents are opening revealing to us some of the most interesting and radical women of our time." She, the radical filmmaker, would tell their story:

> They are part of the largest all-female communal organization in the world. Devotion to God has not always been the primary motivation, but rather a reaction to society's oppression of women at any given time. Among other reasons, women have entered convents to seek the only education available to them, a decent standard of living, participation in female community life and to avoid unwanted marriages.[119]

Kathleen Shannon accepted the proposal and allocated budget funds for research. Demers would eventually write and narrate the film script following an exhaustive period of research that took the partners to archives and religious communities across North America and Europe.

Filmed in Canada, the United States, Ireland and Italy, the two-part film with a running time of 130 minutes offers an exhaustive portrait of nuns through history. It was "the first film ever to record from a global perspective the turbulent history and remarkable achievements of women in religion, from pre-Christian Celtic communities to the radical sisters of the 1980s,"[120] Studio D promotional literature promised. Part One explores the experiences of contemporary nuns. We see members of the Order of Little Sisters of Jesus working in the secular world, in a poverty- and crime-ridden Chicago tenement district. We also see nuns sequestered in the Trappist cloister in their mother house outside of Rome, which opened its doors to Westcott's camera crew and revealed the power of quiet service (harvesting crops, preparing food) at the heart of spiritual rejuvenation. Tempering this affirmative portrait runs a darker theme: the power of the patriarchal Church, the ensuing polemic championing the nuns' goodness (and powerlessness) at the hands of a sometimes ruthless and male hierarchy.

Part One creates a portrait of the contemporary conditions of nuns' lives, using details from sisters in several religious orders as evidence. Featuring the classic talking-head technique, the camera technician focuses closely on the women speaking about their experiences: their personal "call" to the religious order, their experiences as novitiates, the tyranny of the traditional habit (one nun likens her old headgear to a vice), ability to conduct (or not) liturgical ceremonies, devotion to their lives of service and a surprisingly frank discussion of sexuality within the vows of celibacy. Through this form of address organized around the voice of the sisters, the nun is rendered *the* authority figure, the authentic interpreter of her life.

Film sequences of nuns in the midst of their religious work or prayer, the soundtrack blending sublime liturgical music with the noise of everyday life, flesh out the portrait of women tailoring their call to the demands of a contemporary secular world. One sequence captures the surprise of a nun whose dance class for female prisoners in the Chicago-area Cook County Jail has taken an unexpected turn. The camera is pointed at the figure of a grinning inmate (modestly captured from the waist up) caught in a spontaneous gyrating solo and being encouraged by the hoots and applause of her fellows. Another sequence captures a young nun, working for minimum wage, flipping burgers on the front line of a Burger King restaurant. Westcott draws from archival film footage, newsreels, photographs and reproductions of religious art to flesh out the context; Demers's narration completes the compelling portrait.

The closing section of Part One harkens back in time, setting the stage for Part Two and its focus on the central role of women in the early Roman Church. The detailing of the lives of early Christian female saints extends the polemic established earlier, proposing a link between the saintly early Christians and the Goddess, mythic deity from ancient times: "There was a time in the earth's ancient history when the life-giving powers of women were revered, when woman was Goddess, her powers revered and worshipped. These ancient beliefs deteriorated as men became the dominant element and the subjugation of women began." Part Two uses extended shots of majestic natural land and seascape in lavish detail — mythic metaphors for female oneness — to invoke the past, visually re-establishing the "power" of women. Images from illuminated manuscripts, catacomb murals and religious art substantiate women's central role in early religious life. Observations by the scholarly Sister Mary McCurtin (filmed in Dublin) present the contemporary point of view, "I was overwhelmed by the masculinity of the Church ... The 'masculine' nature [was] hard to reconcile with my own understanding." Not all women agreed with the film — one woman wrote to the minister responsible for the Status of Women that the film was a mixture of "fact and fantasy" and a waste of tax payers' dollars. However, Joan Pennefather, commissioner and chairperson of the NFB, defended it as "one of the most active films in our catalogue,"[121] emphasizing the film's careful pre-screening process with a wide number of organizations within the Church.

If *Behind the Veil* proposes religious equality for women, *Kathleen Shannon: On Film, Feminism & Other Dreams* extends an elegiac homage to the retired head of Studio D. Shot at the moment when the NFB announced the Studio's closure, the film opens with footage from a 1996 York University convocation exercise where Shannon and her contribution to feminism is being recognized with an honourary doctorate. The balance of the film is shot on location at her home in the mountains of Kelowna, BC, the year before her death on January 9, 1998. The film is a frank and loving portrait of the feminist visionary, and it concentrates on Shannon's retelling of her life's experiences and her visionary work with Studio D, constructed faithfully in line with Shannon's original plan (women in their own space, recounting their experiences in front of cameras operated by women). Detailing her entry into filmmaking at age seventeen, the trauma of sexual harassment, her battle with alcohol, personal frustration with the differences between "the culture of women and the culture of men," anger at the power of patriarchy and faith in the promise of social change by women working in the company of like-minded women, the film pays tribute to her triumph in the feminist film studio that operated for more than two decades. Shannon remembers her excitement at the consciousness-altering discussions following the screening of films that demonstrated "the brilliance of ordinary people." The film concludes with a panoramic view of the mountains in autumnal colour, Shannon at peace with her world.

*

In her account of second-wave feminism in *Feminism in the Heartland,* Judith Ezekiel has observed that the successes of the women's movement came from its most radical idea and practice — the consciousness-raising group — that provided the link between the personal and the political in a dynamic, utopian dream of transformation. Without the utopian vision, she argues, movements for social change are doomed.[122] With this idea in mind, I am encouraged to return to the earlier debate in feminist filmmaking. A number of theorists now question the value of dividing feminist film theory into two moments. They argue that to do so creates an artificial dualism that splits off feminist political demands from feminist artistic production in an unproductive "tug of war,"[123] where the valuing of the avant-garde is accompanied by "a concurrent erasure of more conventional political documentary practice."[124] These "two moments" may not, in fact, be so distinct from one another. Rather than pitting the social realism of Studio D documentaries against the more intellectually grounded works of Canadian independent feminist filmmakers (names like Kay Armatage, Brenda Longfellow, Janine Marchessault, Midi Onodera and Mina Shum come to mind), a richer reading is possible if the utopian possibilities of the collection are taken as a whole. To adopt this approach sidesteps the troubling comparison between "naive" realism and a "progressive, sophisticated" aesthetic, proposing instead the concept of a combined legacy arising from this period of feminist engagement. And so, my reading of Studio D is a conscious attempt to work against the "erasure" of its documentary practices in the light of Shannon's belief that the best thing is when women come together to exchange stories, because "we hear each other well."

CHAPTER 5

WHAT ARE WE SAYING TO EACH OTHER? FEMINIST NARRATORS TELL THEIR STORIES

When we women offer our experience as our truth,
as human truth, then all the maps change.
— URSULA LE GUIN, *DANCING AT THE EDGE OF THE WORLD*

We knew how to snatch defeat from the jaws of victory.
— DOROTHY TODD HÉNAUT

The world's earliest archives or libraries
were the memories of women.
— TRINH T. MINH-HA, *WOMAN, NATIVE, OTHER*

STUDIO D APPROACHED ITS PROJECT FROM A POLITICAL PLACE THAT COULD only have been given life in 1970s Canada, invoking, for the most part, the notion of women as an international sisterhood. Its films proposed the same tenet over and over — that scrutiny into women's lives would reveal the extent to which "the personal is political." If women understood their lives as politically constructed, they would be empowered to build fresh, more advantageous constructions. Feminist theorists have emphasized that linking these concepts together creates the vital mechanism that provides women with a sense of the direction they need to take so they can act together to bring about change. Without this overview tying together the scattered details of women's experiences, some have argued, women would have remained in "a continued sense of isolation and helplessness."[1]

The filmmakers in Studio D were committed to recording "women's different experience" by reclaiming women's stories and, thus, allowing these women to "speak in their own voices." By doing so, they challenged the hegemony and universality of male-centred discourse. During Studio D's lifetime, dominance became integral to the condition of difference within the women's movement. It created a particular set of tensions for white, liberal, heterosexual, middle-class feminists seeking to understand the significance of "women who were 'different' from the dominant female norm by virtue of race, class, sexuality, and/or disability"[2] and who insisted on being heard in *their* own voices. Ideas arising from life-writing theory are useful for examining the relationship between dominance and the representation of difference in Studio D documentaries. These ideas offer suggestions for unravelling the ways in which *all* women's lives are implicated in patriarchal structures and actions. What draws me to this line of thinking is the potential for considering how the stories told to me by the women of Studio D are related to the documentaries they produced. Studio D's filmography can be read as a collection of individual voices telling particular stories (of course, their version). Thus, this is not so much a story about getting it "right" but, more importantly, about letting a collection of voices "sound" in the "silent space"[3] where previously women's voices had only been faintly heard.

In this chapter, I examine specific Studio D documentaries to more deeply explore the value of women's narratives as an important format for telling their stories. By combining notions arising from life writing as a genre *and* consciousness-raising, a particular practice encouraged through feminist narratives emerges offering insights that make Studio D's work relevant for feminists today. In fact, the assertion of the feminist narrative structure is one of the most significant theoretical discourses transcoded into Studio D documentaries. By definition, the film translates feminist narratology into a visual form, challenging patriarchal social practices and stories. Feminist narratives rewrite the traditional narrative, resituating women as subjects who pose their own questions and conduct their own inquiries, reinvigorating and reconfiguring the terms of their narration.

Studio D's contribution to this form makes it possible "to systematize what is meant by narrative 'in the feminine'"[4] to some extent and to circulate such a notion as a means of potentially enhancing a sense of community within the Canadian women's movement. As Susan Knudson writes: "[A] plurality of voices fill[ing] our world, and structuralist analysis of narrative, combined with feminist consciousness, may help us to understand what we are hearing and saying to each other."[5] Such ideas endow the stories emanating from Studio D with a particularly rich resonance. The story of the Studio itself and the collected stories of women captured in its documentaries become a feminist "coming of age" story. Studio D's feminist approach distinguishes between narrative content and traditional form to reveal the gender–power relations encoded in narrative form, which feminist narratology (Studio D's rendering of the story) may have the power to break:

> Canadian feminist writing [I include Studio D work in this category regarding filmmaking analogous to "writing"] exemplifies a double strategy which contests binary gender definition in narratives while reclaiming the hero/subject position for women. Binary resolution is undermined through nominative, repetitive forms which are open-ended and spiralling rather than linear. At the same time, women are heroes of their own stories … Stories are focalized by characters who draw on what women have collectively learned. At the level of language, women speak to each other.[6]

IMAGINING FEMINIST COMMUNITIES

Great Grand Mother

One of the earliest documentaries produced by Studio D and directed by Anne Wheeler, the award-winning *Great Grand Mother* (1975), rewrites the story of how the Canadian nation was built. The film collects and records memories of European women who settled the Canadian Prairies early in the twentieth century, giving women today a glimpse of the legacy from one group of our foremothers. Their stories yield a unique collection of portraits that are drawn from their letters and diaries and from newspapers of the day, material missing from most official historical accounts of western settlement from that period. Personal accounts of early immigration experiences (hard physical work, birthing, caring for families in extreme isolation during long Prairie winters) and political activity (Prairie women were among the first women in Canada to receive provincial franchise) offer rich evidence of their particular struggles and achievements. One former suffragist remembers the sweetness of political victory but notes with some regret that members of her generation ought to have pressed for greater social and polical automony rather than "resting on their laurels" — a message still resonant today.

Historical space in *Great Grand Mother* is sutured together with a series of documentary techniques. The directors deploy "talking heads" in a feminist strategy to represent the women, now seniors, as voices of authority. Women face the camera directly as they recount their memories, enumerating valuable details, pronouncing and judging through personal experience. The background, a woman's kitchen or parlor, reinscribes the offical space (most often the television studio or the professional office) usually reserved for traditional talking heads and asserts the authority of the domestic sphere. Archival photographs culled from personal collections depict these women giving detailed and vital historical clues about settlers' lives. By including historical film clips from NFB documentaries produced for the Ministry of Transport and Immigration, *Great Grand Mother* creates a counterversion and demonstrates how the "official" record missed the realities of these women's lives. The stories the women tell paint a new picture in which women are the major subjects, their voices rewriting the historical script.

The structure of *Great Grand Mother* sets a prototypic form to which the majority of Studio D films would adhere (the much-acclaimed *Forbidden Love: The Unashamed Stories of Lesbian Lives* provides a notable exception), a practice that earned Studio D the reputation for making formulaic films — "craft" rather than "art"[7] — among some feminist film theorists and film critics. Are there ways, then, that this form might be considered to take up a "writing beyond the ending"? Even though many of Studio D films use a combination of talking heads, direct camera address, films clips from other documentaries, photographs and flashback techniques, the filmmakers of *Great Grand Mother* use this material in fresh ways. The talking head that links the past to the future, the story that doubles back on itself, the iconography of women at the kitchen table and other such familiar features of Studio D film effects a looping and linking of women's lives that deviates from the standard linear narrative. Indeed, women's multiple conversations create significant touchstones for fresh conversations and create archeological tracings that invite new generations of women into the conversation.

Speculating on such possibilities for "reading beyond the ending" allows me to frame a response to the critique of reductionism that Studio D's philosophy of "unity in difference" has invited. While the very form of these realist feminist documentaries encourages a sense of the unified subject, they also invite a radical, new and politicized reinterpretation of the position of the woman as subject. The memories themselves as "experience" furnish a rich source of detail about women's lives and identify issues that affected those lives deeply: the difficulties with respect to health care, the nature and value of women's work (in one section a woman remembers how one of her neighbours, highly educated and in possession of a genteel upbringing, is, nonetheless, harnessed along with the oxen to help clear the land of stumps and rocks), the vital role these women played in sustaining family life and in fostering a sense of community.

Through its representation of women and nation, the film draws a regional, historic, feminist portrait that, in effect, instructs many Canadian spectators about themselves and their country and the fundamental role these Prairie women played in creating it. *Great Grand Mother* was released in the same year that the United Nations declared International Women's Year and three years after the establishment of the National Action Committee on the Status of Women (NAC). Its focus on the conditions of women's lives illustrated the intergenerational nature of women's concerns and delivers a message of resistence and community to contemporary Canadian feminists from a century back in time. In Kathleen Shannon's mind, "the circumstances [for women] hadn't really changed,"[8] making the portrait that much more relevant.

Under the Willow Tree

If the stories told through *Great Grand Mother* can be read as a kind of life writing[9] encouraging intergenerational consciousness-raising about women's circumstances linking then and now, *Under the Willow Tree* (1997) enjoins women to search out those voices of women muffled through time. In *Under the Willow Tree*, directed by Dora Nipp, a remarkable example of feminist narratology surfaces in the history of Chinese women in Canada. The film reveals a new account of "gender as nation" that is more than 100 years old and missing from the official historical record, a reminder of the value *and* urgency of telling women's stories. The cinematic representations of these pioneer Chinese women — mainly in Vancouver, Toronto and Montreal — through old photographs and through the memories and experiences of their daughters, nieces and granddaughters demonstrate the ability of the Eurocentric historical discourse to obliterate and eliminate questions of difference. This Canadian story of settlement, erased through questions of language, culture and gender, has remained largely hidden, precisely because of its specific socio-cultural circumstances. The telling entrenches such experiences in history, fuelling a particular account of Canadian cultural identity that likewise "provides the under girding foundation for filmic representation."[10] Further, women's stories in both films function "'practically and symbolically' revealing rich insights into the nature of political community-making,"[11] nationally as well as among women.

Under the Willow Tree also uses a series of photographs, talking heads, female voice-overs, evidence gleaned from diaries, postcards and footage from newsreels and old NFB documentaries. Though its form is vintage NFB (and Studio D), its story is astonishing in originality and specificity, setting down an unprecedented historical record of the lives of a generation of women who immigrated to Canada from China at the turn of the nineteenth century. A classic example of the first moment of second-wave feminist documentary filmmaking, *Under the Willow Tree* exhibits the best of that moment — "an interest in history and a concern with the experiences of women" — grounded in the assumption that "the truth of women's experience *can* be known and that the source of this truth lies in the experiences of women themselves."[12]

Through the testimony of daughters, sisters, granddaughters and nieces, we hear stories about the first generation of Chinese Canadians, the majority of whom spoke little or no English: stories of the cold-blooded Head Taxes imposed in 1885 and 1904; of the brutality of the *Chinese Exclusion Act* passed on July 1, 1923, known among Chinese Canadians as the "Day of Humiliation"; of fierce loyalties, deprivation and pride. Augmented by vintage documentary footage, these stories reveal a history of national pride and responsibility on the part of the Canadian Chinese community — a community that raised large sums of money to aid the war effort from 1939 to 1945, even though Chinese citizens were denied the right to vote in Canada until 1947 and Chinese Canadian women lost their Canadian citizenship the moment they married a Chinese immigrant.

A symbolic moment occurs towards the end of the film when Jean Lumb, the first Chinese-Canadian recipient of the Order of Canada, recounts events of decades-long lobbying efforts by the Chinese Canadians to effect family reunification, finally possible with the 1947 repealing of the *Exclusion Act*. Encouraged by MPP Roland Michener to travel to Ottawa with her lobby group in 1957 on the grounds that a woman's presence might strengthen the Chinese community's case with immigration minister Ellen Fairclough, Lumb finds herself seated on the "good ear" side of the partially deaf prime minister John Diefenbaker. Unable to hear the arguments being put forward by the delegate on his "bad" side, Diefenbaker turns to Lumb for assistance. Serendipitously, Lumb becomes the "unofficial spokesperson" (the subject in terms of feminist narratology) for the whole delegation, successfully presenting its case. Lumb wears her Order of Canada proudly in the film, although her anecdote suggests, tellingly, that for a hundred years, the Canadian nation had only been half listening, not really wanting to hear.[13]

While the cultural identity emerging from women's reality celebrates Chinese-Canadian experience and demonstrates a struggle against hegemonic political structures, a dynamic construction of identity is "constituted within, not outside representation." The feminist narrative of the personal as national and cultural —"not the so-called return to roots but a coming-to-terms-with our 'routes'" [14] — renders the constructing of a social identity an act of power. Alongside *Great Grand Mother*, *Under the Willow Tree* performs an expansionist function, breaking the silence that separates generations of women from each other, encouraging and empowering the spectator "to make her own meaningful story as she reads."[15] Helen Buss imagines "true" history as the compilation of everyone's biography, a "difficult ideal to achieve, but certainly [shaping] the richest cultural cradle."[16] These films of our ancestors tell women that the personal *is* the political *as well as* the "nation" and invite us, in turn, to consider how our stories fit into the whole.

Women at the Well

Dionne Brand's *Women at the Well* series (1989–1993) not only breaks a silence for Black women in Canada but also marks an important moment in the Canadian women's movement. I refer, of course, to the moment when Black feminists confronted racism within the women's movement itself, illuminating in vivid detail the complex interconnections between racism and sexism. This moment, as Enakshi Dua points out, brought into question the very foundations of Canadian society — its "whiteness"[17] — thereby opening up a particular complexity for Studio D. The *Women at the Well* series breaks fresh ground, capturing fragments of Black Canadian history that are revealed through women's voices, previously eclipsed by a "Eurocentric lens." The series is made up of three films: *Older, Stronger, Wiser* (1989) is drawn from Brand's research published in *No Burden to Carry: Narratives of Black Working Women in Ontario 1920s to 1950s*; *Sisters in the Struggle* (1991), documents Black women's activism in labour and political organizing; *Long Time Comin'* (1993) celebrates Black women artists. Together, the films inaugurate a composite portrait of social and cultural identity generated by the very expression of "lived human lives."

In the series, a powerful "dialogic" potential emerges, made possible, in part, through Studio D's interactive audience relations, which were grounded in its philosophy of the personal as political and of women as an international community. The dialogue, however, launched by the voices of Black women, opens up the stage so new conversations can take place and previously obscured issues can take prominence, effectively shifting feminist debates into new territory:

> The cultural bond that joins these geographically and ethnically diverse cinematic statements is the artistic and political desire to develop innovative, relevant, and authentic relationships between cinematic representation and cultural identity. The effect of filmic representations contextualized by historical trajectories is a powerful icon which resists marginality, promotes survival strategies, and, potentially, transforms audiences into proactive, socially-conscious viewers.[18]

Older, Strong, Wiser

Older, Stronger, Wiser, another ancestor narrative, compiles life stories of five Black women who are mentors, role models, political activists and spiritual leaders. Insights drawn from their experiences of racism and sexism prefigure issues that would later be theorized in post-colonial theory, offering an early and astute analysis. Rina Fraticelli was familiar with Dionne Brand as a scholarly writer who was attentive to the unique thematic and ideological terrain unearthed when Black experience is foregrounded. She also knew Brand was an accomplished poet and author of fiction. Fraticelli invited Brand into Studio D to take a leading role in the *Women at the Well* series. Brand was in the midst of finalizing her book, *No Burden to Carry*, a historical account of Black working women in Ontario from the 1920s to the 1950s. She had collected the oral histories of fifteen women in an unprecedented "excavation of Black women's history in Canada"[19] absent from any literature of that period. Drawing from her research, Brand wrote the script for the film, which featured a number of the women from her book: Addie Aylestock (b. 1909), ordained as a Methodist minister, the first Black pastor in Canada; Gwen Johnston (b. 1915) who founded Third World Books with her husband Lennie; and, Grace Fowler (b. 1915) who made a successful career farming.

Fraticelli's invitation to represent Black women's lives from *their* point of view (the *only* kind of film Brand wanted to consider), allowed Studio D to bridge the gap between feminist communities divided by questions of race and racism. Such "political declarations"[20] represent a particularly significant shift of power relations (remember that Studio D had just undergone an internal upheaval with Fraticelli dispersing the team of in-house directors). *Older, Stronger, Wiser* was directed by Claire Prieto and documents the lives of Black women elders — the three mentioned above, as well as a union activist and a community organizer/teacher — told in their own voices. Their recounted experiences reveal stories that analyse the politics of their time and speak about what it meant "to be Black in a predominantly white society, with its incumbent difficulties." As a researcher, Brand knew that the material she had recovered had the power to "influence the approach of feminist research"[21] and that it was well-suited for Studio D as the rare site where struggles of this nature could be recorded in the medium of documentary film.

Although oft criticized for exerting "a reductive pressure"[22] on the shifting definitions of feminism, Studio D gave Brand the forum in which to articulate the much-needed cultural perspective. In doing so, she projected the primary principles of Black women's cinema: asserting that Black women worldwide share a history of patriarchal oppression; validating their experiences as real and significant; investigating their cultural history, including the survival techniques Black women use to resist oppression and (re)formulate concepts of self; and acknowledging and respecting alternative knowledge systems and the means by which Black women "recall and recollect."[23]

Indeed, the idea behind the series at that particular juncture in Canadian feminism was generated by the urgency of that particular historical moment and by Brand's sense of her own duty in circulating ideas regarded as highly contentious by many, including some feminists, "about the condition of being Black women ... as one means in the effort to change our conditions and to surmount the notion that women could not speak as authorities."[24] Brand's assessment is borne out in the response from the women involved in making the three films. She discovered that the subjects who appeared in *Older, Stronger, Wiser* were enthusiastic about sharing their memories and visions with the next generation, a similar reaction for those involved in *Sisters in the Struggle,* directed by Brand and Ginny Stikeman.

Sisters in the Struggle

Sisters in the Struggle grew out Brand's own activist experiences and her desire to empower Black women, to say to them, "Here we are, on screen." The film is organised around the personal testimonies and insights of a number of Black women who had taken leading roles as community organizers, politicians, labour and feminist organizers. Their insights effectively linked their struggles to the pervasive climate of racism and systematic violence against women and people of colour, more generally.

One of the figures to appear in the film is the activist Sherona Hall. Hall had been involved in the deportation of women who had come from Jamaica as domestic workers. Originally, these women had come to Canada, encouraged by the Canadian government, looking for a workable solution to address the demands for daycare mounted by (white) women in the paid labour force. All had been fine until the economy declined, at which point the government decided to find ways to deport these women. Consequently, government officials began to scrutinize their papers, "discovering" that they had children they had not declared. As

Hall testified, these were children they had been encouraged *not* to declare. When the travesty became public knowledge (the film documents this material faithfully), many members of Canadian society — the Black community, mothers and citizens of conscience of all stripes — rose up against the injustice.

Using Studio D's hallmark techniques (action filmed in real time, women addressing the camera directly, clips spliced from television news footage and from other documentaries to provide background and context, female narration, Brand reading her own script), the film reveals in angry detail how Black women resist hegemonic discrimination that is institutionalized by government policy and enforced by the police they hire. Scenes of political resistance, foregrounding questions of experience, history, culture and identity, reveal how Eurocentric ideas in Canada are "employed to construct the idea of the nation, motherhood, and morality."[25] If the film effectively dismantles any notion of "essentializing" women's experiences, the entire series takes on the tyranny of whiteness, deconstructing "the discursive understanding of race"[26] in Canadian society. Brand's motive was clearly to locate and deconstruct sites of ambiguity and indeterminacy by rewriting the stories of Black women. Here were highly politicized women, members of the Black community, engaged in a wholly Black feminist endeavour to improve Canadian society — for all. *Sisters in the Struggle* effectively records their protest, capturing that particular anti-racist labour demonstration, preserving it for the historical record, and in doing so proposes that change is possible through the radical sounding of voice.

Long Time Comin'

If British filmmaker Pratibha Parmar's work is celebrated for expanding notions of nation where "there ain't no Black women and no one seems to have thought about lesbians at all,"[27] Brand's *Long Time Comin'* furnishes a Canadian example of and pays homage to the power of the artist as cultural creator. *Long Time Comin'* is primarily a portrait and celebration of artists Faith Nolan and Grace Channer and functions as a vital historical document. Identifying themselves as Black lesbians (Nolan is fifth generation Canadian, born in Halifax and raised in Toronto's Regent Park; Channer is first generation Canadian from Jamaica and Britain), the two interpret their art practices (music and painting) as artistic and political expressions of "the people, the culture, the time."[28] Richly layered, the film highlights the friendship between the two women and portrays them as artists at work, at the same time capturing moments of radical feminist activism: a Take Back the Night March and women building a political education centre (Camp Sis) for women and children. The humour and life-affirming portraits that infuse the film incorporate history, myth and experience through words, sound and images (Nolan is responsible for the music in this film as well as the two others in the series). The artists' manifesto, derived from "an uncompromising drive to know themselves, recreate themselves, and connect with others,"[29] projects a unique example of life-writing and feminist narratology as well as capturing an urgent political project. The film opens with Faith Nolan in concert, thanking the crowd for coming: "This is a great evening for me, probably the highlight of my life — I mean it. This is really important to me — more important than most of the things I do." She then dedicates the opening number "Sister Hold My Hand" to Grace, "my bosom buddy." The refrain "I don't want to walk this race alone" pays tribute to a shared artistic vision as it invites in audience members and film spectators alike. When Nolan asserts, "This is our time to rewrite, to recreate ourselves," she lays out the ideological groundwork of the film.

Performance scenes are intercut with shots of the artists explaining their art anecdotally or speaking directly into the camera lens and participating in informal discussions at workshops. As Canner explains, "The importance of the artist in the Black community is to give voice to the community as a whole." The personalizing of her work sets out a radical manifesto, inserting a Black feminist presence into the traditional realm of Western art history, captured in the sequencing of the film. In one scene filmed in her studio, Channer speaks directly into the camera and says, "I'm in the process of revolution, in the process of liberation as a woman. The official history of art didn't hold a lot of information for me." Here, she speaks of university classes where she faced racism and homophobia and "a lot of white, male professors teaching about their world." Channer, of course, wanted to know about Africa and Asia but encountered no teachers who "represented that." The film cuts to another scene of Channer at work in her studio, fabricating a sculpture — a "tree woman" from found material, a knot of wood the head, and twigs her body — as she explains her work to a group of children.

In a similar sequence, Nolan describes herself as a Black lesbian musician needing to sing what is authentic to her. Describing how Black female singers were often deprived of musical instruments, she sits, tuning her guitar and talks of her love of the Blues: "Love songs weren't for me but the Blues spoke directly to how we live as Black people. I listened to it like the Bible — it held fundamental truths for me." The camera sequencing, shifting from concert stage to rehearsal space to artist's studio and, in one section, to Nolan's kitchen, offers dynamic evidence of her particular artistic resistance and creativity, inviting spectators to contemplate their own political positions. As they speak, Channer and Nolan address important political issues: what does it mean to grow up in racist society? what does it mean to name yourself an artist, a lesbian?

Overall, the *Women at the Well* series are "films in their time,"[30] constructing a roadmap to radical social change through recovered historical testimony. They "perform" anger that has been transformed into political action, creating a celebration of art as personal and cultural validation as well as capturing a moment in Canada's cultural history. But how and in what ways might a rereading of these films be of contemporary as well as historical relevance? Author and poet NourbeSe Philip offers a key to accessing their deeper significance through a construct she calls an "*i-mage*":

> Fundamental to any art form is the image, whether it be the physical image as created by the dancer and choreographer, the musical image of the composer and musician, the visual image of the plastic artist, or the verbal image, often metaphorical, of the writer and poet ... The word "image" ... conveys what can only be described as the irreducible essence ... likened to the DNA molecules at the heart of all life. Use of unconventional orthography, *i-mage,* in this instance, does not only represent the increasingly conventional deconstruction of certain words, but draws on the Rastafarian practice of privileging the "I" in many words.[31]

Thus, the *i-mage* speaks to "the essential being of the people among whom and for whom the artist creates." This, however, presents a challenge to the artist with a colonial origin, since New World language effectively strips her of her original language "denying the voice power to make and simultaneously to express the i-mage."[32] Philip implies that such stories (embodied in such Studio D documentaries) become vehicles "to subvert, turn upside down, inside out and even sometimes erase"[33] ethnocentric representations that distort and silence. Channer's account of how her art (part of a show of collected work) was marginalized and misread by the gallery curators is "corrected" by camera footage revealing Channer in her studio, working on a piece of sculpture — the full-length figure of a Black woman composed of found natural objects — reclaiming through language, the material language of the artist, telling her own story in her own voice. Thus, as Philip writes, language becomes a powerful political instrument, "more than a distillation … the truest representation, the mirror *i-mage* of the experience."[34] Philip's approach, then, combines with the portraits of these Black women artists to offer rich analytic opportunities for "reading" the stories of women who come from a non-European background and told through Studio D documentaries:

> For the many like me, Black and female, it is imperative that our writing [filmmaking] begins to recreate our histories and our myths, as well as integrate that most painful of experiences — loss of our history and our word. The reacquisition of power to create in one's own *i-mage* and to create one's own *i-mage* is vital to this process.[35]

REVISIONING NATION

If the goal was to mark territory for feminist change, Studio D documentaries, as a whole, identified a particular constellation of women's issues and feminist resistance to the status quo. I have already discussed how such films as *Not a Love Story* (1981) and *If You Love This Planet* (1982) contributed to the catalytic proliferation of feminist (and political) debates in Canada and abroad, shaping the nature of these debates to a certain degree by virtue of their institutional authority. Heated discussions arising from questions about pornography and censorship unleashed by reactions to *Not a Love Story*, in fact, led to valuable insights on the subject about which some feminists and society, in general, had been only superficially aware. *If You Love This Planet* clearly identified the urgent public need to speak out against nuclear armament in uncompromising and transparent terms easily grasped by the "ordinary" spectator. That the film presented only one point of view was its strength, in director Nash's view, since an argument *in favour* rightly seems "an insane 'no-brainer.'"[36] Its insistence on the single "point of view" focused attention on the ability of a feminist documentary to advance a different and persuasive rhetorical mode.

A number of Studio D documentaries proposed a sweeping reworking of the traditional narrative. Beverly Shaffer's portrait of Shirley Turcotte determined to reinvent her story captured in *To a Safer Place* (1987), for instance, implicitly proposes social transformation. As the determined survivor of incest, Turcotte retracing her memories, questions her mother, her sister and brother, her old nextdoor neighbours. How can children be taught to protect themselves against violent parents? How can women extricate themselves and their children from damaging domestic lives? What responsibilty do neighbours — or film spectators, for that matter — have to intervene? Fundamental elements of incest as a social problem in Canada are revealed as *To a Safer Place* throws down its challenge for feminist change to audiences.

If *To a Safer Place* reconfigures the territory around incest, *If You Love This Planet* forces us to shift our thinking about nuclear arms. Using feminist transformative thinking in an unorthodox (but compelling) approach and refusing to comply with diplomatic policy (never to embarrass the political leader of another country or to ruffle political feathers), the film underscores the ability of a feminist documentary to undermine traditional patriarchal values on military and state matters. Widely popular at the time, the film also caught the eye of one highly placed spectator. After viewing the film, Prime Minister Pierre Elliott Trudeau invited Dr. Caldicott — a medical doctor, a member of Physicians for Social Responsibility and the film's central figure — to a Liberal Party policy session on international affairs. He mentioned her often thereafter, fuelling speculation that she may well have played a "small but instrumental role"[37] in the genesis of Trudeau's own peace initiative. Today, *If You Love This Planet* remains a powerful endictment of nuclear armament, a message of renewed poignancy in the light of current political discussions.

Dorothy Todd Hénaut's triptych, *Firewords: Louky Bersianik, Jovette Marchessault, Nicole Brossard* (1986), created in the classic Studio D style, offers one of its most radical feminist propositions: social transformation to a woman-centred world through art and language. The film's ethos reflects Brossard's description of the artists' collective approach to feminist writing instigated through a radical language practice:

> You have to write two kinds of pages almost at the same time: one on which you try to understand and uncover the patriarchal lies; and another

> on which you try to give your new values, your utopias, and everything you find positive about yourself and about women. You have to write an unedited version, something that is totally new, to shape it. You bring in thoughts that have never been thought, use words in ways that they have never been used. You want to bring your anger but also your utopia and your connection and solidarity with other women.[38]

The film details the writers' call for women to emerge from the silence imposed on them by patriarchal society by inventing a new reality and a new language that reflects their own values and identities. The three half-hour segments, edited so they can be viewed singly or as a whole, present an intimate portrait of three Quebec avant-garde and deeply radical writers and, at the same time, capture a significant moment in Canadian literary (and feminist) history. The writers speak and read from their works in both French and English; the English subtitles by the accomplished translator Susanne de Lotinière-Harwood convey the rich textual meaning to English-speaking spectators, allowing them access to the aural richness of the texts in their original form.

Hénaut's film responds to what is sometimes regarded as a blind spot in Anglo-Canadian feminism. As Quebec historian Micheline Dumont points out, feminists in English Canada either forget about *la scène québéeçoise*, present distorted views or announce at the outset that they will not discuss Quebec.[39] *Firewords* effectively opens a window into the world of French artists and writers. It explores some of the tenets of *écriture féminine* as articulated in its particular Quebec experience, illuminating an important development in feminist theorizing. *Firewords* grew out of personal relationships and political aspirations Hénaut had developed over the years. Even though she was "theoretically challenged," Hénaut recognized that the writing was powerful and significant for feminism; she was willing to tread into this complicated territory, albeit with help:

> I always dreamed of being a bridge between English and French Canada. I had one foot in each culture and dreamed of being a bridge so I thought this could be a useful thing. It took me a year to do the research. I read twenty-seven books, some of them several times. It was *slow-going.* I had a counsellor to explain just what Nicole was really saying. I hired a consultant, the writer Gail Scott, who had feet in both camps, and Louise Forsythe, who taught French and feminism at the University of Western Ontario in London, was another of my counsellors. I really needed help. It was challenging intellectual theory.[40]

In retrospect, what makes this film particularly valuable is the way it captures performances of specific works while at the same time identifying the writers' preoccupations and capturing their everyday experiences as women. The section on Louky Bersianik features a dramatized segment from *L'Euguélionne,* Bersianik's groundbreaking and highly popular feminist novel. Performed by the illustrious Pol Pelletier, the segment displays the astonishment of a female Christ figure who descends to earth (searching for the male of her species) and encounters the bizarre world of "gender." Bersianik's satirical, subversive script gleefully attacks the bastions of tradition — philosophy, the law and government — offering up new archetypes as she dismantles the old. In another section, Bersianik tells Brossard that she has invented the word "gynicity" a joyous transgression into patriarchal language to capture the essence of female virility.

The Marchessault segment captures some of the artist's work (paintings, sculptures, masks of "tellurique" women), introducing it to spectators and also drawing on dramatizations to create insights into the artist's life and to reveal her literary work. The first dramatization pays homage to Marchessault's beloved grandmother. The sequence, enhanced by an animation overlay graphically celebrating both the matrilinear bond and women's culture, re-enacts an early "drawing lesson" narrated in Marchessault's own voice. The radical lesbian feminist, proud of her Aboriginal heritage and the spiritual traditions she traces through her "grand'mère," attributes her persistence as an artist to her early champion, "who has been encouraging me all along." Later, shots of Marchessault's outdoor mask-sculptures illustrate "the commitment to arts and crafts articulated through the traditional ideology of rural women,"[41] a distinctive marker of Quebec feminism.

In one particularly moving scene, Marchessault describes how she discovered one of her own canvasses (*Un Riopelle, un Chagall et un Marchessault*) [42] hanging on the boardroom wall of a corporate suite. An impoverished artist, Marchessault worked as a night concierge, cleaning offices in Place Bonaventure to be able to afford art supplies. Her story, shocking and revelatory, stands in sharp contrast to the opulence of her canvas on screen. Overcome by this experience, Marchessault relates how she quit her job, retreating to the country to take up writing. Her account of sharing a Puss 'n Boots meal with her cats is hilarious but also deeply shocking; a stark reminder of the plight of many women living in poverty and how they sometimes have to manage their difficult circumstances.

Zoe Dirse's skillful cinematography throughout *Firewords* mimics the avant-garde nature of the literary works she films, capturing the spirit of Marchessault's monologue *Night Cows* (performed brilliantly by Pol Pelletier) or illustrating Brossard's "mathematics of the imaginary" by playing with focus, splitting images or panning so closely over an object its meaning is blurred. The exploring eye of the camera in her hands seems to suggest, as does Brossard, that fresh interaction between subjects produces new meaning, untethering "manifold potentialities for transformation."[43]

Listening for Something (1996), one of the last documentaries produced by Studio D, brings together two well-known feminist literary figures, Dionne Brand and Adrienne Rich. The film, ostensibly a portrait of two North American feminists strategizing across difference, suggests a much broader geography. As the women read their poetry and engage in conversation, the film's landscapes alternate between Trinidad, Canada and the American Mid-west. The camera "listens in" on their discussion as they exchange ideas on racism, sexism and the 1990s radical swing of politics to the right, reminding me afresh of the time-honoured tradition of "women sitting around the kitchen table" that projects an image of the familiar, the inclusive in the politics of consciousness-raising.

Exploring the difficult discourse on "race" for Black and white feminists, they exemplify the power of ideas in mutual exchange. Rich speaks of the difficulty of being "a white woman in a racist world and wanting to be blameless ... to claim freedom from ... culpability" in response to Brand's critique of the concept of nation as one of "leaving out" Black women. Both agree that the right wing has been "far more alert to the power of feminism than feminists themselves." The fabric of ideas emerging remains current today — invigorating, challenging ideas, mapping possibilities for further theorizing, further activism — even though the film was produced as Studio D was being dismantled.

STORIES THAT CHALLENGE

In considering Studio D's pursuit of feminist issues, its "challenge" for change and ability to generate a certain measure of critical response to the feminist issues it chose to raise, the Studio could be credited with a durable contribution to developing Canadian feminist thought. I am struck by the similarity of approach and intention outlined by theorist Beverley Skeggs when she speaks about her research into feminist cultural theory in relation to the ways Studio D filmmakers spoke about their work:

> The research we do is not just a matter of where we come from and where we are located but also where we look to. Our work is motivated by our political aspirations. Behind each contribution stands a clear desire for change. It ranges through my idealistic desire to change the world, to challenge categories of "common knowledge," to deconstructing the representations which damagingly position women, to change theory. Because the work occurs in the academy does not mean it is not political.[44]

In fact, the work of producing both film and theory exhibits many parallels. Through the representation of women's experiences, Studio D offered its audiences opportunities to consider the disjunctures between women's individual experience and the representations offered by mainstream texts. Attempts of theory and film, however, are sometimes frustrated in their articulation. Skeggs notes, for example, that while the abstract interrogation of concepts is fundamental to feminist politics for its ability to challenge the very categories of knowledge available to us, the deconstruction of the term "woman" has led some feminist theorists into an impasse, wondering where to go if the central and certain object of their attentions has disintegrated.[45] Likewise, Studio D films, though realist in nature, from time to time set out models for feminist discussion and analysis.

Thus, the documentaries of Studio D require deconstructing and decoding, too, since the presentation of subjects is necessarily informed by the constitutive experiences of the filmmakers. As Skeggs suggests, we need to consider how representations and interpretations come to be produced because they embody power relations. To do so allows us all to "add to our knowledge of the production of the category woman, to feminist understandings."[46]

Overall, then, although operating as an instrument of the state presented Studio D with a series of benefits and difficulties, its position as a significant, if occasionally contentious, component of second-wave feminism is undeniable. Perhaps the words of Dorothy Todd Hénaut capture its position most accurately:

> You desire the collective, but your responsibility is to your superiors. Within an institution like the Film Board "equality" was impossible — the executive producer had the power. You can't hand that responsibility over to somebody else because it's *yours.* So you just live with it and say, "That's the way it is — we're going to do this as fairly as we can and not pretend that issues of power don't exist." Kathleen's energy came from her anger at injustice. In fact, I don't think that the Studio as a whole or Kathleen ever learned to deal with victory when we had it.[47]

While Studio D never relinquished its imagining of women as a global community, even though it adopted a "hands-off" attitude regarding theory, the Studio's documentary production played a unique role in recording a particular feminism within Canada. But what does it mean to engage in cultural production as a woman *and* as a Canadian? Coral Ann Howell argues for a powerful subjective presence for nationality and gender in Canadian women's fiction. Howell notes that the colonial mentality and Canada's relatively recent emergence from it holds close affinities with women's perceptions of themselves. If the early days of the women's movement created the conditions for change in women's consciousness as they struggled to find their own voices, Howell contends that the ability to challenge old notions contains fresh opportunities:

> Women's writing [filmmaking] has always been characterized by the urge to "throw the storyline open to question" and to implement "disarrangements which demand new judgements and solutions" … Such awareness of instability undermines traditional structures of political authority, making it possible to envisage "new solutions" where opposition is discredited in favour of a more pluralistic approach to questions of social and cultural order.[48]

If writers can be concerned with exploration and survival, crossing boundaries, challenging limits and glimpsing new prospects, problematizing theoretical issues by "writing in the instabilities,"[49] so too can Studio D documentaries. While some might have wished for alternative analyses and the interrogation of different sets of instabilities and greater theoretical or structural complexity, many of Studio D documentaries stand, nonetheless, as important artefacts that chart the very territory of evolving feminist inquiry and subsequent theorizing.

Indeed, when women engage in rethinking and revising their stories by inventing narrative strategies that transcend the traditional Oedipal drama, they offer a fresh consciousness and realign the components of "female identity."[50] Consciousness concerned with the "nature and locus of female power — and powerlessness"[51] becomes the ground for speculative narratives that "go beyond the ending." Thus, consciousness becomes the site of potential change. Such stories, according to Rachel Blau DuPlessis have the power to function as "quests" of consciousness: "These quests of consciousness have, moreover, as their major action the changing of seeing, perceiving, and understanding for characters."[52] To create such stories that include future vision, however crudely formed, is to break the reproduction of the status quo. If we consider documentaries as stories that encompass memoirs, confessions, journals and letters, indeed all auto/biographical acts involved in the collection and editing of oral histories and archival accounts, then we can see that Studio D documentaries are an enduring legacy to be read and reread by fresh generations of feminists seeking to make sense of women's lives.

CHAPTER 6

TURMOIL WITHIN AND WITHOUT: REACHING THE BREAKING POINT

Everybody didn't love Studio D, but many did.
— CLAIRE PRIETO, NIF PRODUCER

I have tried to write this thing calmly
even as its lines burn to a close.
— DIONNE BRAND, *NO LANGUAGE IS NEUTRAL*

"The moon is coming," said Evie. "Don't give in."
—LARISSA LAI, *SALT FISH GIRL*

TOWARDS THE END, JUST AS STUDIO D BEGAN TO INTEGRATE "DIFFERENCE" into its documentary work, it was beset by turmoil from both within and without. Kathleen Shannon, awarded the Order of Canada "for her extensive contribution to women's role in filmmaking"[1] in 1986, retired from the Studio for good in 1992, worn down by too many battles. In the early 1990s, external criticisms mounted against the "national treasure" as film critics and a number of feminists deemed Studio D work repetitious, boring and, in notable cases, riddled with historical inaccuracies (*The Burning Times)* and unforgivable Eurocentricities (*Goddess Remembered).* Tarel Quandt, reviewing *Goddess Remembered* for the feminist newspaper *Kinesis,* expressed concern about its essentialist representation of women as well as its "North American appropriation of other cultures":

> *Goddess Remembered* leads the audience down a slippery path towards embracing the female as superior because of her biological capabilities ... The dinner scene is quite bizarre — women reclaiming and embracing ancient cultural practices, calling the differing goddesses their own, as they sit around a lavish dinner table with all the trimmings.[2]

Other critics labelled Studio D "a cabal of 'bourgeois fascists' ... [still] others a vehicle for feminist propaganda."[3] Indeed, Studio D had drawn heavily from a number of high-profile, "popular" American feminists in many of its films, a practice roundly criticized as promoting a simplistic and essentialist attitude that privileged a Western middle-class feminist consciousness. Such ideas would be expressed by the feminist "expert" herself in a talking-head cameo, her argument integrated seamlessly into the fabric of the documentary. Like most features of Canadian social and political life, the Canadian women's movement at that time drew its most salient relationships with its counterpart in the United States,[4] even though Canadian feminists looked to the state as the primary instrument of change, readily accepting state funding in contrast with radical American feminists who regarded relations with the state as "hopeless and beside the point." Meanwhile, Canadian feminists maintained a low profile on the North American stage — women in Canada did not declare themselves, nor were they declared, speakers of the movement on the whole.[5]

This explains, in part, the appeal for Studio D of popular American feminists such as Betty Friedan, Andrea Dworkin, Gloria Steinem, Robin Morgan, Susan Griffin, Starhawk, and later Catherine McKinnon and Naomi Wolfe, or international figures like Germaine Greer and Simone de Beauvoir, whose publications were translated into English. After all, many Canadian women were reading their works. Their voices, however, caused Studio D's film to project a brand of liberal feminism, intended or not. Studio D's refusal to engage in the complexities of these critical concerns (questions of representation, gendered subjectivity, identification and spectatorship practices) coupled with its activist agenda created an inadvertent ideological exclusivity, contradicting the inclusive image the Studio held of itself. As Dorothy Todd Hénaut recalls:

> We never became too theoretical because we were really concerned with our [breadth of] audience. If you become too specialized, you end up with audiences at film festivals only. We *never* finished a film without testing it with typical audiences. We wanted women, people, to think about the issues, so they [the issues] had to be accessible.[6]

Here, perhaps, critiques of the social realist feminist documentary as naive do ring true. It may well be the case that the theoretical consequences of adopting particular approaches — even "anti-theoretical" ones — was not well thought out.

However, in the light of its mandate "to make films by and about women" in a Canadian context, Studio D became an easy target in its failure to incorporate Canadian feminists as authoritative voices. The most notable example of this is when Thelma McCormack — a professor of sociology at York University and an anti-censorship spokesperson — penned a letter to NFB commissioner James de Beaujeu Domville following the release of *Not a Love Story* to express annoyance at being edited out of the final version.[7] McCormack had given a six-hour interview to the Studio D film crew only to be dropped in favour of American feminists Susan Griffin and Robin Morgan, although McCormack's name appears in the credits at the end of the film. By drawing on American experts, a phenomenon that might equally be read as another example of American influence on Canadian life, Studio D was, in fact, situating its concept of "women" within the broader North American context. In his response to McCormack's critique of Studio D, Domville — who had, no doubt, consulted with Studio D — pointed out that the "culture [of pornography] is a North American phenomenon, and the filmmakers approached it as such."[8] However, while it appears that members of Studio D were more familiar with Morgan's popular *Sisterhood is Powerful* than McCormack's more scholarly work, the Studio's emphasis on American and international feminist figures might be read as evidence of its ideological commitment to women as members of an international community with a preference for a more populist view.

Hénaut, the producer of *Not A Love Story*, remembered the events in a different light:

> It took two years to make [the film] and two years to distribute. I thought I could produce that and work on my own film, something on nutrition. But the film just swallowed us whole. It just ate us up. It was hard to keep our heads above water because pornography was such a deadening subject. I had some of the pornography magazines in my office. They were like a malevolent presence because they showed so much hate towards women and, in fact, towards men. I had to get them out of my office and put them in the cutting room where they had all that stuff. The editor went [away] several times just to get back her strength to work on that

> film ... there was so little written on pornography [at that time]. Susan Griffin had done some writing [as well as] a couple of the other women but there was *very little* done on it.[9]

Hénaut's description of pornography as "such a deadening subject" coupled with Domville's defence of Studio D's approach leads me to conclude that the Griffin material was included both because its author was in agreement that pornography was, indeed, deadening and because the filmmakers felt that Griffin's presence endowed the film with a greater international authority.

When Studio D films were screened in commercial theatres, they had to contend (as did all feminist films) with reviewers who were not necessarily knowledgeable or sympathetic to the feminist idiom, underscoring the difficulty feminist films still face to a certain degree. When *Five Feminist Minutes,* a compilation of sixteen short films, was premiered in Montreal in 1989 as part of the Women's International Film and Video Festival, respected culture critic Stephen Godfrey typified it as "an uneven rollercoaster ride of talent, with a half a dozen terrific segments."[10] While Godfrey deemed *Prowling by Night* "an extraordinary example of the kind of work Studio D can foster,"[11] he deemed that the film as a whole tried to be all things to all people, apparently ignoring its appeal to the women's communities for which it was made.

Familiar criticisms, openly hostile to a feminist agenda, labelled Studio D's film work tiresome, predictable and opinionated. As one reviewer wrote, "balanced arguments are not what it strives for." In a review of *No Longer Silent* (a film that travels to India to explore the abuses of the traditional dowry system, including the question of wife-burning) and *Speaking of Nairobi* (the film documenting the unofficial conference attended by 14,000 to 16,000 women held at the same time as the official 1985 UN Conference on Women in Nairobi, Kenya, which was attended by 2,000 delegates),[12] Frank McKie griped that the films were "bombarded with feminist lingo — more time seems to have been spent on creating polemical works than worrying about these movies as films."[13] Of course, the "need" to adhere to a balanced approach in feminist arguments is a classical feature of (patriarchal) rhetorical practice that only fuels feminist incredulity at being expected to play by such rules. Take for example Terre Nash's outspoken refusal to defend nuclear armament in *If You Love This Planet.* The labels, nonetheless, had an impact.

INTERNAL CRITICISMS

Shannon's early vision of a vigorous and thriving feminist collective was severely blunted by the reorganization of Studio D in 1989 culminating in the reallocation of six Studio D filmmakers to other NFB studios and seriously damaging its morale. Rina Fraticelli was forced to grapple with an unsignalled NFB policy change that, in effect, cut Studio D's production budget by roughly $100,000, imperilling its plan to launch ten films that year. The situation caused at least one press report to suggest that Studio D was finished:

> Reduced federal government funding has claimed another victim at the National Film Board of Canada. Studio D, the award-winning women's studio — will disband as of April 1. Six filmmakers on staff will join other NFB studios. Studio D with a production budget of $795,000 will remain a source of funding for women freelance filmmakers across Canada.[14]

Fraticelli laid blame squarely at the government's doorstep. She criticized its lack of vision *and* its privatization of culture, referring to its new focus on private-sector film and video industries in Canada in which the NFB was to participate:

> It is no mystery that the NFB is radically underfunded by the federal government and that it is on a collision course with its own mandate as a public filmmaker ... the NFB cannot hope to serve its mandate while being governed by the laws of the marketplace.[15]

Agreeing to refocus its efforts on developing partnerships with the private sector, the NFB unsuccessfully bid for a specialty channel license. The cost of the proposal was in excess of $800,000 and caused the NFB to table a large budget deficit in 1987–1988.

Fraticelli was frustrated that broken government promises of increased funding created false expectations among independent filmmakers who looked to Studio D with the expectation that employment equity programs, for instance, might lead to film contracts or even longer-term associations with the Studio. She noted, "[Their] expectations grow in light of government rhetoric as *our* means to fulfill these expectations are diminished."[16] Fraticelli, of course, was right, and there are many examples that support her statement. In one instance, independent filmmaker Midi Onodera applied for production assistance to complete *The Displaced View*. She was confident that her film fit Studio D's newly published film proposal guidelines perfectly. Studio D's "Guidelines for Film Proposals" stated that "preference would be given to Canadian women filmmakers and to films relevant to Canadian women demonstrating a conscious effort to be representative of Canadian racial/cultural realities."[17] What Onodera didn't know was that behind her rejection letter was the fact that Studio D's five-year budget had just been slashed. Although Onodera received subsequent funding "for a project on multiculturalism" through the Secretary of State, Studio D's refusal left her feeling rankled.[18]

Less than one year later in 1990, Fraticelli, fed up with administrative struggles, resigned her position and left Studio D just short of its fifteenth anniversary. In a press interview with Stephen Godfrey of the *Globe and Mail*, she spoke of the "resentment" from both male and female Canadians against the Studio: "I think people are uncomfortable with the idea that we are outside the mainstream, questioning the status of women and how they are treated."[19] Referring to the shocking murder of fourteen young women at l'École Polytechnique at l'Université de Montréal in 1989, still dominating public imagination at the time, Fraticelli argued that since the murders "everything has changed but nothing has changed":

> There's this idea that we [women] have to compensate for having taken so much when, really, so little has been given. The fact is women as a group are no further ahead economically than they were before. The tensions between these two perspectives is explosive, and Studio D has to continue working on two fronts as a result; both with men in mainstream fields that haven't been traditionally open to women, but also on our own, as women, to keep questioning the assumptions on which society works.[20]

Meanwhile, within Studio D, New Initiatives in Film (NIF), responsible for the successful *Women at the Well* series, would run aground at the very moment it created unprecedented opportunities for Aboriginal women and women of colour to tell their stories. Structured to balance institutional support with more grassroots methods, NIF had three main components: a Resource Bank that provided a computerized listing of "Women of Colour and Women of the First Nations across Canada" involved in filmmaking; an internship program offering valuable production experience for interning filmmakers in Studio D; and Summer and Fall Institutes that offered scholarships and annual film seminars to women across the country.[21] Although some expressed concern that NIF would become just another form of cultural ghettoization, it was grounded in the stated principle that minority women needed "independence and authority" over their own creativity. However, when Renée Du Plessis (NIF co-ordinator from April to December 1991) was fired, the long-standing murmurs that Studio D held a tight rein on the "proper" (its *own* view) approach to feminist filmmaking became more public. Sun-Kyung Yi, a Toronto-based writer and filmmaker, observed at the time:

> In the past, Studio D has been criticized for being a propaganda tool that caters only to those who conform to its political agenda, and making films in the same predictable form that is becoming known as the "NFB documentary style." Studio D executives have been also accused of having a narrow perspective that prevents them from fully understanding or appreciating women from differing perspectives of race, class, or sexual orientation.[22]

Moreover, Du Plessis herself reported that during the 1991 Summer Institute, the Studio became a battleground where "women of colour were pitted against the studio's white executives; entry-level and advanced filmmakers were locked in a power struggle; conflicting feminist views took precedence over filmmaking."[23]

Legally classified as "coloured" in South Africa, her country of origin, Du Plessis felt that she was trapped in essentialist notions of race and colour and was regarded as not "dark" enough and too "upper-class." As a consequence, she was accused by NIF's advisory board and by Studio D of being inflexible and insensitive to women of colour and of contributing to systemic racism.[24] The dispute divided the feminist filmmaking community into those who feared that Studio D was simply unprepared for the diversity of feminist ideologies and cultures and those who regarded this as just another example of Studio D insisting that women in general and women of minority groups, in particular, be portrayed as victims. One sobering reality to emerge was that women were reluctant to speak openly about this issue unless anonymity was assured since Studio D was "the only [funding] game in town" for their own projects. One filmmaker, insisting on anonymity, stated:

> Their [Studio D executives] view is oppression, oppression, oppression. There's no celebration of feminism or acknowledgement of its successes. Studio D hasn't progressed in the last 20 years. They've been making the

> same damn films that carry the same message: women are victims. At first, white women made them, now they're getting women of colour to make the same thing.[25]

In spite of the reluctance on the part of some critics to speak openly, the Studio was nevertheless represented in some published reports in unflattering terms as an implacable dictator with a lamentably narrow vision, catering only to those who would conform to its vision. Executive producer Ginny Stikeman cautioned, "I have to remind people that we can't do it all. We have to choose. It's not our mandate to exclude women. It's just that we can't include them all."[26] In doing so, she was clearly referring to the long-standing funding drought as the overriding circumstance, although few were prepared to cede to her account.

When NIF was first launched, Rina Fraticelli, who had been hired with an express mandate to bring a revitalized vision to Studio D, envisioned it as a catalytic haven for non-white women wanting to make films in the historical footsteps of Studio D, describing the relationship thus: "as Studio D to the NFB; so NIF to Studio D."[27] Sensitive to questions of race, Fraticelli issued a memo (dated 22 August 1988 [NFBA]) in which she cautioned members of the feminist studio on "the subject of racial politics in our lives and in our work," calling for a meeting to "consider some of the practical steps we can take around anti-racist consciousness-raising." The call for the meeting was in direct response to correspondence Fraticelli had received from a member of the Women's Marketing Development Group. The woman (of Chinese origin) had respectfully raised the issue of essentialism, pointing out that *Goddess Remembered* recognized only Euro-Western experience, ignoring the other three-quarters of the world. However, when the NIF conflicts arose, it might be argued that NIF found itself implicated in a hierarchical relationship with Studio D, replicating the very struggles Studio D had experienced as the "other" studio within the Film Board. The irony, as Burgess points out, is almost too cruel to contemplate: "The mainstream [Studio D] is positioned to be merely tolerant of the goals and achievements of the minority group [NIF], without having to engage in substantive change."[28]

Other filmmakers would express frustrations similar to those of Du Plessis. A few years later, filmmakers Aerlyn Weissman and Lynne Fernie, working on an ambitious international project to detail the "history of lesbian from day one,"[29] encountered resistance from Studio D when it proposed narrowing the focus to Canada only. Their research into the 1950s and 1960s had unearthed a wealth of Canadian material, a vital but hidden aspect of gay history, that would culminate in the acclaimed Studio D documentary *Forbidden Love* (1992), an unabashed celebration of lesbian sexuality. Having tapped into a rich vein of oral history, their intent was to focus on the butch–femme relationship. The roles as a defining device of lesbian identity set in significant historical context became the sticking point. As Weissman declared:

> They [Studio] wanted nice stories. Despite butch/femme being the lesbian style of the '50s, they were uneasy with it. I think Lynne particularly understood that some of the problems the people at Studio D were having were indicative of their own lack of political evolution.[30]

INTERNAL POWER STRUGGLES

Stories like these make it obvious that throughout its history, Studio D suffered through some of the same tensions experienced in the women's movement at large — debates around sexuality, pornography and censorship,[31] recognition of race- and class-bound gender formations, the perceived "divide" between activist and "theoretical" feminisms, indeed, the recognition of different feminisms, played out occasionally through personal (and personally injurious) fights between women. Perhaps Studio D's insistence on the notion of "gender-as-monocause and sisterhood-as-monocure,"[32] as well as its admitted unwillingness to "subscribe" to theory and its protected (isolating? constricting?) institutional site meant that — by its very location — it was encouraged in the blindness of privilege, a criticism that feminists have levelled at men. Certainly, as I argue earlier, Studio D's position within an institution dictated a necessary adherence to NFB standards and procedures, in spite of the fact that its primary interest lay in fulfilling the mandate of making films for women. This contradiction placed it in a perpetually strained Janus-head stance, like the Roman god looking forwards and backwards.

The NIF dispute might also be understood through what Biddy Martin describes as "our ideological struggles with and against one another, particularly in the context of identity politics and representation."[33] Clearly, if all of the NIF and Studio D principals had been able to step back and consider how tensions around power politics often work to pit feminists against each other, the outcome might have been more positive.

Reframing Wendy Brown's argument about power, Martin contends that "the failure to understand how power works inevitably leads to ever more hyperbolic claims to injury on all sides and fewer efforts to negotiate social and political relations."[34] With respect to the NIF tangle, the larger question of women's tenuous hold on any real power within its institutional structure was eclipsed by the legal action launched by Du Plessis, an action eventually settled out of court, leaving a residue of rancour and bad public relations in its wake.

However, strife is both inevitable *and* desirable when women attempt to reconfigure power relations. As Audre Lorde has pointed out about feminist struggles over racism, for instance, "mainstream communication does not want women, particularly white women, responding to racism." Rather, we are encouraged to accept racism as "an immutable given." When struggles to come to grips with divisive issues ensue, she writes, anger among women is an inevitable result:

> So we are working in a context of opposition and threat, the cause of which is certainly not the angers which lie between us, but rather, that virulent hatred leveled against all women, people of Colour, lesbians and gay men, poor people — against all of who are seeking to examine the particulars of our lives as we resist our oppressions, moving toward coalition and effective action.[35]

Lorde's proposition to positive change in the midst of internecine dispute is that women must necessarily recognize the real roots of their anger and use it as a form of energy. As she says, any anger that stands between women "must be used for clarity and mutual empowerment."[36] The unsympathetic who look in from the outside may be scandalized by what they perceive as feminists "tearing each other down" (gender socialization has ensured that anger is a difficult emotion for women to express effectively) when, in fact, the strife is all about trying to negotiate a workable path to feminist change, where the germination of different kinds of ideas suggests a variety of ways forward: "But the strength of women lies in recognizing differences between us as creative, and in standing up to those distortions which we inherited without blame, but which are now ours to alter."[37] So ideas and strategies must be fought over. Not to engage in such a struggle is, in effect, to allow tradition and traditional institutions to crush any feminist dissent and discussion. Thus, "intelligent" struggle yields the promise that "the angers of women can transform difference through insight into power."

Ironically, in its final five years, the documentary releases demonstrated that, at least at the level of the film texts themselves, the Studio had responded in a productive way to many of the feminists debates of the 1990s and had begun to produce films demonstrating a satisfying complexity in content and form. *Forbidden Love*, for instance, was organized around the genres of documentary and melodrama to explore how "a satisfactory relationship between personal and cultural notions of identity"[38] might be negotiated. The *Women at the Well* series celebrated the presence of Black women as Canadian nation, setting out their stories and constructing a unique historical document organized around "experience" that confronted the legacy of racism and sexism in its definitive terms. *Hands of History* and *Keepers of the Fire* realized a similar accomplishment, reclaiming the cultural heritage and artistic prowess of First Nations women artists, including filmmaker Loretta Todd.[39]

Equally ironic is the fact that Kathleen Shannon's initial inclusive and radical vision is fleshed out more fully in two releases setting out new stories of "women and Canadian nation" after Studio D had been formally disbanded — *Under One Sky: Arab Women in North America Talk about the Hijab* and *Beyond Borders: Arab Feminists Talk about Their Lives … East and West*[40]— even though their making was a less than smooth process.

In 1996, Studio D closed its doors (see chapter 3 for a fuller discussion of these details). At that time, the Film Board pledged its commitment to women and filmmaking with an equity policy whereby specially mandated teams (the four Western provinces, Ontario, Quebec and the Atlantic Provinces) would advise on the three new documentary streams that the NFB planned to implement, although a number of filmmakers and producers expressed doubt about the viability of such a plan given that the new teams would have no production money. The reorganization was massive and was based on a strategy to reduce NFB numbers radically in the face of a $20-million budget cut the Film Board had received at the hands of the government. "Diversity" became the new catch word, as the Board announced that productions would be increasingly reflective of a diverse Canadian society, in both the content and the personnel who would create them. Women's voices as a category were effectively subsumed.

Meanwhile, the closure of Studio D also ended NIF, which by that time had trained close to two dozen First Nations women and women of colour (including Dora Nipp).[41] I leave the work of summing up the overall loss to the words of Kathleen Shannon:

> Looking at what we've lost with [Studio D's] passing ... [I see] several things [we've lost]. Within the Film Board, it's a loss of place for women to meet and strategize. Outside the Film Board, it's a loss of possibilities for communities outside the dominant culture to make films, because Studio D's been the only place with that kind of commitment — that's gone beyond words. And then there's the loss for women audiences. There's a travelling film festival that's coming through BC right now, and I looked at the program ... [there is only] one women co-director. Out of the short films, there are maybe about a quarter of them made by women. So this is about as bad as it was back in the seventies. I think the really critical thing for everyone though, is that this is a loss of a perspective that's different from the corporate culture.[42]

IT'S A WRAP, OR IS IT?

What is to be made, then, of the story of Studio D told through the voices of its members, its documentaries and traces of its history as found in official records and media sources? For more than two decades Studio D managed, often under duress, to produce a significant body of documentary films that focused on major issues debated by Canadian feminists. In collaboration with other government agencies, mainly the Federal Women's Film Program, Studio D produced an additional constellation of documentaries that explored women's experiences in unprecedented breadth, creating a focus on their particular lives, circumstances and problems that has no parallel in film history. In retrospect, Studio D can be understood as a dynamic, innovative organization; as a site of competing discourses, contradictions and struggles inextricably linked to the state and the women's movement; and as a singular contributor to feminist culture through its feminist film practices and aesthetics.

Ironically, during a period when Studio D ought to have been positioned favourably to make a trenchant contribution to emerging, sometimes heated debates through its documentary production, it, along with many other feminist initiatives, fell victim to successive rounds of government "cutbacks." Feminists in many areas found themselves struggling to retain a foothold in a political landscape that had veered sharply to the right, radically reducing women's opportunities generally. By now, political analysts traced how this trend was put into motion a mere five years after Studio D's inception in 1974 when Margaret Thatcher was elected prime minister of Britain. Her neo-conservative approach, much admired by both Ronald Reagan (elected U.S. president in1980) and Brian Mulroney (elected Canadian prime minister in 1984), launched a policial tragectory that, in Canada, replaced a public concern for social issues with a heavy emphasis on increasingly global business interests. A growing body of feminist scholarship is now examining the worrying impact of this trend that has ushered in a number of closures of government services for women, quietly dismantling women's rights.

Cuts to the NFB and the closure of Studio D must be read within this larger political and economic context. The budget-cutting era of the 1990s was a period indelibly marked by what Sylvia Bashevkin calls "the money crunch"[43] — a pattern of state-generated policy changes designed to reduce public spending and government regulation throughout Canada. While the consequences of this money-crunch resulted in "a fraying of the broader social fabric that had been woven since the era of the Great Depression,"[44] the disappearance of Studio D as a particular "voice" for women becomes an example of how women in the general public are disproportionately impoverished.

When the Mandate Review Committee (Juneau Report) tabled its report (January 12, 1996), it called for a three-year budget cut of $350 million to Canada's largest cultural producers — the CBC, the Canada Council for the Arts and the NFB (its cut was roughly $20 million) —and identified "pervasive structural problems at the NFB,"[45] including general inefficiencies. The NFB countered with a cost-cutting plan, proposing increased reliance on freelance personnel, a restructuring of branches and programming. Closing Studio D became simply "part of the move towards a leaner, more streamlined NFB"[46] with women filmmakers scattered throughout the Film Board structure. The voices of women would now be filtered through Film Board productions reflecting, more generally, "the diversity of Canadian society."[47] An integrationist approach of this nature, however, encourages a public attitude that is "merely tolerant of the goals and achievements of [*any*] group, without having to engage in substantive change."[48] It effectively dismantles "women" as a distinct category.

Anticipating her address on the occasion of receiving an honorary doctorate from York University in 1996, Kathleen Shannon expressed her frustration with a system that, in her view, persisted in hampering women in their struggles for change although Studio D had, she believed, put its best effort into identifying problems and raising social consciousness to promote a climate of change:

> I'm talking about that in what I'm going to say on Saturday. That whole crap that women are just like everyone else now. But who is everybody? There is a real betrayal in that statement. Who is everybody else? And just which women are like this "everybody"? When you look at it, you know that one of the ostensible reasons for the creation of Studio D was the status of women in the country and basically that's not changed.[49]

If Ruth Roach Pierson's contention that the "reality" of the past is knowable, albeit "imperfectly and incompletely,"[50] the narrative of Studio D embedded in the host of women's stories constitutes an archive of inestimable value. If theorizing about feminist narratives sets out women's stories as political texts, reading a documentary film that tells the story of a woman's life becomes an exercise in consciousness-raising — that is, as an investigation into the past or into contemporary societal structures in order to interrogate the present reality and configuration of women's concerns. Consciousness-raising of this order promises not just the feminist "click — a key opening a lock, a button pushed — to be activated,"[51] as a result of gaining insight into women's secondary status, but a coming of age, of new forms of freedom accompanied by a keen awareness of the "danger of choosing to stay right where we are."[52]

Studio D's insistence on telling stories, and my own insistence on foregrounding stories, helps to bridge the gap between feminist activism and theorizing. After all, "the validation of women's experience, and the social, political, and intellectual changes necessary to accommodate women's experience — was the impetus for the rise of the women's movement,"[53] responsible, in part, for social, political and cultural "advances" for women, including the establishment of women's studies as a legitimate area of study.

Documentaries such as those of the *Women at the Well* series (an exploration of Black women's lives in Canada), *Under the Willow Tree* (a recuperation of Chinese history in Canada as told by English-speaking daughters and granddaughers of Chinese women "pioneers"), *Under One Sky* (that looks at Arab women's concerns and the wearing of the hijab) and *Beyond Borders* (a cogent analysis of East–West politics) bring to light significant insights about women's lives and provide fresh scrutiny of such issues as citizenship and entitlement within a properly functioning democracy. Others, such as *Firewords* (a celebratory portrait of Canadian feminist writers Louky Bersianik, Jovette Marchessault and Nicole Brossard), *Forbidden Love* (a brilliant and pro-sex "writing" of lesbian history) and the *Women and Spirituality* series, draw attention to the richness and value of a woman-centred culture and its ability to enhance and enlarge traditional constructions.

As the body of films produced by Studio D tracked and configured the territory of Canadian women's concerns in particular ways in the latter third of the twentieth century, it bears testimony to past struggles that may encourage later generations of women to avoid "reinventing the feminist wheel."[54] Writes historian Cathy L. James:

> One of the strengths of historical films is their ability to bring the past to life to recreate, through visual images, narrations, and dramatizations, the look and feel of an earlier time; the power of a visionary idea, or the strength of a deeply held political conviction. The apparent immediacy of film can draw viewers into the past through the experience of the individuals on screen; by this means ... documentaries can introduce ideological positions ... in a manner that is easily accessible. Moreover, film can integrate analytical categories: such as race, class, and gender that written texts often fragment.[55]

Studio D fulfilled a unique mandate through its films by and for women that "explored the circumstances of women's past and present existence and fostered the movement towards gender equality"[56] and it fulfilled the activist role that Studio D envisioned for itself. Studio D's record exists as a rich source for contemporary theorizing about the nature of this form of "realist"' feminist documentary, about this unique example of state "accommodation" to women's demands.

In 2001, these points coalesced in my mind with certain poignancy as I sat combing through Studio D archives in the NFB's Montreal headquarters. Sorting through files, I came across my signature affixed to a petition I had composed in 1996. It was signed by students and members of the teaching team of my women's studies course at York's Glendon College, urging NFB officials to keep Studio D in operation. I had come full circle. Once, I was "outside" feminism, reading and asking questions about women's lives, my own included. Now I was "inside," still reading, still asking questions about women's lives, now working in that space between theory and action.

There are lessons to be gleaned, then, from the "messy assemblage"[57] that was Studio D. As I ask at the beginning of this book, what happens when a feminist film studio, working within a nation-building institution, engages in cultural production on behalf of Canadian women? Teresa de Lauretis's hunch that self-expression and communication with other women leads to "the creation/invention of new images and the creation/imaging of new forms of community"[58] leads me to circle back to the following question: What does the closing of Studio D imply about agency and citizenship for the women of Canada? The recent shift to the political right by much of the world has resulted in a growing chasm between state responsibility and social need. Bashevkin's research into women's groups in Canada, for instance, reveals that under the national political leadership of such figures as Brian Mulroney (and, more recently Stephen Harper) women paid a huge price: "most activists and feminist movements operated in a defensive posture to stop rollbacks and keep what they had previously won."[59] While Studio D may have been hamstrung, its own story and its portrayal of women's issues offer a significant and invaluable record of Canadian feminist political engagement.

Perhaps one of Studio D's most forward-looking legacies is its view of women as a global community. The initial impulse of the NFB to "interpret Canada to Canadians and the world" retains its currency. Given Canada's vast geographic reality and constantly shifting nation, the need for telling each other stories about ourselves is vital if Canada is to remain a coherent whole. In envisioning its mandate — "our goal is to make films that encourage discussion and dialogue among women, and that promote action aimed at improving the status of women in society"[60] — Studio D set the stage for its imagining of women as a global nation at the same time rendering more porous the notion of nation, the notion of borders. Indeed, its documentary work, demonstrating a praxis of "recuperation and reconstruction" invites a reconsideration of women's stories that in turn invite a fresh opportunity for reflexivity — "that is self-awareness and self-criticism."[61]

Rather than disrupting "dominant discourses of nationhood, national identity and national unity,"[62] I see Studio D extending and refining these discourses, refiguring notions about nation and women to locations that encourage fresh examination. In this respect, Studio D broke new territory by producing documentaries in an era of intensified globalization, unprecedented in world history. If feminists need to develop a "new global ethic and consciousness in the world today" to negotiate "the relations of antagonism and tension"[63] arising within the political, economic and the cultural realms that globalization encompasses, we need look no further than the Studio D documentaries, which offer themselves as models for analyses of women's lives and circumstances.

With respect to the criticisms that Studio D received from theorists lamenting that it rarely departed from the simplicity of the social realist film, I am reminded of Alexandra Juhasz's trenchant observation that the "tension between theory and practice seems most tense for theorists." Prompting us to remember the value of the political realist documentary, Juhasz suggests it remains a genuine tool for achieving change:

> Because women who watch and make political documentary share beliefs, feminist positions, or a political agenda, viewers use their identification with women on the screen as do women in consciousness-raising groups; not to form a complete sense of self, but to cross through individual identity so as to unify a collective, ideological agenda.[64]

A journal entry by one of the students in my feminist film course in 2002, speaks precisely to this point underscoring, incidentally, the value of Jennifer Kawaja's films, among Studio D's last productions:

> For myself as a South Asian Muslim woman, Jennifer Kawaja's political documentary *Beyond Borders* serves as an example of this. There were powerful images of educated, articulate, beautiful Muslim women who spoke about the detrimental effects of Western foreign policies on Arab nations. Without fixing an essentialist identity on myself or the women on the screen, I was able to produce new and useful identities by what I saw on the screen and relate it to my political organizing.[65]

Is there a way, I asked at the beginning of this book, to assess the efforts of "liberal feminism" more generously through a productive examination of Studio D and its work? As a particular voice of, by and for women, Studio D, a cultural producer mediating between the state and its women, navigated uncharted territory testifying to the kind of struggle women face when they tell their own stories in the name of "changing the world." If this goal dwells in the realm of the hyperbolic, perhaps it can be said, then, that Studio D offered notions to "disrupt prevailing arrangements, challenge and/or change relationships of power — where there are new possibilities, but never any guarantees."[66] In this context, Studio D surely deserves credit for challenging the status quo and advancing its own version of "a feminist democratic project,"[67] however vexed in the execution.

*

What does Studio D's closure imply for the concept "women as nation" or our entitlement as citizens? As I was finishing up the writing of this book, I spent some time navigating through the NFB website looking for old Studio D titles. I discovered that a number of its films are no longer listed and that those films listed and produced by Studio D are now identified as NFB productions. Studio D's name has disappeared from the electronic credits, which led me to ask, "What of the presence and role of women in the Film Board today?" This is surely a question for ongoing feminist scholarship.

Shortly after Kathleen Shannon's appointment as executive producer of Studio D, she and Linda Roberts (who was in charge of distributing the *Working Mothers* films), organized a celebration of women who had worked at the NFB in its early years. The result was 4 Days in May (May 6 to 9, 1975), a series of film screenings, workshops and a "sharing and exchange of ideas" that included presentations from many of the women[68] who had worked at the Film Board through the war years. Everyone who was employed by the NFB was invited to attend, among them a number of Studio D women: Dorothy Todd Hénaut, Margaret Pettigrew, Ginny Stikeman and celebrated cinematographer Susan Trow. Clearly, the voices of women from a previous era at the Film Board inspired this new generation, underscoring the value of women's contribution to documentary film and challenging them to carry on.

If the survival of feminism as "an ongoing history-in-process" depends, in part, on our ability to reproduce ourselves in subsequent generations and to pass on what we have learned so that the wheel does not need to be reinvented every generation,[69] the existence of Studio D and its extended body of feminist documentary film constitute a valuable legacy. If the experiences of women (captured in Studio D's story and its documentary films) provide the foundation of women's knowledge as claimed by many feminist theorists,[70] a concrete and valid epistemology emerges to compete with and to resist dominant forms of knowledge. To paraphrase Carolyn Heilbrun's words, Studio D's particular brand of feminist narratology, whether deployed "unconsciously, and without recognizing or naming the process,"[71] produced new knowledge about the politics of telling stories about women's lives. Thus, rather than treating its stories as "fixed truths" to be handed down like precious heirlooms,"[72] I think of Studio D's legacy as a rich and open-ended body of ideas that offers new generations of feminists material for ongoing resistance and change. While filmmaking remains a male-dominated field, the social realist documentary has become a political tool that women use globally to illuminate their stories. Studio D, now gone, stands as a vibrant example of women filming, editing and producing feminist documentaries, in "a room of their own," remaining faithful in its belief that if women were to identify themselves as "community" and to discuss their problems *as* women, positive change would come. This is an image we should "cherish … like a certitude and a wound showing sign of healing."[73]

NOTES

INTRODUCTION

1 "Studio D Commemorates 20 Years of Groundbreaking Feminist Documentaries," News Release, National Film Board of Canada, 12 May 1994. National Film Board Archives (hereafter NFBA).

2 Ibid.

3 Canada, Department of Canadian Heritage, *Making Our Voices Heard: Canadian Broadcasting and Film For the 21st Century* (Hull, QC: Minister of Supply and Services Canada, 1996). It was prepared by Pierre Juneau, a member of the federal Liberal government's Privy Council and chair of the Mandate Review Committee; Catherine Murray, associate professor of communications at Simon Fraser University and a former vice-president at Decima Research; and Peter Herrndorf, chair and CEO of TVOntario.

4 Ibid., summary of chapter 3, "The National Film Board," 1.

5 Ray Conlogue, "NFB Should Accept 25% Budget Cut, Juneau Report Says," *Globe and Mail* (Toronto), 1 February 1996, D1.

6 The term "state" generally refers to the organized political community under any given government. Canadian feminist political analysts (Jill Vickers and Sylvia Bashevkin, among others) have criticized the contemporary Canadian state for perpetuating a rhetoric of "participatory democracy" when, in fact, women's voices are muffled in the central process of political and economic policymaking.

7 Jessica Johnston, "Enough Already," *This Magazine* (January/February 2007), 4.

8 Elizabeth Anderson, "Studio D's Imagined Community: From Development (1974) to Realignment (1986–1990)," in *Gendering the Nation: Canadian Women's Cinema,* ed. Kay Armatage, Kass Banning, Brenda Longfellow and Janine Marchessault (Toronto: University of Toronto Press, 1999), 43.

9 Judy Rebick, "Where Are Women's Voices?" *Canadian Forum* (April 1997), 24.

10 Philinda Masters recalls the outrage of Winnipeg artist Sharon Zenith Corne when she learned that the Winnipeg Art Gallery was planning to use a $10,000

International Women's Year federal grant to mount a show exploring ways women had been perceived and portrayed in art from the nineteenth and early twentieth centuries, an exhibition of work rendered by men that was bound, in Corne's view, to celebrate stereotypic images of women. Philinda Masters, "Women, Culture and Communications," in *Canadian Women's Issues,* Vol. 1, *Strong Voices: Twenty-Five Years of Women's Activism in English Canada*, ed. Ruth Roach Pierson, Marjorie Griffin Cohen, Paula Bourne and Philinda Masters (Toronto: James Lorimer, 1993), 398.

11 Sheila Rowbotham, *Women's Consciousness, Man's World* (Harmondsworth, UK: Penguin Books, 1973), 28.

12 My use of this phrase "Canadian women's movement" in no way represents a clearly defined monolith, but rather refers to the version of distinctive Canadian feminism that is generally understood to overlap many of the concerns of American feminism. Canadian feminist struggles against gender oppression blended with other "liberation" struggles, including civil rights and the right to promote peace initiatives were associated largely with English-speaking women, influenced by traditions of liberalism. More recent developments in feminist thinking, particularly those of postmodern feminism, offer a much more politically nuanced and richer form of analysis.

13 Anderson, "Studio D's Imagined Community," 42.

14 The "first wave" of the women's movement generally refers to the first concerted effort to seek reforms with respect to women's social and legal inequalities in the nineteenth and early twentieth centuries. Their major achievements include gaining access to higher education for women, entrenching property rights for married women (*Married Women's Property Act*, Britain, 1870) and obtaining the vote for women. Linda Nicholson's *The Second Wave* (London: Routledge, 1997) describes the second wave in the United States as a movement initially composed largely of professional (white) women who began putting pressure on state institutions to end discrimination against women in relation to waged employment; it also advanced a radical questioning of gender roles. Similarly in Canada, a group of professional women lobbied the federal government to establish a Royal Commission to investigate women's needs.

15 The mandate articulated in *The National Film Act* of 1950 updated John Grierson's (first NFB commissioner) original language "to make and distribute films designed to help Canadian in all parts of Canada to understand the ways of living and the problems of Canadian in other parts." The 1950 version created a much more expansive articulation of the concept "national interest," its scope an invitation to Studio D to interpret it in the name of feminist interests.

16 Chris Scherbarth, "Why Not D? An Historical Look at the NFB's Women's Studio," *Cinema Canada* 139 (1987), 10.

17 Chris Scherbarth, "Canada's Studio D: A Women's Room with an International Reputation," *Canadian Woman Studies/les cahiers de la femme* 8, no. 1 (1987), 25.

18 Ibid.

19 Ibid.

20 Ibid.

21 Teresa de Lauretis, "Rethinking Women's Cinema: Aesthetics and Feminist Theory," *Issues in Feminist Film Criticism,* ed. Patricia Erens (Bloomington: Indiana University Press, 1991), 296.

22 Here, I refer to Timothy Brennan's discussion of the novel as an instrument of "nation" creation, which I apply to documentary film. Organized around Benedict Anderson's concept of nation as imagined community, Brennan says of the novel that is has the power to objectify "the 'one, yet many' of national life ... by mimicking the structure of the nation, a clearly bordered jumble of languages and styles ... helping to standardize language, encourage literacy, and remove mutual incomprehensibility." "The National Longing for Form," in *Nation and Narration*, ed. Homi Bhabha (London: Routledge, 1990), 49.

23 Trinh T. Minh-ha, "'Who is Speaking?' Of Nation, Community, and First-Person Interviews," in *Feminisms in the Cinema*, ed. Laura Pietropaolo and Ada Testaferri (Bloomington: Indiana University Press, 1995), 44.

24 bell hooks, *Talking Back: Thinking Feminist, Thinking Black* (Boston, MA: South End Press, 1989).

25 Sara Suleri, "Woman Skin Deep: Feminism and the Postcolonial Condition," in *The Post-Colonial Studies Reader*, ed. Bill Ashcroft, Gareth Griffiths and Helen Tiffin (London: Routledge, 1995), 278.

26 Ibid., 273.

27 Michel Foucault, "The Subject and Power," in *Power: Michel Foucault*, ed. James D. Faubion, trans. Robert Hurley and others (New York: New Press, 2000), 329.

28 Ibid.

29 Ruth Roach Pierson, "Introduction," *Writing Women's History: International Perspectives*, ed. Karen Offen, Ruth Roach Pierson and Jane Rendall (Bloomington: Indiana University Press, 1991), 81.

30 Ibid., 90.

31 Ibid., 80.

32 Ibid., 79.

33 Linda Carty, "Combining Our Efforts: Making Feminism Relevant to the Changing Sociality," in *And Still We Rise: Feminist Political Mobilization in Contemporary Canada*, ed. Linda Carty (Toronto: Women's Press, 1993), 18.

34 Françoise Lionnet, *Autobiographical Voices: Race, Gender, Self-Portraiture* (Ithaca, NY: Cornell University Press, 1989), xii.

35 Sheila Rowbotham's landmark study *Hidden from History: 300 Years of Women's Oppression and the Fight against It* (London: Pluto Press, 1973) emphasizes the need of preserving the cultural presence of women to prevent their stories from being lost to the historical record.

36 Lionnet, *Autobiographical Voices*, xi.

37 In her essay "Combining Our Efforts: Making Feminism Relevant to the Changing Society," Linda Carty notes specifically that, unfortunately, the failure to make linkages mars much of Canadian feminist theorizing.

38 Alexandra Juhasz, "Introduction," *Women of Vision: Histories in Feminist Film and Video* (Minneapolis: University of Minnesota Press, 2001), 2.

39 I draw on Laura Marks's notion in her study of cinema and embodiment in *The Skin of the Film* (Duke University Press, 2000), xv.

40 In her study on literacy released in International Literacy Year (1990), Horsman discusses how she sat around many kitchen tables listening to the intimate stories "illiterate" women had to tell about their lives. Horsman was determined to expose the myths about illiteracy and to point out inequalities in the social system, an effective strategy in shedding light on the social constructedness of illiteracy. She asks a compelling question: How can women think their own stories are important if they have no sense of their own self-importance if their "stories" are always told by "others"? Her conclusion: Deriving a sense of one's own identity (and a sense of agency) is the vital outcome, since the language of others and influencing social structures work to render their stories invisible.

CHAPTER 1

1 Adrienne Rich, "Toward a Woman-Centered University (1973–74)," *On Lies, Secrets, and Silences: Selected Prose 1966–1978* (New York: W.W. Norton, 1979), 126.

2 Joan Kelly's foundational essay "Did Women Have a Renaissance?" argues that the rise of the modern state, early forms of capitalism and separation between public and private realms associated with the Renaissance combined, diminishing and constraining women's personal and social lives while at the same time increasing their dependency on their male counterparts. See her *Women, History, and Theory: The Essays of Joan Kelly* (Chicago: Chicago University Press, 1984), 19–50.

3 Chris Scherbarth, "Why Not D? An Historical Look at the NFB's Woman's Studio," *Cinema Canada* 139 (1987), 9.

4 Diane Burgess, "Leaving Gender Aside: The Legacy of Studio D?" in *Women Filmmakers: Refocusing,* ed. Jacqueline Levitin, Judith Plessis and Valerie Raoul (Vancouver: UBC Press, 2003), 418.

5 Kathleen Shannon, internal memo, 1 April 1974, 4. National Film Board Archives (hereafter NFBA).

6 Ruth Roach Pierson, *Canadian Women and the Second World War* (Ottawa: Canadian Historical Association, 1983), 19.

7 "Women's Program," internal memo, 22 May 1974. NFBA.

8 Joyce Nelson, *The Colonized Eye: Rethinking the Grierson Legend* (Toronto: Between the Lines, 1998), 77.

9 Elizabeth Sussex, *The Rise and Fall of British Documentary: The Story of the Film Movement Founded by John Grierson* (Berkeley: University of California Press, 1975), 86.

10 At the landmark NFB 4 Days in May Conference held in Montreal, May 6–9, 1975, the contributions of women who had worked at the Film Board were celebrated. Being there no doubt inspired Shannon and stiffened her resolve when a number of these women returned to speak of their accomplishments and trials.

11 Barbara Halpern Martineau, "Before the Guerillières: Women's Films at the NFB during World War II," in *Canadian Film Reader,* ed. Seth Feldman and Joyce Nelson (Toronto: Peter Martin Associates, 1977), 62.

12 Kathleen Shannon, personal interview with the author, 12 June 1996.

13 Chris Scherbarth, "Canada's Studio D: A Women's Room with an International Reputation," *Canadian Woman Studies/les cahiers de la femme* 8, no. 1 (1987), 24.

14 Julia Lesage, "The Political Aesthetics of the Feminist Documentary Film," in *Issues in Feminist Film Criticism,* ed. Patricia Erens (Bloomington: Indiana University Press, 1990), 223.

15 Shannon memo, 1 April 1974. NFBA.

16 Scherbarth, "Canada's Studio D," 10.

17 Scherbarth, "Why Not D?" 10.

18 Kathleen Shannon, internal memo, "Women's Program (English) 1975–80,"1 April 1974. NFBA.

19 It is hard to tell when the name of the Studio changed from "Unit D" to "Studio D." It is referred to as Unit D in the early memos that refer to the women's studio; by 1975 "Unit" is dropped altogether.

20 Kathleen Shannon, memo to Bob Verrall, director of English Production on the formation of Unit D, 4 June 1974. NFBA.

21 Ibid.

22 Kathleen Shannon, *INTERLOCK,* no. 1 (January/February 1975), 27.

23 Editorial, *INTERLOCK,* no. 1 (January/February 1975), 2.

24 Scherbarth, "Canada's Studio D," 10.

25 Nancy Adamson, Linda Briskin and Margaret McPhail, *Feminist Organizing for Change: The Contemporary Women's Movement in Canada* (Toronto: Oxford University Press, 1988), 51.

26 Roberta Hamilton, *Gendering the Vertical Mosaic: Feminist Perspectives on Canadian Society* (Toronto: Copp Clark, 1996), 51.

27 Ibid., 50.

28 Adamson, Briskin and McPhail, *Feminist Organizing for Change*, 51.

29 Marjorie Griffin Cohen, "The Canadian Women's Movement," in *Canadian Women's Issues,* Vol. 1, *Strong Voices*, ed. Ruth Roach Pierson, Marjorie Griffin Cohen, Paula Bourne and Philinda Masters (Toronto: James Lorimer, 1993), 6.

30 Monique Bégin, "The Royal Commission on the Status of Women in Canada: Twenty Years Later," in *Challenging Times: The Women's Movement in Canada and the United States,* ed. Constance Backhouse and David H. Flaherty (Montreal: McGill-Queen's University Press, 1992), 27.

31 Shannon, "Women's Program (English)," 3.

32 Kathleen Shannon, "Implementation of Unit D (English)," 23 July 1974. NFBA.

33 Hamilton, *Gendering the Vertical Mosaic*, 51.

34 Cerise Morris, "'Determination and Thoroughness': The Movement for a Royal Commission on the Status of Women in Canada," *Atlantis* 5, no. 2 (1980), 11.

35 Signe Johansson, personal interview with the author, 1 May 1997.

36 Dorothy Todd Hénaut, personal interview with the author, 1 September 2000.

37 Lisa Bryn Rundle, "Who Needs NAC?" *This Magazine* (March/April 1999), 26.

38 Ibid., 28.

39 Gerry Rogers, personal interview with the author, 11 February 2002.

40 *Studio D: The Women's Studio of the National Film Board of Canada*, undated promotional brochure, NFB.

41 Terre Nash, personal interview with the author, 2 May 2002.

42 Hénaut interview, 1 September 2000.

43 On April 17, 1982, the government added section 28 which stated, "Notwithstanding anything in this Charter, the rights and freedoms referred to in it are guaranteed equally to male and female persons," a clause that feminists have been able to draw on to effectively secure equality rights for women.

CHAPTER 2

1 Chris Scherbarth, "Why Not D? An Historical Look at the NFB's Women's Studio," *Cinema Canada* 139 (1987), 10.

2 Dorothy Todd Hénaut, personal interview with the author, 1 September 2000.

3 Graeme Turner, *National Fictions: Literature, Film and the Construction of Australian Narrative*, 2nd ed. (St. Leonards, Australia: Allen and Unwin, 1993), xiii.

4 Beverly Shaffer, personal interview with the author, 31 August 2000.

5 Ibid.

6 For fuller discussions of this provocative issue see Joyce Nelson, *The Colonized Eye: Rethinking the Grierson Legend* (Toronto: Between the Lines, 1988); Scott Forsyth, "The Failure of Nationalism and Documentary," *Canadian Journal of Film* 1, no. 1 (1990); and Zoë Druick "'Ambiguous Identities' and the Representation of Everyday Life," in *Canadian Identity: Region, Country, Nation. Selected Proceedings of the 24th Annual Conference of the Association for Canadian Studies, June 6–8, 1997*, ed. Association for Canadian Studies (Montreal: Association for Canadian Studies, 1998), 125–137.

7 Toby Miller, *The Well-Tempered Self: Citizenship, Culture and the Postmodern Subject* (Baltimore: Johns Hopkins University Press, 1993), 16.

8 Jan Jindy Pettman, "Boundary Politics: Women, Nationalism and Danger," in *New Frontiers in Women's Studies: Knowledge, Identity and Nationalism,* ed. Mary Maynard and June Purvis (London: Taylor and Francis, 1996), 187.

9 To make this point, Miller uses Tony Bennett's definition of culture from "Putting Policy into Cultural Studies," in *Cultural Studies,* ed. Lawrence Grossberg et al. (New York: Routledge, 1992), 50.

10 Miller, *The Well-Tempered Self*, 15.

11 Ibid., ix.

12 Philosophically, Western culture derives its notion of citizenship from Plato who sets the classic example in his preface to *The Republic* when he specifies that the citizen is a land-owing male, specifically excluding women and slaves.

13 Miller, *The Well-Tempered Self*, 4.

14 Beverly Thiele identifies mechanisms of "male-stream" thought (exclusion, pseudo-inclusion, alienation, tricks of the trade, decontextualization, universalisms, naturalisms, dualisms and appropriation and reversal) that combine to make women "disappear" from historical accounts of culture and society in her essay "Vanishing Acts in Social and Political Thought: Tricks of the Trade," in *Defining Women: Social Institutions and Gender Divisions*, ed. Linda McDowell and Rosemary Pringle (London: Polity Press in association with Open University Press, 1992).

15 Sylvia Bashevkin, *True Patriot Love: The Politics of Canadian Nationalism* (Toronto: Oxford University Press, 1991), 4.

16 Ibid., 28.

17 Ibid., 4.

18 J.L. Granatstein, *The Ottawa Men: The Civil Service Mandarins* (Toronto: Oxford University Press, 1982), 273–274.

19 Mike Gasher, "From Sacred Cows to White Elephants: Cultural Policy Under Siege," in *Canadian Cultures and Globalization: Proceedings of the Twenty-third Annual Conference of the Association for Canadian Studies, June 1–3, 1996*, ed. Joy Cohnstaedt and Yves Frenette (Montreal: Association for Canadian Studies, 1997), 13.

20 Ted Magder *Canada's Hollywood: The Canadian State and Feature Films* (Toronto: University of Toronto Press, 1993), 248.

21 Ibid., 4.

22 Ibid., 82.

23 This phrase has been used repeatedly since the NFB's inception through the *National Film Act* (2 May 1939) to describe its mandate.

24 Nelson, *The Colonized Eye*, 12.

25 Cerise Morris, "'Determination and Thoroughness': The Movement for a Royal Commission on the Status of Women in Canada," *Atlantis* 5, no. 2 (1980), here quoting Grierson in an article by Thelma Lecocq, "Propaganda Maelstrom," *Maclean's*, 1 June 1943.

26 Ibid., 37.

27 Ibid., 32.

28 Magder, *Canada's Hollywood*, 54.

29 As a student at the University of Glasgow and later at the University of Chicago, Grierson was influenced by Walter Lippmann who argued in *Public Opinion* (New York: Harcourt, Brace, 1922) that ordinary people, being irrational, need to be manipulated by knowledgeable leaders who have access to knowledge not readily accessible to the public, hence the term "manufacturing consent."

30 Morris, "'Determination and Thoroughness,'" 28.

31 In *Public Opinion*, Lippmann advances the concept of "pictures in the public head" suggested by symbolic images.

32 Bill Nichols, *Representing Reality: Issues and Concepts in Documentary* (Bloomington: Indiana University Press, 1991), 3.

33 Gasher, "From Sacred Cows to White Elephants," 15.

34 Manjunath Pendukur, *Canadian Dreams and American Control: The Political Economy of the Canadian Film Industry* (Detroit: Wayne State University Press, 1990), 143.

35 Gasher, "From Sacred Cows to White Elephants," 23.

36 In 1950, the NFB moved its head office from Ottawa to Montreal *precisely* in order to create distance between itself and the bureaucracy of the federal government. As Gary Evans recounts in his chronicle of the Film Board, "Civil-service Ottawa was filled with stereotypical conservative and conventional people … [whereas] the Film Board was an operation whose success depended on the effectiveness of its creative core." NFB commissioner Arthur Irwin engineered the move, believing that the "obvious thing was to get [the Film Board] somewhere it wouldn't be so bloody conspicuous." Gary Evans, *In the National Interest: A Chronicle of the National Film Board of Canada from 1949 to 1989* (Toronto: University of Toronto Press, 1991), 17.

37 Ibid.

38 Diane Burgess, "Leaving Gender Aside: The Legacy of Studio D?" in *Women Filmmakers: Refocusing,* ed. Jacqueline Levitin, Judith Plessis and Valerie Roaul (Vancouver: UBC Press, 2003), 420.

39 Ibid.

40 Ibid., quoting Alison Beale, "Cultural Policy as a Technology of Gender," in *Ghosts in the Machine: Women and Cultural Policy in Canada and Australia,* ed. Alison Beale and Annette Van Den Bosch (Toronto: Garamond Press, 1998), 233.

41 Andrew Higson, "The Concept of National Cinema," *Screen* 30, no. 4 (1990), 37.

42 Turner, *National Fictions*, 2.

43 Jill Vickers, Pauline Rankin and Christine Appelle, *Politics as if Women Mattered: A Political Analysis of the National Action Committee on the Status of Women* (Toronto: University of Toronto Press, 1983), 50.

44 Historian Jill Vickers uses this phrase to identify how the Canadian state responds to feminist demands without instigating any genuine political shift in power.

45 Roberta Hamilton, *Gendering the Vertical Mosaic: Feminist Perspectives on Canadian Society* (Toronto: Copp Clark, 1996), 112, 7.

46 Hénaut interview, 1 September 2000.

47 Veronica Strong-Boag, Sherrill Grace, Avigail Eisenberg and Joan Anderson, eds., *Painting the Maple: Essays on Race, Gender, and the Construction of Canada* (Vancouver: University of British Columbia Press, 1998), 7.

48 Gerry Rogers, telephone interview with the author, 11 February 2002.

49 Barbara Halpern Martineau, "Before the Guerillières: Women's Films at the NFB during World War II," *Canadian Film Reader,* ed. Seth Feldman and Joyce Nelson (Toronto: Peter Martin Associates, 1977), 58. Barbara Halpern Martineau is the penname of Sara Halprin. From 1970 to 1983, she wrote numerous articles under this name on documentary film and video, popular films and women's media which appeared in the following journals: *Cinema Canada, Film Quarterly, Jump Cut, Take One* and *Women & Film.* She also had anthology pieces in *The*

Canadian Film Reader, Cartoon Animation, Show Us Life, The Jump Cut Reader, The Broadside Reader and *Women and the Cinema.* Sara Halprin died in November 2006.

50 Marsh and Grierson clashed over who should be producer for the popular and politically significant war propaganda films. Although Marsh was the obvious choice, Grierson was appointed.

51 Martineau, "Before the Guerillières," 62.

52 Ibid.

53 Terre Nash, "Against the Grain," *This Magazine* (May/June 1998), 37.

54 Ibid.

55 Ibid.

56 Burgess, "Leaving Gender Aside," 424.

57 Nelson, *The Colonized Eye*, 164.

58 Grierson is appropriating Bertolt Brecht's famous quote, "Art is not a mirror to hold up to reality, but a hammer with which to shape it." From "Art in Action," Grierson Archive, File G4: 21:2.

59 Kathleen Shannon, "'D' is for Dilemma," *Herizons* (Summer 1995), 26.

60 Rogers interview, 11 February 2002.

61 Kathleen Shannon, personal interview with the author, 12 June 1996.

62 Sue Findlay, "Facing the State: The Politics of the Women's Movement Reconsidered," in *Feminism and Political Economy: Women's Work, Women's Struggles,* ed. Heather Jon Maroney and Meg Luxton (Toronto: Methuen, 1987), 32. See also Nicos Poulantzas, *Political Power and Social Classes* (London: Verso, 1978).

63 Findlay, "Facing the State," 33.

64 Ibid., 48.

65 Letter from Studio D signed by Joy Johnson, audience researcher soliciting outside support, 21 December 1982. National Film Board Archives (hereafter NFBA).

66 Kathleen Shannon, Presentation to the Standing Committee on Communications and Culture, 10 May 1983, 2. NFBA.

67 Undated memo, 2, 3. NFBA.

68 "Studio D Statement in Response to the Applebaum-Hébert Report and Recommendations," 21 December 1982, 2. NFBA.

69 Kay Armatage quotes the introductory section of the *Summary of Briefs and Hearings* in "Film: Winter of Discontent," *The Canadian Forum* (May 1982), 41.

70 Ibid., 39. Armatage cites statistics from the Canada Council and the Ontario Arts Council. In the category "Film and Video," no woman had received an "A" grant for the past seven years; in the "B" grant, 17 women compared to 60 men had received grants in the past seven years. With the Ontario Arts Grants, women filmmakers had received only 18 per cent of the grants awarded between 1970 and 1980.

71 Ibid. Emphasis in original.

72 Ibid., 41.

73 Ibid., 39.

74 Findlay, "Facing the State," 34.

75 Vickers, *Politics as if Women Really Mattered*, 51.

76 *Studio D of the National Film Board of Canada Guidelines for Film Proposals*, undated publication. NFBA. Emphasis added.

77 Ramsay Cook, *The Maple Leaf Forever: Essays on Nationalism and Politics in Canada* (Toronto: Macmillan of Canada, 1997), 6.

78 Ibid., 9.

79 Scott Lauder, "A Studio with a View," *The Canadian Forum* (August/September 1986), 14.

80 Shannon interview, 12 June 1996.

81 Chris Scherbarth, "Studio D of the National Film Board of Canada: Seeing Ourselves through Women's Eyes" (MA thesis, Carleton University, 1986), 1.

82 Shannon, "'D' is for Dilemma," 26.

83 Brenda Longfellow, "Globalization and National Identity in Canadian Film," *Canadian Journal of Film Studies/Revue canadienne d'études cinématographiques* 5, no. 2 (Fall 1996), 14.

84 Chantal Mouffe, "Feminism, Citizenship, and Radical Democratic Politics," in *Feminists Theorize the Political,* ed. Judith Butler and Joan W. Scott (New York: Routledge, 1992), 381, 384.

CHAPTER 3

1 I use this phrase cautiously to identify the "English-speaking" women's movement of the 1970s, aware of various criticisms that challenge labels such as this term for being reductive and imprecise.

2 Constance Backhouse, "Contemporary Women's Movements: An Introduction," *Challenging Times: The Women's Movement in Canada and the United States,* ed. Constance Backhouse and David H. Flaherty (Montreal: McGill-Queen's University Press, 1992), 5.

3 Ibid.

4 Chris Scherbarth coins the phrase "women's room" applying it to Studio D in direct reference to Virginia Woolf's insistence that women gain "the habit of freedom" when they possess such a space, a central theme in Woolf's well-known essay "A Room of One's Own." See Scherbarth, "Studio D of the National Film Board of Canada: Seeing Ourselves through Women's Eyes" (MA thesis, Carleton University, 1986).

5 Kay Armatage, "The Evolution of Women Filmmakers in Canada," in *Changing Focus: The Future for Women in the Canadian Film and Television Industry* (Toronto: Toronto Women in Film and Television, 1991), 137.

6 Elizabeth Anderson, "Studio D's Imagined Community: From Development (1974) to Realignment (1986–1990)," in *Gendering the Nation: Canadian Women's Cinema*, ed. Kay Armatage, Kass Banning, Brenda Longfellow and Janine Marchessault (Toronto: University of Toronto Press, 1999), 42.

7 One of the first models arising from the "second-wave," liberal feminism (typically associated with middle-class white women) operates within the structures of mainstream society (government, the law) to gain rights for women. Rooted in principles of liberalism, it is commonly regarded as a conservative framework for change. Conceiving of politics as the pursuit of individual rights, it looks to reform "liberal" practices in society, rather than advocating for wholesale revolutionary change. Liberal feminists focus on gender issues, lack of affordable day care for working mothers and gender stereotyping as the main sources of inequality.

8 I draw on definitions of humanism taken from *The Columbian Dictionary of Modern Literary and Cultural Criticism* (New York: Columbia University Press, 1995), 141, and *The Oxford Companion to Philosophy* (New York: Oxford University Press, 1995), 375.

9 Andrew Higson, "The Concept of National Cinema," *Screen* 30, no. 4 (1990), 42.

10 *National Film Act*, 1950.

11 Kathleen Shannon, "'D' is for Dilemma," *Herizons* (Summer 1995), 24.

12 Government Memorandum/Note de service, 6 August 1974, signed by Kathleen Shannon. National Film Board Archives (hereafter NFBA).

13 Chris Scherbarth, "Canada's Studio D: A Women's Room with an International Reputation," *Canadian Woman Studies/les cahiers de la femme* 8, no. 1 (1987), 25.

14 Government Memorandum, 1.

15 Ibid.

16 "Implementation of Unit D (English)," Internal NFB Memo, 23 July 1974. NFBA.

17 "Implementation of Unit D (English), Appendix: Ad Hoc List of Films to be Produced by Unit D," 23 July 1974, 5. NFBA.

18 "Implementation of Unit D (English)," 23 July 1974, 3. NFBA.

19 Kathleen Shannon, personal interview with the author, 12 June 1996.

20 Scott Lauder, "A Studio with a View," *The Canadian Forum* (August/September 1986), 12.

21 Ginny Stikeman, personal interview with the author, 2 May 1997.

22 Signe Johansson, personal interview with the author, 1 May 1997. The abortion film referred to is Studio D's *Abortion: Stories from North and South,* dir. Gail Singer (1984).

23 Stikeman interview, 2 May 1997.

24 Ibid.

25 Chris Scherbarth, "Why Not D? An Historical Look at the NFB's Women's Studio," *Cinema Canada* 139 (1987), 10.

26 Julia Lesage, "The Political Aesthetics of the Feminist Documentary Film," in *Issues in Feminist Film Criticism*, ed. Patricia Erens (Bloomington: Indiana University Press, 1990), 222.

27 Shannon, "'D' is for Dilemma," 26.

28 Scherbarth, "Why Not D?" 10.

29 Shannon interview, 12 June 1996.

30 Shannon, "'D' is for Dilemma," 28.

31 Shannon interview, 12 June 1996.

32 Gary Evans, *In the National Interest: A Chronicle of the National Film Board of Canada from 1949 to 1989* (Toronto: University of Toronto Press, 1991), 219.

33 Shannon interview, 12 June 1996.

34 Evans, *In the National Interest*, 283, 299.

35 Shannon, "'D' is for Dilemma," 27.

36 Jill Vickers, Pauline Rankin and Christine Appelle, "The Intellectual and Political Context for the Development of NAC," in *Open Boundaries*, ed. Barbara A. Crow and Lise Gotell (Toronto: Prentice Hall, 2000), 122.

37 Ibid., 121.

38 Benedict Anderson's argument, in his study of nationalism *Imagined Communities* (London: Verso, 1991), has become a classic for theorists inquiring into the ideological and cultural construction of community — of almost any kind.

39 Stuart Hall, "Cultural Identity and Cinematic Representation," in *Film and Theory*, ed. Robert Stam and Toby Miller (Malden, MA: Blackwell, 2000), 714.

40 B. Anderson, *Imagined Communities*, 7.

41 Hall, "Cultural Identity and Cinematic Representation," 714.

42 "Notes to the Federal Cultural Review Committee," Studio D memo, undated, 8. NFBA. Known officially as the Report of the Federal Cultural Policy Review Committee, the Applebaum-Hébert Commission proposed that the government relinquish its role as owner, producer and distributor of culture and advocated, instead, for a free-enterprise model for Canadian cultural industries that would have strangled the CBC, the Canada Council for the Arts and the NFB.

43 Gary Evans notes how Gail Singer, a freelance filmmaker working in Studio D, brings women together in a cross-cultural survey from Ireland, Japan, Thailand, Peru, Columbia and Canada to demonstrate how the ability to obtain abortions remains a constant historical hardship linking women against impediments from powerful patriarchal structures such as the church, the state and the medical profession. Evans, *In the National Interest,* 299.

44 Ibid., 211.

45 Brenda Longfellow, "Un cinéma distinct: stratégies féministes dans les films canadiens," in *Les cinémas du Canada*, ed. Jean-Paul Passek with Sylvain Garel and André Pâquet (Montreal: Centre Georges Pompidou, 1992), 221. Translated from the French by the author.

46 Diane Burgess, "Leaving Gender Aside: The Legacy of Studio D?" in *Women Filmmakers: Refocusing*, ed. Jacqueline Levitin, Judith Plessis and Valerie Raoul (Vancouver: UBC Press, 2003), 418.

47 In "The Intellectual and Political Context for the Development of NAC," Vickers, Rankin and Appelle note that Americans like Marlene Dixon (hired to teach sociology at McGill University in 1969) and Bonnie Kreps (who had presented a brief explaining radical feminism to the Royal Commission on the Status of Women in 1968) supported quite opposite propositions that nonetheless were recognized as radical feminist approaches (124).

48 Ibid., 125.

49 Margaret Westcott, personal interview with the author, 21 August 2006.

50 Vickers, "The Intellectual and Political Context for the Development of NAC," 124.

51 Ibid., 121.

52 Ibid., 124.

53 Roberta Hamilton, *Gendering the Vertical Mosaic: Feminist Perspectives on Canadian Society* (Toronto: Copp Clark, 1996), 1. Emphasis added.

54 Nancy Adamson, Linda Briskin and Margaret McPhail, eds., *Feminist Organizing for Change: The Contemporary Women's Movement in Canada* (Toronto: Oxford University Press, 1988), 206.

55 Bonnie Sherr Klein, personal interview with the author, 18 August 1999.

56 Stikeman interview, 2 May 1997.

57 Ibid.

58 "Highlights of 1975–76: Studio D," undated internal report. NFBA.

59 Ibid., 2.

60 *INTERLOCK* acted as an industry resource guide, publishing reviews, interviews, distribution information, articles on technical questions as well as a directory of women working in various aspects of filmmaking.

61 Klein interview, 18 August 1999.

62 Ibid.

63 *INTERLOCK* , nos. 4 & 5 (1976).

64 Beverly Shaffer, personal interview with the author, 31 August 2000.

65 Internal memo from Kathleen Shannon, Executive Producer of Studio D, to André Lamy, NFB Commissioner, 9 October 1975. NFBA.

66 Shannon interview, 12 June 1996.

67 Gerry Rogers, telephone interview with the author, 22 February 2002.

68 Terre Nash, personal interview with the author, 24 February 2001.

69 Shannon interview, 12 June 1996.

70 Dorothy Todd Hénaut, personal interview with the author, 1 September 2000.

71 Shaffer interview, 31 August 2000.

72 Klein interview, 18 August 1999.

73 Johansson interview, 1 May 1997.

74 Lauder, "A Studio with a View," 12.

75 Stikeman interview, 2 May 1997.

76 Shannon interview, 12 June 1996.

77 Ibid.

78 Hénaut interview, 1 September 2000.

79 Shannon interview, 12 June 1996

80 Johansson interview, 1 May 1997.

81 Stikeman interview, 2 May 1997.

82 Scherbarth, "Why Not D?" 12.

83 Shannon interview, 12 June 1996.

84 The IC represented Labour Canada, Women's Bureau; Secretary of State, Women's Program; Treasury Board, Equal Opportunities for Women; Public Service Commission, Equal Opportunities for Women; Employment and Immigration: Women's Employment Division and Affirmative Action Division; Canadian Human Rights Commission; Status of Women Canada; Health and Welfare Canada; Agriculture Canada; and Transport Canada.

85 Studio D memo (untitled draft), 6 April 1982. NFBA.

86 Anita Taylor, "The National Film Board of Canada's Studio D: Feminist Filmmakers," in *Women and Media: Content/Careers/Criticism*, ed. Cynthia M. Lont (Belmont, CA: Wadsworth, 1995), 298.

87 Nash interview, 24 February 2001.

88 Taylor, "The National Film Board of Canada's Studio D," 297.

89 Internal memo, 20 February 1986, 2. NFBA.

90 "Studio D of the National Film Board of Canada: Starting the Second Decade," NFB Press Release, April 1985. NFBA.

91 Internal NFB document, "'We Are What We See': Thoughts on the N.F.B. from Studio D," 18 February 1985, 21. NFBA.

92 The Employment Equity Program was created by the federal government in 1986, parallel to the Federal Contractors Program. Both programs were designed to ensure workplace equity.

93 Meeting notes taken by Studio D, 15 January 1986, 1. NFBA.

94 Ibid., 2.

95 Ibid., 5.

96 Meeting notes, Advisory Group Meeting, NAC office, Toronto, 3 February 1986, 2. NFBA.

97 Canada, House of Commons, *Debates (Hansard)*, 17 April 1986 (43:26).

98 Ibid. (43:5, 26).

99 Ibid.

100 Government of Canada Memorandum, 22 May 1986, 2. NFBA. Emphasis in original.

101 Ibid., 3.

102 Ibid., 4.

103 Government of Canada Memorandum, 10 July 1986, 1. NFBA.

104 Margaret MacGee, letter to François Macerola, 10 July 1986. NFBA.

105 Ina Warren, "Future Bleak for Famed Studio D," *Globe and Mail*, 30 July 1986 (Montreal), C8.

106 Michele Landsberg, "Studio D: A Rare Source of Images from Canadian Culture," *Globe and Mail* (Toronto), 13 September 1986, A2.

107 Doris Anderson, "Studio D's Films Garner Few Financial Rewards," *Toronto Star*, 22 February 1986, L1.

108 The 1986 Caplan-Sauvageau Report on Canadian Broadcasting Policy was the result of a task force chaired by Gerald Caplan and Florian Sauvageau. The report signalled a crisis in Canadian culture with Canada's voice diminishing in a broadcast world being reshaped by new electronic technologies.

109 Chaviva Hosek, letter to François Macerola, 2 October 1986. NFBA.

110 Joan Pennefather, *Action and Communications Plan: Women, November 1986 to April 1987*, 17 November 1986. NFBA.

111 Anne Usher, letter to members of the Advisory Committee, 6 October 1986. NFBA.

112 Dorothy Todd Hénaut, "Notes on Studio D's Financial Situation," internal memo, 3 October 1996. NFBA.

113 Sharon Wickham-Foxwell, "If You Love This Studio," October 1986. Publication not identified. NFBA.

114 Sue Findlay's account of the confrontation is found in her essay "Problematizing Privilege: Another Look at the Representation of 'Women' in Feminist Practice," in *And Still We Rise: Feminist Political Mobilization in Contemporary Canada*, ed. Linda Carty (Toronto: Women's Press, 1993), 207–224. Fraticelli was well placed to instigate a more systemic anti-racist practice, designed to increase the representation of women of colour, integrating this group more fully into feminism in Canada.

115 R.E.A.L. Women, which stands for Realistic, Equal, Active for Life, is a group of mainly middle-class white women. In the 1980s, many of its members had direct political connections to the Progressive Conservative Party in power at the time. In 1989, public opinion on abortion was polarized by the well-publicized *Daigle vs. Tremblay* trial. Although the Canadian Charter of Rights and Freedoms had declared abortion laws invalid in 1988, the Quebec Court of Appeal had upheld an injunction obtained by Daigle's boyfriend to prevent her from seeking an abortion. Aided by LEAF, which argued that reproductive rights are fundamental to women's equality, Daigle appealed to the Supreme Court of Canada. The Court unanimously overturned the injunction, ruling that a fetus is not a legal "person," effectively entrenching women's right to control their own bodies.

116 Lois Sweet, "Studio D Faces Big Job Small Budget," *Toronto Star*, 4 May 1987, C1.

117 Ina Warren, "Head of Women's Film Unit Faces Big Task," *Ottawa Citizen*, 20 June 1987, C6.

118 Rina Fraticelli, "The Story So Far," Studio D Press Release (draft), undated. NFBA.

119 Evans, *In the National Interest,* 313.

120 Ina Warren, "NFB Disbands Women's Studio," *Ottawa Citizen*, 13 February 1989, C6.

121 *Blinkity Blank* (Fall 1987). This was an NFB publication for teachers. NFBA.

122 Kathleen Shannon, "Studio D Becomes a National Programme," personal memo, 13 February 1989. NFBA.

123 Diane Burgess, "Leaving Gender Aside: The Legacy of Studio D?" in *Women Filmmakers: Refocusing*, ed. Jacqueline Levitin, Judith Plessis and Valerie Raoul (Vancouver: UBC Press, 2003), 426.

124 Shannon, "'D' is for Dilemma," 29.

125 Sylvia Hamilton and Rina Fraticelli, "New Initiatives in Film, Working Document," April 1989, 1. NFBA.

126 Hamilton, co-directing with Claire Prieto, had just released *Black Mother, Black Daughter* (1989), which tells the story of generations of Black women in Nova Scotia.

127 Anderson, "Studio D's Imagined Community," 51. These filmmakers produced a body of work creating a new hybrid form playing with film techniques from fiction film and the social realist documentary: *Speak Body* and *Striptease* (Armatage, 1979, 1980); *The Central Character* (Gruben, 1977); *Breaking Out* and *Our Marilyn* (Longfellow, 1984, 1987); *Ten Cents a Dance (Parallax)* and *The Displaced View* (Onodera, 1985, 1988). As Elizabeth Anderson points out, sexuality, interpretations of history and the fluidity of racial, ethnic and gender identity take centre stage.

128 Undated press material, Studio D. NFBA

CHAPTER 4

1 Michel Foucault, "The Subject and Power," in *Power: Michel Foucault*, ed. James D. Faubion, trans. Robert Hurley and others (New York: New Press, 2000), 426.

2 Ibid., 427.

3 Jill Dolan, *The Feminist Spectator as Critic* (Ann Arbor: University of Michigan Press, 1991), 3.

4 Ibid.

5 Teresa de Lauretis, "*Guerrilla* in the Midst: Women's Cinema in the 80s," *Screen* 31, no. 1 (1990), 9.

6 Anneke Smelik, "Feminist Film Theory," in *The Cinema Book,* ed. Pam Cook and Mike Berniuk (London: British Film Institute, 1999), 353.

7 The two critical studies most often cited in feminist film history are Marjorie Rosen's *Popcorn Venus: Women, Movies and the American Dream* (New York: Avon Books, 1973) and Molly Haskell's *From Reverence to Rape: The Treatment of Women in the Movies*, rev. ed. (Chicago: University of Chicago Press, 1987).

8 Smelik, "Feminist Film Theory," 353.

9 Kass Banning, "The Canadian Feminist Hybrid Documentary," *Cinéaction*, nos. 26/27 (1992), 109.

10 Terre Nash, personal interview with the author, 24 February 2001.

11 Tania Modleski, "On the Existence of Women: A Brief History of the Relations between Women's Studies and Film Studies," *Women's Studies Quarterly* 30, nos. 1/2 (2002), 15-16.

12 Annette Kuhn uses John Grierson's definition to define this genre of filmmaking in *The Woman's Companion to International Film* (London: Virago Press, 1990), 123.

13 Sue Thornham, "Introduction," *Feminist Film Theory: A Reader*, ed. Sue Thornham (New York: New York University Press, 1999), 10.

14 Julia Lesage, "The Political Aesthetics of the Feminist Documentary Film," in *Issues in Feminist Film Criticism,* ed. Patricia Erens (Bloomington: Indiana University Press, 1990), 223.

15 Thornham, "Introduction," 2.

16 Alexandra Juhasz, "They Said We Were Trying to Show Reality — All I Want to Show Is My Video: The Politics of the Realist Feminist Documentary," in *Collecting Visible Evidence,* ed. Jane M. Gaines and Michael Renov (Minneapolis: University of Minnesota Press, 1999), 191.

17 Simone de Beauvoir, *The Second Sex,* trans. H.M. Parshley (New York: Knopf, 1953), 260.

18 See Shulamith Firestone, *The Dialectic of Sex: A Case for Feminist Revolution* (New York: Morrow, 1970).

19 Patricia White, "Feminism and Film," in *The Oxford Guide to Film Studies,* ed. John Hill and Pamela Church Gibson (New York: Oxford University Press, 1998), 129.

20 Janet McCabe, *Feminist Film Studies: Writing the Woman into Cinema* (London: Wallflower Press, 2004), 7.

21 Haskell, *From Reverence to Rape,* xviii.

22 Lesage, "The Political Aesthetics of the Feminist Documentary Film," 222.

23 Janet Walker and Diane Waldman, "Introduction," *Feminism and Documentary,*

ed. Diane Waldman and Janet Walker (Minneapolis: University of Minnesota Press, 1999), 8.

24 NFB promotional brochure, *Kathleen Shannon on Films, Feminism & Other Dreams* (1997). National Film Board Archives (hereafter NFBA).

25 Kay Armatage, "The Evolution of Women Filmmakers in Canada," in *Changing Focus: The Future for Women in the Canadian Film and Television Industry* (Toronto: Toronto Women in Film and Television, 1991), 135.

26 Ibid., 136.

27 Patricia Erens, "Women's Documentary Filmmaking: The Personal Is Political," in *New Challenges for Documentary*, ed. Alan Rosenthal (Berkeley: University of California Press, 1988), 555.

28 Library and Archives Canada, "Celebrating Women's Achievements, Canadian Women in Film: Kathleen Shannon," retrieved from www.collectionscanada.ca/women/ 002026-714-e.html.

29 Kathleen Shannon, personal interview with the author, 12 June 1996.

30 Vickers rejects the idea of a rupture inherent in the concepts of "first-wave and second-wave feminism," arguing instead that feminists must recognize "the forces of continuity in those movements across time" that encourage an intergenerational exchange of ideas." See "The Intellectual Origins of the Women's Movements in Canada," in *Challenging Times: The Women's Movement in Canada and the United* States, ed. Constance Backhouse and David H. Flaherty (Montreal: McGill-Queen's University Press, 1992), 39–60.

31 Shannon interview, 12 June 1996.

32 Dorothy Todd Hénaut, personal interview with the author, 1 September 2000.

33 Colin Low's *Fogo Island Communications Experiment*, a series of twenty-six short films made in 1967 and 1968, was developed in close collaboration with the citizens of Fogo Island, one of several federal-provincial resettlement projects. The settlement was split into two rival forces — the poor residents and the established authorities. Low began by discussing the issues with local people who were reluctant to appear on camera. He gained their trust by promising to show the footage to the locals and gaining their consent before airing it elsewhere. With villagers' permission, Low took the films to St. John's where he screened them to a group of academics in a discussion seminar at Memorial University. Low filmed the seminar session, returning to Fogo Island and sharing his footage containing the discussion with the local residents. The outcome was substantial. Hearing their concerns discussed with respect made residents feel vindicated. The film series established a new relationship between director, filmmaker and film subject. The use of *cinéma direct* techniques allowed the filmmaker to obliterate the class-based subject–object relation that inevitably exists between the middle-class filmmaker and working-class subject.

34 Gary Evans, *In the National Interest* (Toronto: University of Toronto Press, 1991), 174.

35 Ginny Stikeman, personal interview with the author, 2 May 1997.

36 Evans, *In the National Interest*, 169. The film captured events (protests, scuffles and arrests) surrounding a blockade of the international bridge between New York and Cornwall by members of the Mohawk Nation protesting infringement of long-held rights. It foreshadowed the events of a similar and much larger protest duplicated in Alanis Obomsawin's *Kanehsatake: 270 Years of Resistance* two decades later.

37 Ibid., 168.

38 *En tant que femmes* was a series of five documentaries developed in 1972 for French-language television by the NFB. Headed by feminist filmmaker Anne Claire Poirier, the series proved to be enormously popular with women in Quebec, presenting clearly defined feminist approaches (to abortion, the needs of single-mothers for good daycare and the feminization of poverty) that allowed even the most conservative of spectators to reappraise the capabilities and situations of women at the time.

39 Laurinda Hart, "Kathleen Shannon: Working Mothers Series," *Cinema Canada* 2, no. 15 (August/September 1974), 55.

40 Shannon quoted in ibid.

41 Evans, *In the National Interest*, 169.

42 Lesage, "The Political Aesthetics of the Feminist Documentary Film," 223.

43 National Film Board of Canada, "Our Collection: Working Mothers: The Film." Available online at www.nfb.ca/collection/films/fiche/?id=18465.

44 *The Spring and Fall of Nina Polanski* (dir. Hutton/Roy, 1974) celebrates the cyclical nature of women's necessary work in the "kitchen" in a whimsical and trenchant portrait.

45 Lesage, "The Political Aesthetics of the Feminist Documentary Film," 224.

46 Lisa Maria Hogeland, *Feminism and Its Fictions: The Consciousness-Raising Novel and the Women's Liberation Movement* (Philadelphia: University of Pennsylvania Press, 1998), i.

47 Joanne Hollows, *Feminism, Femininity and Popular Culture* (Manchester: Manchester University Press, 2000), 43.

48 Bill Nichols, in *Representing Reality: Issues and Concepts in Documentary* (Bloomington: Indiana University Press, 1991), coins this term to identify such documentary films as examples of *cinema verité* that "hinge on the ability of the filmmaker to be unobtrusive" (39).

49 Nichols uses this term to "stress images of testimony or verbal exchange ... that demonstrate the validity ... of the witnesses ... [as] their comments and responses provide a central part of the film's argument" (ibid., 44).

50 Brian Winston, "The Tradition of the Victim in Griersonian Documentary," in *Image Ethics: The Moral Rights of Subject in Photographs, Film, and Television*, ed. Larry Gross, John Stuart Katz and Jay Ruby (New York: Oxford University Press, 1988).

51 Ibid., 35, 45.

52 Lesage, "The Political Aesthetics of the Feminist Documentary Film," 223.

53 Roberta Hamilton, *Gendering the Vertical Mosaic: Feminist Perspectives on Canadian Society* (Toronto: Copp Clark, 1996), 56.

54 Anne Crocker, *Equal Times* (October 1975).

55 Mary Anne Doane, Patricia Mellencamp and Linda Williams, "Feminist Film Criticism: An Introduction," in *Re-vision: Essays in Feminist Film Criticism* (Frederick, MD: The American Film Institute, 1984), 5.

56 Signe Johansson, personal interview with the author, 1 May 1997.

57 Stikeman interview, 2 May 1997.

58 Hénaut interview, 1 September 2000.

59 While this title is my own creation, I note that Alexandra Juhasz uses one identical in her essay "They Said We Were Trying to Show Reality — All I Want to Show Is My Video,"198.

60 Armatage, "The Evolution of Women Filmmakers in Canada," 136.

61 Christl Verduyn, "Reconstructing Canadian Literature: The Role of Race and Gender," in *Painting the Maple: Essays on Race, Gender, and the Construction of Canada*, ed. Veronica Strong-Boag, Sherrill Grace, Avigail Eisenberg and Joan Anderson (Vancouver: University of British Columbia Press, 1998), 102.

62 Julia Lesage, "Feminist Documentary: Aesthetics and Politics," in "*Show Us Life*": *Toward a History and Aesthetics of the Committed Documentary*, ed. Tom Waugh (Metechen, NJ: Scarecrow Press, 1984), 223.

63 Teresa de Lauretis, "Rethinking Women's Cinema: Aesthetics and Feminist Theory," in *Issues in Feminist Film Criticism,* ed. Patricia Erens (Bloomington: Indiana University Press, 1991), 288.

64 McCabe, *Feminist Film Studies*, 10.

65 Thornham, "Introduction," 12.

66 Claire Johnston, "Women's Cinema as Counter-Cinema," in *Feminist Film Theory: A Reader*, ed. Sue Thornham (New York: New York University Press, 1999), 40.

67 McCabe, *Feminist Film Studies*, 10.

68 Ibid., 11.

69 Modleski, "On the Existence of Women," 16.

70 Shannon interview, 12 June 1996.

71 Ibid.

72 Diane Burgess, "Leaving Gender Aside: The Legacy of Studio D?" in *Women Filmmakers: Refocusing*, ed. Jacqueline Levitin, Judith Plessis and Valerie Raoul (Vancouver: UBC Press, 2003), 428.

73 Terre Nash, "Against the Grain: Kathleen Shannon in Memoriam," *This Magazine* (May/June1998), 37.

74 Studio D undated memo, "Notes to the Federal Cultural Review Committee," 4. NFBA.

75 Smelik, "Feminist Film Theory," 353.

76 Bonnie Sherr Klein, personal interview with the author, 12 August 1999.

77 Beverly Shaffer, personal interview with the author, 30 August 2000.

78 Hénaut interview, 1 September 2000.

79 Ibid.

80 See, for example, Beverley Skeggs, "Introduction," *Feminist Cultural Theory: Process and Production*, ed. Beverley Skeggs (Manchester: Manchester University Press, 1995), 7.

81 Beverly Shaffer, personal interview with the author, 31 August 2000.

82 Ibid.

83 Smelik, "Feminist Film Theory," 359.

84 Bonnie Sherr Klein, personal interview with the author, 18 August 1999.

85 Kathleen Shannon, "Real Issues in a Reel World," *Media & Values* (Winter 1989), 49, 15.

86 Joan Kelly, "Early Feminist Theory and the Querelle des Femmes, 1400–1789," in *Women, History and Theory: The Essays of Joan Kelly* (Chicago: University of Chicago Press, 1984), 79.

87 Nash, "Against the Grain," 37.

88 Gloria Steinem quoted in ibid., 38.

89 Anita Taylor, "The National Film Board of Canada's Studio D: Feminist Filmmakers," in *Women and Media: Content/Careers/Criticism*, ed. Cynthia M. Lont (Belmont, CA: Wadsworth, 1995), 303.

90 Studio D's protected location insulated it — to a certain extent — from outside criticism, demonstrating that privilege, however restricting in nature, is accompanied by a certain "blindness," an established feminist complaint of patriarchal structures.

91 Nash interview, 24 February 2001.

92 Ibid.

93 Ibid.

94 Hamilton, *Gendering the Vertical Mosaic*, 106.

95 Nash interview, 24 February 2001.

96 Ibid.

97 Evans, *In the National Interest*, 283.

98 Burgess, "Leaving Gender Aside," 424.

99 Nancy Adamson, Linda Briskin and Margaret McPhail, eds., *Feminist Organizing for Change: The Contemporary Women's Movement in Canada* (Toronto: Oxford University Press, 1988), 3.

100 Kathleen Shannon, "'D' is for Dilemma," *Herizons* (Summer 1995), 27.

101 Burgess, "Leaving Gender Aside," 425. That it wasn't uncontested is argued in B. Ruby Rich's "Anti-Porn: Soft Issue, Hard World," in *Gendering the Nation: Canadian Women's Cinema,* ed. Kay Armatage, Kass Banning, Brenda Longfellow and Janine Marchessault (Toronto: University of Toronto Press, 1999), which credits the film for signalling an important issue but finds its direction wanting on ideological grounds.

102 "Studio D," undated selected chronology of Studio D. NFBA.

103 Elizabeth Anderson, "Pirating Feminisms: Film and the Production of Post-War Canadian National Identity" (PhD diss., University of Minnesota, 1996), 195.

104 Ibid.

105 Sid Adilman, "Movie about Porn Trade Packs a Punch," *Toronto Star*, 4 September 1981, D3; Jay Scott, "Not a Love Story: A Sleazy Peek at Women and Porn," *Globe and Mail* (Toronto), 7 September 1981, C13.

106 B. Ruby Rich, "Anti-Porn: Soft Issue, Hard World," *The Village Voice,* 20 July 1982, 16. Her article was subsequently published in *Gendering the Nation: Canadian Women's Cinema*, ed. Armatage, Banning, Brenda and Marchessault.

107 Susan Barrowclough, "Not a Love Story," *Screen* 23, no. 5 (1982), 36.

108 Anderson, "Pirating Feminisms," 196.

109 Linda Williams, *Hard Core: Power, Pleasure and the "Frenzy of the Visible"* (Berkeley: University of California Press, 1989), 265.

110 Robert Fulford, "NFB Film Ignites Anti-Porn Movement," *Toronto Star*, 5 June 1982, F3.

111 B. Ruby Rich, *Chick Flicks* (Durham, NC: Duke University Press, 1998), 256.

112 Linda Nicholson, ed., *The Second Wave: A Reader in Feminist Theory* (New York: Routledge, 1997), 1.

113 Burgess, "Leaving Gender Aside," 424.

114 Brenda Longfellow, "Making Documentary Films," in *Women Filmmakers: Refocusing*, ed. Jacqueline Levitin, Judith Plessis and Valerie Raoul (Vancouver: UBC Press, 2003), 212.

115 Kathleen Shannon, "Studio D and the National Film Board Women's Program," 28 August 1978, 3. NFBA.

116 Kathleen Shannon, *INTERLOCK* (ca. 1975), 26. NFBA.

117 Westcott, personal interview with the author, 21 August 2006.

118 Wikipedia, "Second Vatican Council." Available online from http://en.wikipedia.org/wiki/Second_Vatican_Council.

119 Margaret Westcott, *Nuns—The Invisible Women*, "Investigates Memo," 15 October 1979. NFBA.

120 NFB publicity brochure, undated. NFBA.

121 Joan Pennefather, personal letter, 23 May 1990. NFBA

122 Judith Ezekiel, *Feminism in the Heartland* (Columbus: Ohio State University Press, 2002).

123 de Lauretis, "Rethinking Women's Cinema," 289.

124 Juhasz, "They Said We Were Trying to Show Reality — All I Want to Show Is My Video," 191.

CHAPTER 5

1 Nancy Adamson, Linda Briskin and Margaret McPhail, eds., *Feminist Organizing for Change: The Contemporary Women's Movement in Canada* (Toronto: Oxford University Press, 1988), 206.

2 Ruth Roach Pierson, "Experience, Difference, Dominance and Voice in the Writing of Canadian Women's History," in *Writing Women's History: International Perspectives*, ed. Karen Offen, Ruth Roach Pierson and Jane Rendall (Bloomington: Indiana University Press, 1991), 93.

3 Chris Scherbarth, "Studio D of the National Film Board of Canada: Seeing Ourselves through Women's Eyes" (MA thesis, Carleton University, 1986), 3.

4 Susan Knudson, "For a Feminist Narratology," *Tessera* 4, no. 3 (1989), 13.

5 Ibid.

6 Ibid., 10.

7 Diane Burgess points out that such critiques carry a troubling pejorative edge because they suggest that films with a social purpose are of less value than others, which works to further marginalize the genre in her essay, "Leaving Gender Aside: The Legacy of Studio D?" in *Women Filmmakers: Refocusing*, ed. Jacqueline Levitin, Judith Plessis and Valerie Raoul (Vancouver: UBC Press, 2003), 422.

8 Kathleen Shannon, personal interview with the author, 12 June 1996.

9 Here I draw on ideas set out by Marlene Kadar in a lecture on life-writing (York University, 24 February 2000) in which she argued that such women's stories fall into the genre of life-writing when they demonstrate the following characteristics: the stories bear witness, write history from an insider perspective, reveal social circumstances from a personal vantage point and perform the political act of "reclamation," re-understanding the implication of "dailiness" in women's lives.

10 Gloria J. Gibson-Hudson, "The Ties that Bind: Cinematic Representations by Black Women Filmmakers," *Quarterly Review of Film and Video* 15, no. 2 (1993), 29.

11 Becky Ross, "A Lesbian Politics of Erotic Decolonization," in *Painting the Maple: Race, Gender, and the Construction of Canada,* ed. Veronica Strong-Boag, Sherrill Grace, Avigail Eisenberg, and Joan Anderson (Vancouver: University of British Columbia Press, 1998), 206.

12 Andrea Bernard, "Experiencing Problems: The Relationship between Women's Studies and Feminist Film Theory," *Women's Studies International Forum* 18, no. 1 (1995), 62 .

13 I am indebted to my colleague Dr. Leslie Sanders for her insights and interpretation of this Studio D documentary and for her attention in considering the questions of gender and nation simultaneously to arrive at a more complex understanding of the dimensions of gender in the inflection of gender and culture we were attempting to excavate through our classroom teaching. In tutorial discussions following the screening of this film, the vast majority of our 130 students, a number with Chinese origins, reported little or no previous knowledge of such stories as those of the women in *Under the Willow Tree.*

14 Stuart Hall, "Who Needs Identity," in *Questions of Cultural Identity*, ed. Stuart Hall and Paul du Gay (London: Sage, 1996), 4.

15 Helen M. Buss, "Writing and Reading Autobiography: Introduction to *Prairie Fire's* 'Life Writing' Issue," *Prairie Fire* 16, no. 2 (1995), 14.

16 Ibid., 15.

17 Enakshi Dua, "Introduction," *Scratching the Surface: Canadian Anti-racist Feminist Thought,* ed. Enakshi Dua and Angela Robertson (Toronto: Women's Press, 1999), 13.

18 Gibson-Hudson, "The Ties that Bind," 26.

19 Dionne Brand, *No Burden to Carry: Narratives of Black Working Women in Ontario 1920s to 1950s* (Toronto: Women's Press, 1991), 13.

20 Gibson-Hudson, "The Ties that Bind," 27.

21 Brand, *No Burden to Carry*, 31, 32.

22 Burgess, "Leaving Gender Aside," 418.

23 Gibson-Hudson, "The Ties that Bind," 27.

24 Brand, *No Burden to Carry*, 34.

25 Dua, "Introduction," 14.

26 Ibid.

27 Tracy Prince, "The Post of Colonial in the Works of Pratibha Parmer: *Kiss My Cuddies*," in *Women Filmmakers: Refocusing*, ed. Jacqueline Levitin, Judith Plessis, Valerie Raoul (Vancouver: UBC Press, 2003) 294.

28 Laurie Soper, "*Long Time Comin'*," *Herizons* (Spring 1994), 45.

29 Ibid.

30 Dionne Brand, personal interview with the author, 29 March 2003.

31 Marlene NourbeSe Philip "The Absence of Writing or How I Almost Became a Spy," *A Geneology of Resistance and Other Essays*, ed. Marlene NourbeSe Philip (Toronto: Mercury Press, 1997), 43.

32 Ibid., 43, 46.

33 Ibid., 49.

34 Ibid.

35 Ibid., 56.

36 Terre Nash, personal interview with the author, 24 February 2001.

37 Gary Evans, *In the National Interest: A Chronicle of the National Film Board of Canada from 1949 to 1989* (Toronto: University of Toronto Press, 1991), 284.

38 Beverly Daurio, "Order and Imagination," *Books in Canada* 20, no. 2 (1991), 19.

39 Micheline Dumont, "The Origins of the Women's Movement in Quebec," *Challenging Times: The Women's Movement in Canada and the United States*, ed. Constance Backhouse and David H. Flaherty (Montreal: McGill-Queen's University Press, 1991), 75.

40 Dorothy Todd Hénaut, personal interview with the author, 1 September 2000.

41 Dumont, "The Origins of the Women's Movement in Quebec," 73.

42 Jean Paul Riopelle (1923–2002) was a renowned Canadian Abstract Expressionist, and Marc Chagall a renowned painter and stained glass artist of Russian-Jewish origin (1887–1985). They were both members of the *École de Paris.*

43 Barbara Godard, "Nicole Brossard," *Profiles in Canadian Literature* 6 (1986), 123.

44 Beverley Skeggs, ed. *Feminist Cultural Theory: Process and Production* (Manchester: Manchester University Press, 1995), 12.

45 Ibid., 13.

46 Ibid., 18.

47 Hénaut interview, 1 September 2000.

48 Coral Ann Howells, *Private and Fictional Worlds: Canadian Women Novelists of the 1970s and 1980s* (London: Methuen, 1987), 4.

49 Ibid., 5.

50 Rachel Blau DuPlessis, *Writing beyond the Ending: Narrative Strategies of Twentieth-Century Women Writers* (Bloomington: Indiana University Press, 1985), 34, 36.

51 Ibid., 196.

52 Ibid., 197.

CHAPTER 6

1 Matthew Hays, "Lament for Studio D: A Conversation with Kathleen Shannon," *Point of View* 29 (Spring 1996), 16.

2 Tarel Quandt, "Does the Goddess Gave a Hidden Agenda?"*Kinesis* (May 1990), 16.

3 "Feminist Broke Ground for Female Filmmakers: Obituary/Kathleen Shannon," *Globe and Mail,* 15 January 1998, S10.

4 Naomi Black, "Ripples in the Second Wave: Comparing the Contemporary Women's Movement in Canada and the United States," in *Challenging Times: The Women's Movement in Canada and the United* States, ed. Constance Backhouse and David H. Flaherty (Montreal: McGill- Queen's University Press, 1992), 95.

5 Roberta Hamilton, *Gendering the Vertical Mosaic: Feminist Perspectives on Canadian Society* (Toronto: Copp Clark, 1996), 53.

6 Dorothy Todd Hénaut, personal interview with the author, 1 September 2000.

7 Elizabeth Anderson, "Pirating Feminisms: Film and the Production of Post-War Canadian National Identity" (PhD diss., Univrsity of Minnesota, 1996), 234.

8 Letter from James De B. Domville to Thelma McCormack, 21 July 1981. NFBA.

9 Hénaut interview, 1 September, 2000.

10 Stephen Godfrey, "A Ride on a Feminist Rollercoaster," *Globe and Mail* (Toronto), 11 October 1989, C1.

11 Directed by Toronto guerrilla artist Gwendolyn, *Prowling by Night* featured cartoon-like cut-out figures that were "self-portraits" the prostitutes had created to give a critical insider view of the occupational dangers of street prostitution.

12 Canada was represented at the UN conference by Walter McLean, the minister responsible for the Status of Women portfolio.

13 Frank McKie, "Feminist NFB Films Boring," *Winnipeg Free Press*, 16 June 1986, 21.

14 "NFB: Studio D Shuffles Staff," *Cinema Canada* 160 (February/March 1989), 49.

15 Ibid.

16 Ibid. Emphasis added.

17 "Guidelines for Film Proposals," Studio D of the National Film Board of Canada (undated). NFBA.

18 Midi Onodera, guest lecture at Glendon College, York University 3 February 2000.

19 Stephen Godfrey, "Through the Eyes of a Woman," *Globe and Mail* (Toronto), 19 January 1990, C1.

20 Ibid.

21 "Studio D Commemorates 20 Years of Groundbreaking Feminist Documentaries," NFB/ONF News Release, 12 May 1994. NFBA.

22 Sun-Kyung Yi, "Trouble in Paradise or Testing the Limits at Studio D," *Take One* 5 (Summer 1991), 40.

23 Ibid.

24 Ibid.

25 Ibid.

26 Ibid.

27 Elizabeth Anderson, "Studio D's Imagined Community: From Development (1974) to Realignment (1986–1990)," in *Gendering the Nation: Canadian Women's Cinema*, ed. Kay Armatage, Kass Banning, Brenda Longfellow and Janine Marchessault (Toronto: University of Toronto Press, 1999), 52.

28 Diane Burgess, "Leaving Gender Aside: The Legacy of Studio D?" in *Women Filmmakers: Refocusing*, ed. Jacqueline Levitin, Judith Plessis and Valerie Raoul (Vancouver: UBC Press, 2003), 430.

29 Cindy Filipenko, "Calling the Shots," *Herizons* (Fall 1996), 18.

30 Ibid., 19.

31 During a telephone conversation on 2 April 2002, Bonnie Sherr Klein referred to critical analyses of her film *Not a Love Story* (1981) that charge the film proposes a pro-censorship stance. She noted with some irony that the concept for the film originated in a discussion group to which she belonged that was exploring possible feminist repositionings of women's sexuality.

32 Rachel Blau DuPlessis and Ann Snitow, "A Feminist Memoir Project," in *The Feminist Memoir Project: Voices from Women's Liberation,* ed. Rachel Blau DuPlessis and Ann Snitow (New York: Three Rivers Press, 1998), 8.

33 Biddy Martin, "Success and Its Failures," *differences: A Journal of Feminist Cultural Studies* 9, no. 3 (Fall 1997), 113.

34 Ibid.

35 Audre Lorde, "Uses of Anger," *Zami, Sister Outsider, Undersong* (New York: Quality Paperback Books, 1993), 128.

36 Ibid., 132.

37 Ibid., 131.

38 Jean Bruce, "Querying/Queering the Nation," in *Gendering the Nation: Canadian Women's Cinema*, ed. Kay Armatage, Kass Banning, Brenda Longfellow and Janine Marchessault (Toronto: University of Toronto Press, 1999), 282.

39 I am indebted to Dr. Allan J. Ryan (New Sun Chair in Aboriginal Art and Culture, Carleton University, Ottawa) for pointing out this insight that the director herself must be included as one of the film's artists.

40 *Beyond Borders* was filmed in the United States, Egypt, Jordan, the West Bank and Gaza, and includes interviews with prominent Arab intellectuals, including Egyptian author Nawal Saadawi.

41 Centeme Zeleke, "That's a Cut: Feds Close Women's Studio," *Herizons* (Summer 1996), 9.

42 Hays, "Lament for Studio D," 7.

43 Sylvia B. Bashevkin, *Women on the Defensive* (Toronto: University of Toronto Press, 1998), 8.

44 Ibid.

45 Canada, Department of Canadian Heritage, *Making Our Voices Heard: Canadian Broadcasting and Film For the 21st Century* (Hull, QC: Minister of Supply and Services Canada, 1996), 163.

46 Burgess, "Leaving Gender Aside," 429.

47 "The National Film Board of Canada in the Year 2000: A Charter for a New Century," unpublished report, 18 March 1996, 2. NFBA.

48 Burgess, "Leaving Gender Aside," 430.

49 Kathleen Shannon, personal interview with the author, 12 June 1996.

50 Ruth Roach Pierson, *Canadian Women and the Second World War* (Ottawa: Canadian Historical Association, 1983), 73.

51 DuPlessis and Snitow, "A Feminist Memoir Project," 9.

52 Carolyn G. Heilbrun, *Writing a Woman's Life* (New York: W.W. Norton, 1988), 131.

53 Andrea Bernard, "Experiencing Problems: The Relationship between Women's Studies and Feminist Film Theory," *Women's Studies International Forum* 18, no. 1 (1995), 61.

54 Alexandra Juhasz, "They Said We Were Trying to Show Reality — All I Want to Show Is My Video: The Politics of the Realist Feminist Documentary," in *Collecting Visible Evidence*, ed. Jane M. Gaines and Michael Renov (Minneapolis: University of Minnesota Press, 1999), 192.

55 Cathy L. James, "Women's History on Film: Requiem for Studio D," *Canadian Historical Review* 80, no.1 (March 1999), 94.

56 Ibid., 93.

57 In *Australian National Cinema* (London: Routledge, 1993), Film theorist Tom O'Regan defines the conflicting elements, strategies and purposes marking national film a messy assemblage.

58 Teresa de Lauretis, "Rethinking Women's Cinema: Aesthetics and Feminist Theory," in *Issues in Feminist Film Criticism*, ed. Patricia Erens (Bloomington: Indiana University Press, 1991), 296.

59 Bashevkin, *Women on the Defensive*, 237.

60 "Studio D Commemorates 20 Years of Groundbreaking Feminist Documentaries," NFB News Release, 12 May 1994. NFBA.

61 Mary Maynard and June Purvis, *New Frontiers in Women's Studies: Knowledge, Identity, and Nationalism* (New York: Taylor and Francis, 1996), 2.

62 Anderson, "Studio D's Imagined Community, 42.

63 Frederic Jameson, "Preface," *The Cultures of Globalization,* ed. Frederic Jameson and Masao Miyoshi (Durham, NC: Duke University Press, 1998), xii.

64 Juhasz, "They Said We Were Trying to Show Reality — All I Want to Show Is My Video," 209.

65 Leila Sarangi, "Critical Commentary" (course journal).

66 Joan Wallach Scott, "Women's Studies on the Edge, Introduction," *differences: A Journal of Feminist Cultural Studies* 9, no. 3 (1997), iv.

67 See my discussion in chap. 2 of Chantal Mouffe's feminist "we" as radical democratic citizens.

68 Among these women were Daphne Lilly Anstey, Beth Bertram, Jane Marsh Beveridge, Laura Boulton, Betty Brunke, Janet Scellen Bull, Red Burns, Margaret Carter, Evelyn Spice Cherry, Judith Crawley, Margaret Ann Elton, Helen Watson Gordon, Margaret Grierson (who worked at the Film Board for six months without salary, so decreed by her husband NFB commissioner John Grierson), Evelyn Horne, Joan Hutton, Eve Lambart, Marion Leigh Leventhal, Dorothy Macpherson, Calais Calvert-Marty, Majorie McKay, Edith Spencer Osberg, Gudrun Bjerring Parker, Margaret Perry, Dalila Barbeau Price and Mary Lyn Twomblay.

69 Susan Stanford Friedman, *Mappings: Feminism and the Cultural Geographies of Encounter* (Princeton, NJ: Princeton University Press, 1998), 215.

70 I refer specifically to such Canadian theorists as Himani Bannerji, Arun Mukherjee, Roberta Hamilton, Rosanna Ng and Margaret O'Brien whose work appears in *Open Boundaries*, ed. Barbara A. Crow and Lise Gotell (Toronto: Prentice Hall, 2000), an assessment of contemporary Canadian feminism and its debates.

71 Heilbrun, *Writing a Woman's Life*, 11.

72 Friedman, *Mappings*, 215.

73 Nicole Brossard, *Yesterday, at the Hotel Clarendon*, trans. Susanne de Lotbinière-Harwood (Toronto: Coach House Press, 2001), 219.

PHOTO CAPTIONS

I am grateful for the assistance of Dorothy Todd Hénaut, Signe Johansson and Ginny Stikeman in helping me to identify faces and places in the photographs.

All Photo Credits: Signe Johansson.

1. Studio D members (Kathleen Shannon, Ginny Stikeman and Elizabeth Prinn on the left) discuss how print images of women can generate and circulate stereotypic notions.
2. Kathleen Shannon checking a camera angle during one of the filming sessions for the *Working Mothers* series.
3. Nesya Shapiro (cinematographer for *Some American Feminists* and later director of her own films) checks lighting.
4. Signe Johansson (centre) raises a point with the Studio D "collective" planning a daycare centre for NFB headquarters in Montreal.
5. Lotte Reiniger pioneer film animator (likely influence on Evelyn Lambart), renowned for cinematic mastery with delicate and intricate paper silhouettes designed through freehand scissor cutting, works with Studio D lighting technician Nesya Shapiro on *Aucassin & Nicolette* (1975) retelling the medieval tale from a feminist perspective.
6. Studio D and associates early in 1987: (front row seated left to right) Dorothy Rosenberg, Ginny Stikeman, Linda Paris Quillinan, Gisèlle Guilbault (Studio administrator), Beverly Shaffer, Chantal Bowen (producer); (second row, sitting) Donna Dudinsky (research), Linda Payette, Susan Huycke, Dorothy Todd Hénaut; (back row) Gloria Demers, Cynthia Scott, Joy Johnson, Kathleen Shannon, Margaret Westcott, unidentified male from technical services, Signe Johansson, Terre Nash, Irene Angelico, Henriette Frey and Gerry Rogers.
7. Anne Henderson (foreground) and Irene Angelico thread a film.
8. Esther Auger adjusts the sound system.
9. Camera captures the image of an animator associated with Studio D.

10. Tiina Soomet (now president of CLARE Media Inc.) working with a strip of film at a rewind table, with a moviola (editing system) in the background.

11. Cinematographer Aerlyn Weissman (now partner in Producers on Davie and mentor at the Gulf Islands Film and Video School) films a discussion in the Studio D meeting room.

12. Studio D members conducting an International Women's Year (1975) workshop at the NFB shooting stage. Anne Henderson (second from the left) and Signe Johansson (extreme right) listen to the speaker, while Kathleen Shannon (fourth from the left) consults her notes.

13. An unidentified sound technician checks the volume as she holds a mike.

14. Ginny Stikeman edits a film using a Steinbeck.

15. Cinematographer Susan Trow (now a professional breeder of award-winning Scottish deerhounds) adjusts her camera lens.

16. Irene Angelico (award-winning Montreal filmmaker and chair of DLI Productions) threads a projector in an NFB screening room.

17. Signe Johansson and Doris Mae Oulton (now CEO, Community Youth Solutions) consult images to be used in a film project. Employed by *Challenge for Change,* Oulton had travelled across Canada polling public interest in the *Working Mother* series. The overwhelmingly positive public response was a major factor in the NFB's decision to create Studio D.

18. Judith Sanderford participates in a collective discussion in the Studio D meeting room.

19. Anne Wheeler, director of *Great Grand Mother,* in discussion in the Studio D meeting room.

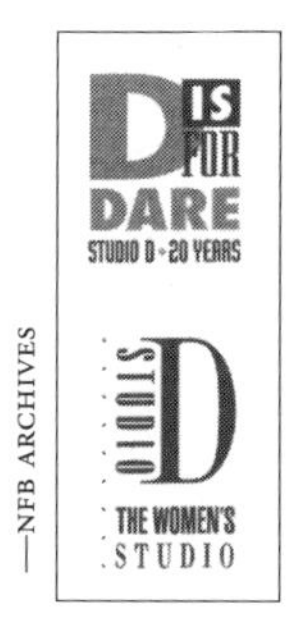

—NFB ARCHIVES

STUDIO D CHRONOLOGICAL FILMOGRAPHY

This is a list of Studio D documentaries, containing titles Studio D co-produced with the Federal Women's Film Program (FWFP), the New Initiative in Film (NIF) program and with a number of regional NFB studios and privately owned film companies. The FWFP was a coalition of federal government departments and agencies committed to producing films, available in both official languages, on women's concerns designed to create an impetus for discussions of social reform.

Extensions of the Family. Dir. Kathleen Shannon, 1974.

It's Not Enough. Dir. Kathleen Shannon, 1974.

Like the Trees. Dir. Kathleen Shannon, 1974.

Luckily I Need Little Sleep. Dir. Kathleen Shannon, 1974.

Mothers Are People. Dir. Kathleen Shannon, 1974.

The Spring and Fall of Nina Polanski. Dir. Joan Hutton and Louise Roy, 1974.

They Appreciate You More. Dir. Kathleen Shannon, 1974.

Tiger on a Tight Leash. Dir. Kathleen Shannon, 1974.

Would I Ever Like a Job. Dir. Kathleen Shannon, 1974.

"... And They Lived Happily Ever After." Dir. Kathleen Shannon, 1975.

Great Grand Mother (with Filmwest Assoc. Ltd.). Dir. Anne Wheeler and Lorna Rasmussen, 1975.

My Friends Call Me Tony. Dir. Beverly Shaffer, 1975.

My Name Is Susan Yee. Dir. Beverly Shaffer, 1975.

Just–A-Minute (compilation of twenty-three short films). Dir. various (Aitkin et al.), 1976.

Maud Lewis: A World Without Shadows. Dir. Diane Beaudry, 1976.

Our Dear Sisters. Dir. Kathleen Shannon, 1976.

Beautiful Lennard Island. Dir. Beverly Shaffer, 1977.

Gurdeep Singh Bains. Dir. Beverly Shaffer, 1977.

How They Saw Us: Women at War; Wings on Her Shoulder; Proudly She Marches; Careers and Cradles; Needles and Pins; Service in the Sky; Is it a Women's World; Women at Work. Dir. Ann Pearson, 1977.

I'll Find a Way. ** Dir. Beverly Shaffer, 1977.

Kevin Alec. Dir. Beverly Shaffer, 1977.

Some American Feminists. Dir. Nicole Brossard, Luce Guilbeault and Margaret Westcott, 1977.

The Lady from Grey County. Dir. Janice Brown, 1977.

Veronica. Dir. Beverly Shaffer, 1977.

An Unremarkable Birth. Dir. Diane Beaudry, 1978.

Benoît. Dir. Beverly Shaffer, 1978.

Eve Lambart. Dir. Margaret Westcott, 1978.

Patricia's Moving Picture. Dir. Bonnie Sherr Klein, 1978.

Sun, Wind and Wood. Dir. Dorothy Todd Hénaut, 1978.

Prairie Album. Dir. Blake James, 1979.

The Right Candidate for Rosedale. Dir. Bonnie Sherr Klein, Anne Henderson, 1979.

Sea Dream (animation). Dir. Ellen Besen, 1979.

Boys Will Be Men. Dir. Donald Rennick, 1980.

Just a Lady. Dir. Susan Trow, 1980.

Laila. Dir. Janice Brown, 1980.

Loved, Honoured and Bruised. Dir. Gail Singer, 1980.

Rusting World. Laurent Coderre, 1980.

The Town Mouse and the Country Mouse (animation, with NFB). Dir. Evelyn Lambart.

After the Axe. Dir. Sturla Gunnarsson, 1981.

Julie O'Brien. Dir. Beverly Shaffer, 1981.

Louise Drouin, Veterinarian. Dir. Margaret Westcott, 1981.

Not a Love Story. Dir. Bonnie Sherr Klein, 1981.

*Four Centuries: The Firearm in Canada.** Dir. Joan Henson, 1982.

*If You Love This Planet.*** Dir. Terre Nash, 1982.

Portrait of the Artist — As an Old Lady. Dir. Gail Singer, 1982.

It's Just Better. Dir. Beverly Shaffer, 1982.

The Way It Is. Dir. Beverly Shaffer, 1982.

*Attention: Women at Work!** Dir. Anne Henderson, 1983.

I Want To Be an Engineer. Dir. Beverly Shaffer, 1983.

Dream of a Free Country: A Message from Nicaraguan Women. Dir. Kathleen Shannon and Ginny Stikeman, 1983.

Flamenco at 5:15 (with NFB).** Dir. Cynthia Scott, 1983.

Abortion: Stories from North and South. Dir. Gail Singer, 1984.

Adèle and the Ponies of Ardmore. Dir. Char Davies, 1984.

Behind the Veil: Nuns. Dir. Margaret Westcott, 1984.

*Head Start: Meeting the Computer Challenge.** Dir. Diane Beaudry, 1984.

On Our Own (with Ciné-Contact). Dir. Laurette Deschamps, 1984.

This Borrowed Land. Dir. Bonnie Kreps, 1984.

Too Dirty for a Woman. Dir. Diane Beaudry, 1984.

The Treadmill (with NFB). Dir. Dagmar Teufel, 1984.

Turnaround: A Story of Recovery (with NFB). Dir. Moira Simpson, 1984.

*Waterwalker.** Dir. Bill Mason, 1984.

The Best Time of My Life: Portraits of Women in Midlife. Dir. Patricia Watson, 1985.

Dark Lullabies (with DLI Productions). Dir. Irene Angelico, 1985.

DES: An Uncertain Legacy. Dir. Bonnie Andrukaitis and Sidonie Kerr, 1985.

Speaking Our Peace. Dir. Bonnie Sherr Klein and Terre Nash, 1985.

Spirit of the Kata (with NFB). Dir. Sharon McGowan, 1985.

A Writer in the Nuclear Age. Dir. Terre Nash, 1985.

*Beyond Memory.** Dir. Louise Lamarre, 1986.

*Children of War.** Dir. Premika Ratnam, 1986.

*Doctor, Lawyer, Indian Chief.** Dir. Carol Geddes, 1986.

Firewords: Louky Bersianik, Jovette Marchessault, Nicole Brossard. Dir. Dorothy Todd Hénaut, 1986.

*First Take Double Take.** Dir. Paula Fairfield, 1986.

The Impossible Takes a Little Longer. Dir. Anne Henderson, 1986.

*Moving On.** Dir. Tina Horne, 1986.

*No Longer Silent.** (with Ciné Sita). Dir. Laurette Deschamps, 1986.

Nuclear Addiction: Dr. Rosalie Burtell on the Cost of Deterrence. Dir. Terre Nash, 1986.

*A Safe Distance.** Dir. Tina Horne, 1986.

Speaking of Nairobi. Dir. Tina Horne, 1986.

*Sylvie's Story.** Dir. Tina Horne, 1986.

*Thin Dreams.** Dir. Suzie Mah, 1986.

A Love Affair with Politics: A Portrait of Marion Dewar. Dir. Terre Nash, 1987.

The Legacy of Mary McEwan (with P.K.W. Productions). Dir. Patricia Watson, 1987.

A Mother and Daughter on Abortion. Dir. Gail Singer, 1987.

To a Safer Place. Dir. Beverly Shaffer, 1987.

The Man Who Stole Dreams (animation). Dir. Kathleen Shannon and Joyce Borenstein, 1987.

Worth Every Minute. Dir. Catherine Macleod and Lorraine Segato, 1987.

*Mile Zero: The SAGE Tour.** Dir. Bonnie Sherr Klein, 1988.

15th Anniversary. Dir. Sidonie Kerr, 1989.

Adam's World. Dir. Donna Read, 1989.

Goddess Remembered. Dir. Donna Read, 1989.

Half the Kingdom (with Kol Ishah Productions). Dir. Francine Zuckerman and Roushell Goldstein, 1989.

Illuminated Lives (animation). Dir. Ellen Besen, 1989.

*In Her Chosen Field.** Dir. Barbara Evans, 1989.

Older, Stronger, Wiser. Dir. Claire Prieto, 1989.

Russian Diary. Dir. Terre Nash, 1989.

Studio D: 15 Years in the Making. Dir. Janice Brown, 1989.

Unnatural Causes. Dir. Maureen Judge, 1989.

Working Nights. Dir. Sarah Butterfield, 1989.

After the Montreal Massacre. Dir. Gerry Rogers, 1990.

The Burning Times. Dir. Donna Read, 1990.

*Fair Trade.** Dir. Barbara Doran, 1990.

*From the Shore.** Dir. Barbara Doran, 1990.

*The Famine Within.** Dir. Katherine Gilday, 1990.

Five Feminist Minutes (compilation of fifteen short films). Dir. various (Annharte-Baker et al.), 1990.

Fragments of a Conversation on Language. Nora Alleyn, 1990.

*Gathering Together.** Dir. Kathleen Shannon, 1990.

*Harmony and Balance.** Dir. Kathleen Shannon, 1990.

*I'll Never Forget You.** Dir. Kathleen Shannon, 1990.

*No Time to Stop.** Dir. Helene Kladowsky, 1990.

*The Power of Time.** Dir. Liette Aubin, 1990.

*Priorities and Perspectives.** Dir. Kathleen Shannon, 1990.

*Texts and Contexts.** Dir. Kathleen Shannon, 1990.

*Through Ignorance or Design: A Discussion of Stereotypes.** Dir. Kathleen Shannon, 1990.

*A Time to Reap.** Dir. Dagmar Teufel, 1990.

Toying with Their Future (with NFB). Dir. Claire Nadon, 1990.

*Where Credit Is Due.** Dir. Barbara Doran, 1990.

*Working Towards Peace.** Dir. Kathleen Shannon, 1990.

Mother Earth. Dir. Terre Nash, 1991.

Sisters in the Struggle. Dir. Dionne Brand and Ginny Stikeman, 1991.

*When the Day Comes.** Dir. Sharon McGowan, 1991.

Wisecracks (with Zinger Films). Dir. Gail Singer, 1991.

Women in the Shadows (with Direction Films). Dir. Norma Bailey, 1991.

*A Balancing Act.** Dir. Helena Cynamon, 1992.

Forbidden Love: The Unashamed Stories of Lesbian Lives. Dir. Aerlyn Weissman,

Lynne Fernie, 1992.

Making Babies (with Cinéfort). Dir. Gwynne Basen, 1992.

Making Perfect Babies (with Cinéfort). Dir. Gwynne Basen, 1992.

Return Home (with Fortune Films). Dir. Michelle Wong, 1992.

Toward Intimacy. Dir. Debbie McGee, 1992.

Long Time Comin'. Dir. Dionne Brand, 1993.

A Web Not a Ladder. * Dir. Bonnie Dickie, 1993.

Hands of History. Dir. Loretta Todd, 1994.

Keepers of the Fire (with OMNI Films). Dir. Christine Welsh, 1994.

Motherland: Tales of Wonder. Dir. Helene Klodawsky, 1994.

Twenty Years of Feminist Filmmaking. Dir. Janice Brown and Cheryl Sim, 1994.

When Women Kill (with MORAG Productions). Dir. Barbara Doran, 1994.

Skin Deep. Dir. Midi Onodera, 1995.

Widening the Circle: A Gathering with Young Women * (with Canadian Advisory Council on the Status of Women and Disabled Persons Secretariat). Prod. Annette Clarke, Nicole Hubbert, 1995.

Asking Different Questions: Women and Science. * Dir. Erna Buffie, 1996.

The Dreams of the Night Cleaners. * Dir. Leila Sujir, 1996.

Listening for Something. Dir. Dionne Brand, 1996.

Taking Charge. * Dir. Claudette Jaiko, 1996.

Alternate Route. * Dir. Denise Withers, 1997.

Kathleen Shannon: On Film, Feminism & Other Dreams. Dir. Gerry Rogers, 1997.

Under the Willow Tree. Dir. Dora Nipp, 1997.

Veronica. Dir. Beverly Shaffer, 1997.

Beyond Borders: Arab Feminists Talk about Their Lives … East and West. Dir. Jennifer Kawaja, 1999.

Under One Sky: Arab Women in North America Talk about the Hijab. Dir. Jennifer Kawaja, 1999.

* Indicates films made in collaboration with the Federal Women's Film Program.

** Indicates films that won an Academy Award.

SERIES

Working Mothers, 1974–1975.

How They Saw Us —Women at Work, 1977.

Just-A-Minute, 1974–1978.

Children of Canada, 1974–1994.

International Youth Year Training Program (Ministry of Culture and Communications), 1986.

Women and Spirituality, 1989–1991.

Women at the Well, 1989–1993.

African Market Women (with MORAG Productions and CIDA), 1991.

Faithful Women (with Vision TV), 1990.

On the Eighth Day (with Cinéfort), 1992.

—NFB ARCHIVES

—NFB ARCHIVES

Poster announcing the premier of
Five Feminist Minutes *in Montreal, 1989.*

CHRONOLOGY OF IMPORTANT DATES FOR FEMINISM AND STUDIO D*

Canadian Political Leadership
Lester B. Pearson (Liberal) 1963–1968 • Pierre Elliott Trudeau (Liberal) 1968–1979 • Joe Clark (Progressive Conservative) 1979-1980 • Pierre Elliott Trudeau (Liberal) 1980–1984 • John Turner (Progressive Conservative) June–September 1984 • Brian Mulroney (Progressive Conservative) 1984–1993 • Kim Campbell (Progressive Conservative) June–November 1993 • Jean Chrétien (Liberal) 1993–2003.

1966
The Committee for the Equality of Women in Canada (CEWC) is founded in Toronto to "pursue the rights of women in Canada" and immediately begins a campaign for a Royal Commission on the Status of Women • Called together by Thérèse Casgrain, a leader in the suffrage movement in the 1930s and 1940s, representatives of women's groups in Quebec form a new coalition, the Fédération des femmes du Québec (FFQ).

1967
A Royal Commission on the Status of Women (RCSW) is established by the Liberal government of Lester Pearson. The Commission holds hearings in fourteen communities in all ten provinces, meets 890 witnesses, and receives 468 briefs and 1,000 letters • The United Nations Declaration on the Elimination of All Forms of Discrimination Against Women is adopted.

1970
More than 200 women from across Canada gather in Saskatoon, Saskatchewan, for the first national conference on the women's

movement. In her keynote address, McGill University sociologist Marlene Dixon argues that race and class divide women too much to build an autonomous women's movement • The Report of the Royal Commission on the Status of Women, including 167 recommendations, is tabled in the House of Commons • Women are 37 per cent of full-time undergraduate students in Canadian universities.

1971
Robert Andras is appointed first Minister Responsible for the Status of Women • The Canadian Women's Educational Press (the Women's Press) is founded in Toronto by several women who recognize the urgent need to publish material "by, for and about Canadian women."

1972
The Ad Hoc Committee on the Status of Women is formed. The words "ad hoc" are later dropped • *Kinesis*, a newspaper published by the Vancouver Status of Women, is founded.

1973
Ms. magazine is first published • A Quebec jury acquits Dr. Henry Morgentaler for the first time on a charge of committing an illegal abortion. He is subsequently acquitted three times by juries in Ontario and Quebec, only to have those acquittals overturned by higher courts. The Supreme Court of Canada eventually finds in Morgentaler's favour, and in January 1988 declares therapeutic abortion committees (TACs) unconstitutional • Rape crisis centres open in Vancouver and in Toronto. They are the first such centres in Western and Central Canada • *Long Time Coming*, Canada's first lesbian newsletter, is published in Montreal • The Canadian Women's Negro Association organizes the first national Conference of Black Women. After seven years of annual meetings, the Association founds the Congress of Black Women of Canada • The Women's Program of the Secretary of State is created. It becomes an important source of funding for women's organizations across the country • The Conseil du statut de la femme (CSF) is founded in Quebec. Its twofold mandate is to advise the government on matters relating to the status of women and to keep women abreast of its analysis and policy positions.

1974
Canadian government adopts United Nations guidelines for International Women's Year • Kathleen Shannon's *Working Mothers* films are met with overwhelmingly positive response from the Canadian public • The NFB opens Studio D as a studio for women, appointing Kathleen Shannon as its first executive producer. Other Studio members are Margaret Pettigrew and Yuki Yoshida.

1975
The United Nations proclaims International Women's Year. NFB misses the deadline to apply for federal funds earmarked for specific initiatives to promote International Women's Year • Kathleen Shannon establishes the *INTERLOCK* newsletter as a resource for women in Canada who want to make documentaries • The NFB hosts 4 Days in May, a conference organized by Kathleen Shannon to celebrate the role women have played in the NFB during its early years. Many of these women return to discuss their experiences • Studio D releases *Great Grand Mother*, a film that tells the stories of some of the pioneering women who helped to settle the Canadian West.

1976
Bertha Wilson becomes the first woman appeal level judge in Canada when she is appointed to the Ontario Court of Appeal • The Canadian Research Institute for the Advancement of Women (CRIAW) is founded to encourage, co-ordinate and disseminate research into women's experiences • Studio D establishes the practice of hiring a full-time audience researcher and meets on a regular basis with community groups to ascertain public interests in feminist issues.

1977
Studio D releases *How They Saw Us*, a series of eight short films featuring archival footage from documentaries shot in the 1940s and 1950s, interpreted from a feminist perspective. The *Canadian Human Rights Act* becomes law. The *Indian Act* is not covered, and consequently status Indian women continue to lose all entitlement to, and all rights and benefits of, registration as Indians upon marriage to non-Indian men.

1978

The first Take Back the Night March in Canada is held in Toronto. Marchers protest violence against women and demand that they be able to walk the streets at night in safety • Beverly Shaffer wins an Academy Award for *I'll Find a Way* and thanks Studio D for its support in front of one of North America's largest television audiences, putting Studio D on the map • The United Nations Human Rights Committee agrees to hear the case of Sandra Lovelace, an Aboriginal woman from the Tobique Reserve in New Brunswick who claims that the *Indian Act* is discriminatory • In 1981, the Committee finds Canada in breach of the Covenant on Civil and Political Rights.

1979

Aboriginal women organize a 100-mile march to Ottawa from Oka, Quebec, to protest housing conditions on reserves and to demand changes to the *Indian Act* • Report by the Organization for Economic Cooperation and Development (OECD) places Canada nineteenth among nineteen industrialized nations when women's wages are compared with men's • *Herizons* founded as a regional feminist newspaper based in Winnipeg.

1980

Studio D proposes to make *The Quilt*, a budget strategy to involve as many women filmmakers as possible • Kathleen Shannon creates the Federal Women's Film Program (FWFP) in collaboration with a number of federal agencies • Alexa McDonough is elected leader of the NDP of Nova Scotia, becoming the first woman leader of a provincial political party in Canada.

1981

Studio D releases *Not a Love Story*, a feminist film about pornography. The Ontario Film Board restricts its presentation in Ontario due to explicit sexual content • Applebaum-Hébert Report (Federal Cultural Review Committee Report) tabled, proposing a more commercial approach to cultural production. Kathleen Shannon writes *Speaking of Women's Culture* in response, rebuking the authors for their limited definition of culture and arguing that women are "doubly colonized" • 1,300 women from across the country gather on Parliament Hill for a national conference on Women and the Constitution, galvanizing women's opposition to proposed changes to the Constitution and mobilizing them to fight such changes • Judy Erola, Sudbury MP, appointed the first woman minister responsible for the Status of Women portfolio.

1982

If You Love This Planet causes an international incident between Canada and the U.S. as director Terre Nash of Studio D wins an Academy Award • Wimmin's Fire Brigade fire-bombs Red Hot Video, a Vancouver video outlet allegedly dealing in porn • Bertha Wilson is appointed to the Supreme Court of Canada, the first woman appointed to the country's highest court.

1983

Shannon makes a formal presentation to the Standing Committee on Communication and Culture, refuting the Applebaum-Hébert Report and defending NFB's ability to produce Canadian culture. She champions the NFB as the "only environment in the country where women have the opportunity to work together to develop their own perspective, professional standard, artistic style and esthetic" and recommends that the NFB receive enough funding to establish a National Women's Film Program led by Studio D. The proposal falls on deaf ears • According to NFB statistics, 60 per cent of Studio D films are in the top 20 per cent most popular titles booked; 35 per cent of Studio D films are in the top 20 per cent of most popular titles sold • Judge Rosalie Abella coins the term "employment equity" and is appointed to lead a one-woman Royal Commission on Equality in Employment. The report is tabled in 1984 • Studio D's *Flamenco at 5:15* wins an Academy Award • 16 of 282 Members of Parliament are women.

1984

Behind the Veil: Nuns and *Abortion: Stories from North and South* gain critical acclaim but irritate conservative women in Canada who lobby politicians to cut off Studio D's funding • Studio D receives 10 per cent of the total Film Board budget in the English division • Using statistics from the Canadian Advisory Council on the Status of Women, NDP MP Margaret Mitchell raises the issue of wife battering in the House of Commons. Male MPs respond with laughter and catcalls • The first, and thus far only, televised debate on women's issues between the three major federal parties is held. Organized by NAC, the event is picketed by R.E.A.L. Women • In the federal election, twenty-seven women are elected to the House of Commons. Six are appointed to the Cabinet.

1985

The Women's Legal Education and Action Fund (LEAF) is founded • Studio D's budget allocation shrinks to 6 per cent by the end of the year • Section 15, the main equality rights section of the Canadian Charter of Rights and Freedoms, comes into effect, entrenching equality rights for women in the Canadian Constitution • Section 12(l)(b) of the *Indian Act* is repealed. Indian women may marry non-Indian men without losing their Indian status • The DisAbled Women's Network (DAWN) is founded • The federal government promises to amend the *Canadian Human Rights Act* to end discrimination against lesbians and gay men but only tables a proposal roundly denounced by human rights activists as inadequate in 1992. Meanwhile, it fights all cases brought forward by lesbians and gay men • Governmental delegates gather in Nairobi, Kenya, to debate and ratify the United Nations *Forward-Looking Strategies for the Advancement of Women* document. A parallel conference, organized by feminists, brings together 13,000 women from around the globe to assess women's progress and to chart strategies for the future • Studio D is proclaimed a national treasure by the Canadian Women's Institute for Women's Culture (London, ON) • *Herizons* begins publishing as a popular feminist magazine across Canada.

1986

Studio D funding shrinks to 2.2 per cent of the total Film Board budget of $69 million, nearly forcing it to close. High-powered feminists form an Advisory Group and lobby successfully for financial support • Kathleen Shannon takes a sabbatical leave but remains on Studio D staff • Shannon awarded the Order of Canada • *Employment Equity Act* passed • Shirley Carr becomes the first woman president of the Canadian Labour Congress • *Chatelaine* Magazine poll reveals that 47 per cent of its readers identify as feminists • 73 per cent of Canadians believe that the "feminist movement" has had a positive impact on Canadian society • Claire L'Hereux-Dubé becomes the first francophone woman appointed to the Supreme Court of Canada.

1987

Rina Fraticelli becomes executive producer of Studio D as budget restraints continue • R.E.A.L. Women protest that NAC does not represent its interests and launches a "muffin-baking" lobby campaign, appealing to the federal government for funding equal to NAC's • Siding with the anti-abortion (so-called pro-life) faction, R.E.A.L. Women launch a letter-writing campaign denouncing Studio D and its documentaries, demanding that its government funding be cut off.

1988

To celebrate its 50th anniversary, the NFB releases *Cinquante Ans—Fifty Years*, containing 109 shots of people, 42 of which are of men only. Shots of women are either stereotypes or are demeaning. Denouncing the racism, sexism and violence in the NFB anniversary film, Shannon releases *Mother Earth* that contains many of the same shots but developed from a feminist perspective • Studio D's *Goddess Remembered* is welcomed by some and criticized by others who fear that the film embraces the notion of female superiority through biology • Rina Fraticelli releases all of Studio D's full-time directors as budgets continue to shrink • A study finds that only 4.5 per cent of the 39,000 works of art in the National Gallery are created by women.

1988

Supreme Court of Canada declares Canada's abortion law unconstitutional on the grounds that it violates a woman's right to life, liberty and security of the person • Justine Blainey plays her first minor-bantam league (boys) hockey game, following a decision by the Ontario Court of Appeal using the Ontario Human Rights Code that determines discrimination in sports on the basis of sex is unconstitutional.

1989

Studio D celebrates its 15th anniversary • The federal government announces a $2-million cut from the Secretary of State's Women's Program • Women's groups mount a partially successful campaign to have their funding restored • Chantale Daigle's successful fight against an injunction prohibiting her from having an abortion goes all the way to the Supreme Court and galvanizes public support for women's right to choose whether or not to bear children regardless of the wishes of the father • 25 Canadian universities have women's studies programs •

Audrey McLaughlin becomes the first woman leader of a federal party (NDP) and is elected to the House of Commons • Geneviève Bergeron, Hélène Colgan, Nathalie Croteau, Barbara Daigneault, Anne-Marie Edward, Maud Haviernick, Barbara Klucznik Widajewicz, Maryse Laganière, Maryse Leclair, Anne-Marie Lemay, Sonia Pelletier, Michèle Richard, Annie St-Arneault, and Annie Turcotte are killed when Marc Lépine opens fire in Montreal's École Polytechnique before turning the gun on himself. The Montreal Massacre provokes national debates about violence against women and gun control • Rina Fraticelli implements NIF, reactivates FWFP and resigns from Studio D.

1990
Studio D releases *Five Feminist Minutes* • Ginny Stikeman becomes executive director of Studio D and is instrumental in developing NIF to respond to the underrepresentation of women of colour and First Nations women in Canadian film • *Wisecracks*, a production of Studio D, is released and puts to rest the laughable notion that feminists have no sense of humour.

1991
The federal government appoints the Canadian Panel on Violence Against Women • York University admits its first students into a PhD program in women's studies, the first of its kind in North America • Canada enters an era of budget constraints and widespread social discontent • Renée DuPlessis, NIF's program co-ordinator, is fired. The women in NIF and the executives of Studio D grapple with conflicting feminist views.

1992
Kathleen Shannon retires for good from Studio D and moves to the Kootenays where she opens a guest house for women • *Forbidden Love* is released and wins a number of awards, including a Genie • Quebec City lawyer Paule Gauthier becomes the first female president of the Canadian Bar Association.

1993
Kim Campbell is sworn in as Canada's first woman prime minister on June 25.

1994
Studio D celebrates 20 years of feminist filmmaking, adopting the slogan D is for Dare to acknowledge the boldness of women in film over the past twenty years and encouraging future daring • Promotional paraphernalia includes a yellow alert whistle.

1996
Studio D releases *Under the Willow Tree* • Sandra MacDonald is appointed NFB commissioner • Barbara Janes is head of English-language production • Sheila Copps is heritage minister, which includes the NFB portfolio • Paul Martin is finance minister when the federal government slashes the NFB budget by $20 million • Studio D closes but manages to complete those films under production • *Point of View* Magazine publishes "Lament for Studio D," a conversation with Kathleen Shannon "on the birth and death of Canada's groundbreaking feminist film studio."

* A number of these entries are inspired by the PAR-L website, www.unb.ca/PAR.L/milestones.htm.

BIBLIOGRAPHY

Archives

John Grierson Archives

National Film Board Archives (NFBA)

Books & Articles

Adams, Mary Louise. “There’s No Place Like Home: On the Place of Identity in Feminist Politics.” *Feminist Review* 31 (1989): 22–33.

Adamson, Nancy, Linda Briskin, and Margaret McPhail, eds. *Feminist Organizing for Change: The Contemporary Women’s Movement in Canada.* Toronto: Oxford University Press, 1988.

Anderson, Benedict. *Imagined Communities.* 2nd ed. London: Verso, 1991.

Anderson, Doris. “Studio D’s Films Garner Few Financial Rewards.” *Toronto Star*, 22 February 1986: L1.

Anderson, Elizabeth. “Pirating Feminisms: Film and the Production of Post-War Canadian National Identity.” PhD diss., University of Minnesota, 1996.

—. “Studio D’s Imagined Community: From Development (1974) to Realignment (1986–1990).” In *Gendering the Nation: Canadian Women’s Cinema*, edited by Kay Armatage, Kass Banning, Brenda Longfellow and Janine Marchessault, 41–61. Toronto: University of Toronto Press, 1999.

Armatage, Kay. “Film: Winter of Discontent.” *The Canadian Forum* (May 1982): 38–41.

—. “The Evolution of Women Filmmakers in Canada.” In *Changing Focus: The Future for Women in the Canadian Film and Television Industry*, 133–141. Toronto: Toronto Women in Film and Television, 1991.

Backhouse, Constance, and David H. Flaherty, eds. *Challenging Times: The Women’s Movement in Canada and the United States.* Montreal: McGill-Queen’s University Press, 1992.

Banning, Kass. “From Didactics to Desire: Building Women’s Film Culture.” *Work in*

Progress, 149–176. Toronto: The Women's Press, 1987.

—. "The Canadian Feminist Hybrid Documentary." *Cinéaction*, nos. 26/27 (1992): 108–113.

Barrowclough, Susan. "Not a Love Story." *Screen* 23, no. 5 (1982): 26–36.

Bashevkin, Sylvia B. *True Patriot Love: The Politics of Canadian Nationalism.* Toronto: Oxford University Press, 1991.

—. *Women on the Defensive: Living through Conservative Times.* Toronto: University of Toronto Press, 1998.

Beale, Alison. "Cultural Policy as a Technology of Gender." In *Ghosts in the Machine: Women and Cultural Policy in Canada and Australia*, edited by Alison Beale and Annette Van Den Bosch, 233–250. Toronto: Garamond Press, 1998.

Bégin Monique. "The Royal Commission on the Status of Women: Twenty Years Later." In *Challenging Times: The Women's Movement in Canda and the United States*, edited by Constance Backhouse and David H. Flaherty, 21–38. Montreal: McGill-Queen's University Press, 1992.

Berenstein, Rhona. "As Canadian as Possible: The Female Spectator and the Canadian Context." *Camera Obscura* 20/21 (May/September, 1989): 40–51.

Bernard, Andrea. "Experiencing Problems: The Relationship between Women's Studies and Feminist Film Theory." *Women's Studies International Forum* 18, no. 1 (1995): 61–65.

Bjornson, Michelle. "Making Documentary Films: Panel Discussion with Nicole Giguère, Brenda Longfellow, Loretta Todd and Aerlyn Weissman." In *Women Filmmakers: Refocusing*, edited by Jacqueline Levitin, Judith Plessis and Valerie Raoul, 208–218. Vancouver: UBC Press, 2003.

Black, Naomi. "Ripples in the Second Wave: Comparing the Contemporary Women's Movement in Canada and the United States." In *Challenging Times: The Women's Movement in Canada and the United States*, edited by Constance Backhouse and David H. Flaherty, 94–109. Montreal: McGill-Queen's University Press, 1992.

Bloom, Ira. "Forward." *Writing Women's History: International Perspectives,* edited by Karen Offen, Ruth Roach Pierson and Jane Rendall. Bloomington: Indiana University Press, 1991.

Brand, Dionne. *No Language Is Neutral.* Toronto: Coach House Press, 1990.

—. *No Burden to Carry: Narratives of Black Working Women in Ontario 1920s to 1950s*. Toronto: Women's Press, 1991

Brennan, Timothy. "The National Longing for Form." In *Nation and Narration*, edited by Homi Bhabha, 44–70. London: Routledge, 1990.

Brossard, Nicole. *Yesterday, at the Hotel Clarendon*. Translated by Susanne de Lotbinière-Harwood. Toronto: Coach House Press, 2001.

Bruce, Jean. "Querying/Queering the Nation." In *Gendering the Nation: CanadianWomen's Cinema*, edited by Kay Armatage, Kass Banning, Brenda Longfellow, and Janine Marchessault, 274–290. Toronto: University Toronto Press, 1999.

Burgess, Diane. "Leaving Gender Aside: The Legacy of Studio D?" In *Women Filmmakers: Refocusing*, edited by Jacqueline Levitin, Judith Plessis and Valerie Raoul, 418–433. Vancouver: UBC Press, 2003.

Buss, Helen M. "Writing and Reading Autobiography: Introduction to *Prairie Fire's* 'Life Writing' Issue." *Prairie Fire* 16, no. 2 (1995): 5–15.

Canada. Department of Canadian Heritage. *Making Our Voices Heard: Canadian Broadcasting and Film For the 21st Century.* Hull, QC: Minister of Supply and Services Canada, 1996.

Carty, Linda, ed. *And Still We Rise: Feminist Political Mobilization in Contemporary Canada.* Toronto: Women's Press, 1993.

Cixous, Hélène, and Catherine Clément. *The Newly Born Woman: Theory and History of Literature*, vol. 24. Translated by Betsy Wing. Minneapolis: University of Minnesota Press, 1986.

Cohen, Marjorie Griffin. "The Canadian Women's Movement." In *Canadian Women's Issues*, Vol. 1, *Strong Voices*, edited by Ruth Roach Pierson, Marjorie Griffin Cohen, Paula Bourne and Philinda Masters, 1–31. Toronto: James Lorimer, 1993.

Conlogue, Ray. "NFB Should Accept 24% Budget Cut, Juneau Report Says." *Globe and Mail* (Toronto), 1 February 1996: D1.

Cook, Ramsay. *The Maple Leaf Forever: Essays on Nationalism and Politics in Canada.* Toronto: Macmillan of Canada, 1977.

Crow, Barbara A., and Lise Gotell, eds. *Open Boundaries.* Toronto: Prentice Hall, 2000.

de Beauvoir, Simone. *The Second Sex.* Translated by H.M. Parshley. New York: Knopf, 1953.

de Lauretis, Teresa. "Rethinking Women's Cinema: Aesthetics and Feminist Theory." In *Issues in Feminist Film Criticism*, edited by Patricia Erens, 288–308. Bloomington: Indiana University Press, 1991.

—. "*Guerrilla* in the Midst: Women's Cinema in the 80s." *Screen* 31, no. 1 (1990): 6–25.

Din, Ravida, and Mutriba Din. "Sisters in the Movement." *Fireweed* 30 (1990): 35–39.

Doane, Mary Anne, Patricia Mellencamp, and Linda Williams. *Re-Vision: Essays in Feminist Film Criticism.* Frederick, MD: The American Film Institute, 1984.

Dolan, Jill. *The Feminist Spectator as Critic.* Ann Arbor: The University of Michigan Press, 1991.

Dorland, Michael. *So Close to the State/s: The Emergence of Canadian Feature Film Policy.* Toronto: University of Toronto Press, 1998.

Druick, Zoë. "'Ambiguous Identities' and the Representation of Everyday Life: Notes towards a New History of Production Policies at the National Film Board of Canada." In *Canadian Identity: Region, Country, Nation. Selected Proceedings of the 24th Annual Conference of the Association for Canadian Studies, June 6–8, 1997,* edited by the Association for Canadian Studies, 125–137. Montreal: Association for Canadian Studies, 1998.

Dua, Enakshi. "Introduction." *Scratching the Surface: Canadian Anti-racist Feminist Thought,* edited by Enakshi Dua and Angela Robertson, 7–31. Toronto: Women's Press, 1999.

Dumont, Micheline. "The Origins of the Women's Movement in Quebec." In *Challenging Times: The Women's Movement in Canada and the United States,* edited by Constance Backhouse and David H. Flaherty, 72–93. Montreal: McGill-Queen's University Press, 1991.

DuPlessis, Rachel Blau. *Writing beyond the Ending: Narrative Strategies of Twentieth-Century Women Writers.* Bloomington: Indiana University Press, 1985.

DuPlessis, Rachel Blau, and Ann Snitow, eds. *The Feminist Memoir Project: Voices from Women's Liberation.* New York: Three Rivers Press, 1998.

Erens, Patricia, ed. *Issues in Feminist Film Criticism.* Bloomington: University of Indiana Press, 1990.

—. "Women's Documentary Filmmaking: The Personal Is Political." In *New Challenges for Documentary,* edited by Alan Rosenthal, 554–565. Berkeley: University of California Press, 1988.

Evans, Gary. *In the National Interest: A Chronicle of the National Film Board of Canada from 1949 to 1989.* Toronto: University of Toronto Press, 1991.

Ezekiel, Judith. *Feminism in the Heartland.* Columbus: Ohio State University Press, 2002.

"Feminist Broke Ground for Female Filmmakers: Obituary/Kathleen Shannon." *Globe and Mail,* 15 January 1998: S10.

Filipenko, Cindy. "Calling the Shots." *Herizons* (Fall 1996): 18–19.

Findlay, Sue. "Problematizing Privilege: Another Look at the Representation of 'Women' in Feminist Practice." In *And Still We Rise: Feminist Political Mobilization in Contemporary Canada,* edited by Linda Carty, 207–224. Toronto: Women's Press, 1993.

—. "Facing the State: The Politics of the Women's Movement Reconsidered." In *Feminism and Political Economy: Women's Work, Women's Struggles,* edited by Heather Jon Maroney and Meg Luxton, 30–53. Toronto: Methuen, 1987.

Firestone, Shulamith. *The Dialectic of Sex: A Case for Feminist Revolution.* New York: Morrow, 1970.

Forsyth, Scott. "The Failure of Nationalism and Documentary: Grierson and Gouzenko." *Canadian Journal of Film* 1, no. 1 (1990): 74–82.

Foucault, Michel. "The Subject and Power." In *Power: Michel Foucault*, edited by James D. Faubion, translated by Robert Hurley and others, 426–448. New York: New Press, 2000.

Friedman, Susan Stanford. *Mappings: Feminism and the Cultural Geographies of Encounter.* Princeton, NJ: Princeton University Press, 1998.

Fulford, Robert. "NFB Film Ignites Anti-Porn Movement." *Toronto Star*, 5 June 1982: F3.

Gasher, Mike. "From Sacred Cows to White Elephants: Cultural Policy Under Siege." In *Canadian Cultures and Globalization: Proceedings of the Twenty-third Annual Conference of the Association for Canadian Studies, June 1–3, 1996*, edited by Joy Cohnstaedt and Yves Frenette, 13–29. Montreal: Association for Canadian Studies, 1997.

Gibson-Hudson, Gloria J. "The Ties that Bind: Cinematic Representations by Black Women Filmmakers." *Quarterly Review of Film and Video* 15, no. 2 (1993): 25–44.

Godard, Barbara. "Nicole Brossard." *Profiles in Canadian Literature* 6 (1986): 121–126.

Godfrey, Stephen. "A Ride on a Feminist Rollercoaster." *Globe and Mail* (Toronto), 11 October 1989: C1.

—. "Through the Eyes of a Woman." *Globe and Mail* (Toronto), 19 January 1990: C1.

Granatstein, J.L. *The Ottawa Men: The Civil Service Mandarins.* Toronto: Oxford University Press, 1982.

Hall, Stuart. "Who Needs Identity?" In *Questions of Cultural Identity*, edited by Stuart Hall and Paul du Gay, 1–17. London: Sage, 1996.

—. "Cultural Identity and Cinematic Representation." In *Film and Theory*, edited by Robert Stam and Toby Miller, 704–714. Malden, MA: Blackwell, 2000.

Hamilton, Roberta. *Gendering the Vertical Mosaic: Feminist Perspectives on Canadian Society.* Toronto: Copp Clark, 1996.

Hart, Laurinda. "Kathleen Shannon: Working Mothers Series." *Cinema Canada* 2, no. 15 (August/September 1974): 55.

Haskell, Molly. *From Reverence to Rape: The Treatment of Women in the Movies.* Rev. ed. Chicago: University of Chicago Press, 1987.

Hays, Matthew. "Lament for Studio D: A Conversation with Kathleen Shannon," *Point of View* 29 (Spring 1996):16–19.

Heilbrun, Carolyn G. *Writing a Woman's Life.* New York: W.W. Norton, 1988.

Higson, Andrew. "The Concept of National Cinema." *Screen* 30, no. 4 (1990): 36–46.

Hogeland, Lisa Maria. *Feminism and Its Fictions: The Consciousness-Raising Novel and the Women's Liberation Movement.* Philadelphia: University of Pennsylvania Press, 1998.

Hollows, Joanne. *Feminism, Femininity and Popular Culture.* Manchester: Manchester University Press, 2000.

hooks, bell. *Reel to Real: Race, Sex and Class at the Movies.* London: Routledge, 1996.

—. *Talking Back: Thinking Feminist, Thinking Black.* Boston, MA: South End Press, 1989.

Horseman. Jennifer. *Something in My Mind besides the Everyday: Women and Literacy.* Toronto: Canadian Scholars' Press, 1990.

Howells, Coral Ann. *Private and Fictional Words: Canadian Women Novelists of the 1970s and 1980s.* London: Methuen, 1987.

James, Cathy L. "Women's History on Film: Requiem for Studio D." *Canadian Historical Review* 80, no. 1 (March 1999): 93–96.

Johnston, Claire. "Women's Cinema as Counter-Cinema." In *Feminist Film Theory: A Reader*, edited by Sue Thornham, 31–40. New York: New York University Press, 1999.

Johnston, Jessica. "Enough Already." *This Magazine* (January/February 2007): 4.

Juhasz, Alexandra, ed. *Women of Vision: Histories in Feminist Film and Video.* Minneapolis: University of Minnesota Press, 2001.

—. "They Said We Were Trying to Show Reality — All I Want to Show Is My Video: The Politics of the Realist Feminist Documentary." In *Collecting Visible Evidence*, edited by Jane M. Gaines and Michael Renov, 190–215. Minneapolis: University of Minnesota Press, 1999.

Kadar, Marlene. *Reading Life Writing.* Toronto: Oxford University Press, 1993.

Kellner, Douglas. *Media Culture: Culture Studies, Identity and Politics between the Modern and the Postmodern.* London: Routledge, 1995.

Kelly, Joan. *Women, History, and Theory: The Essays of Joan Kelly.* Chicago: University of Chicago Press, 1984.

Knudson, Susan. "For a Feminist Narratology." *Tessera* 4, no. 3 (1989): 10–13.

Kuhn, Annette, ed., with Susannah Radstone. *The Women's Companion to International Film.* London: Virago Press, 1990.

Lai, Larissa. *Salt Fish Girl.* Toronto: Thomas Allen, 2002.

Landsberg, Michele. "Studio D: A Rare Source of Images from Canadian Culture." *Globe and Mail* (Toronto), 13 September 1986: A2.

Lauder, Scott. "A Studio with a View." *The Canadian Forum* (August/September 1986): 12–15.

Le Guin, Ursula. *Dancing at the Edge of the World.* New York: Grove Press, 1989.

Lesage, Julia. "The Political Aesthetics of the Feminist Documentary Film." In *Issues in Feminist Film Criticism*, edited by Patricia Erens, 222–237. Bloomington: Indiana University Press, 1990.

—. "Feminist Documentary: Aesthetics and Politics." In *"Show Us Life": Toward a History and Aesthetics of the Committed Documentary*, edited by Tom Waugh, 223–251. Metechen, NJ: Scarecrow Press, 1984.

Lionnet, Françoise. *Autobiographical Voices: Race, Gender, Self-Portraiture.* Ithaca, NY: Cornell University Press, 1993.

Lippmann, Walter. *Public Opinion.* New York: Harcourt, Brace, 1922.

Longfellow, Brenda. "Un cinéma distinct: stratégies féministes dans les films canadiens." In *Les cinémas du Canada*, edited by Jean-Loup Passek with Sylvain Garel and André Pâquet, 221–233. Montreal: Centre Georges Pompidou, 1992.

—. "Globalization and National Identity in Canadian Film." *Canadian Journal of Film Studies/Revue canadienne d'études cinématographiques* 5, no. 2 (Fall 1996): 3–16.

Lorde, Audre. *Zami, Sister Outsider, Undersong.* New York: Quality Paperback Books, 1993.

Magder, Ted. *Canada's Hollywood: The Canadian State and Feature Films.* Toronto: University of Toronto Press, 1993.

Marks, Laura. *The Skin of the Film.* Duke University Press, 2000.

Masters, Philinda. "Women, Culture and Communication." In *Canadian Women's Issues,* Vol. 1, *Strong Voices: Twenty-Five Years of Women's Activism in English Canada*, edited by Ruth Roach Pierson, Marjorie Griffin Cohen, Paula Bourne and Philinda Masters, 394–417. Toronto: James Lorimer, 1993.

Martin, Biddy. "Success and Its Failures." *differences: A Journal of Feminist Cultural Studies* 9, no. 3 (1997): 102–131.

Martineau, Barbara Halpern. "Before the Guerillières: Women's Films at the NFB during World War II." In *Canadian Film Reader*, edited by Seth Feldman and Joyce Nelson, 58–67. Toronto: Peter Martin Associates, 1977.

Maynard, Mary, and June Purvis. *New Frontiers in Women's Studies: Knowledge, Identity, and Nationalism.* New York: Taylor and Francis, 1996.

McCabe, Janet. *Feminist Film Studies: Writing the Woman into Cinema.* London: Wallflower Press, 2004.

McKie, Frank. "Feminist NFB Films Boring." *Winnipeg Free Press,* 16 June 1986: 21

Miller, Toby. *The Well-Tempered Self: Citizenship, Culture and the Postmodern Subject.* Baltimore: Johns Hopkins University Press, 1993.

Millet, Kate. *Sexual Politics.* New York: Avon, 1971.

Minh-Ha, Trinh T. *Woman, Native, Other: Writing Postcoloniality and Feminism.* Bloomington: Indiana University Press, 1989.

—. "'Who Is Speaking?' Of Nation, Community, and First-Person Interviews." In *Feminisms in the Cinema*, edited by Laura Pietropaolo and Ada Testaferri, 41–59. Bloomington: Indiana University Press, 1995.

Mitchell, Penni. "Women's Policy Units Wiped Out." *Herizons (*Summer 2002), 6.

Modleski, Tania. *Feminism Without Women: Culture and Criticism in a "Postfeminist" Age.* New York: Routledge, 1995.

—. "On the Existence of Women: A Brief History of the Relations between Women's Studies and Film Studies." *Women's Studies Quarterly* 30, nos. 1/2 (2002): 15–24.

Morgan, Robin, ed. *Sisterhood is Powerful: An Anthology of Writings from the Women's Liberation Movement.* New York: Vintage, 1970.

Morris, Cerise. "'Determination and Thoroughness': The Movement for a Royal Commission on the Status of Women in Canada." *Atlantis* 5, no. 2 (1980): 1–21.

Mouffe, Chantal. "Feminism, Citizenship, and Radical Democratic Politics." In *Feminists Theorize the Political,* edited by Judith Butler and Joan W. Scott, 69–84. New York: Routledge, 1992.

Nash, Terre. "Against the Grain: Kathleen Shannon in Memoriam." *This Magazine* (May/June 1998): 36–39.

Nelson, Joyce. *The Colonized Eye: Rethinking the Grierson Legend.* Toronto: Between the Lines, 1988.

"NFB: Studio D Shuffles Staff." *Cinema Canada* 160 (February/March 1989): 49.

Nichols, Bill. *Representing Reality: Issues and Concepts in Documentary*. Bloomington: Indiana University Press, 1991.

Nicholson, Linda, ed. *The Second Wave: A Reader in Feminist Theory*. New York: Routledge, 1997.

Offen, Karen, Ruth Roach Pierson, and Jane Rendall, eds. *Writing Women's History: International Perspectives.* Bloomington: Indiana University Press, 1991.

O'Regan, Tom. *Australian National Cinema.* London: Routledge, 1993.

Pendakur, Manjunath. *Canadian Dreams and American Control: The Political Economy of the Canadian Film Industry.* Detroit: Wayne State University Press, 1990.

Pettman, Jan Jindy. "Boundary Politics: Women, Nationalism and Danger." In *New Frontiers in Women's Studies: Knowledge, Identity and Nationalism*, edited by Mary Maynard and June Purvis, 187–202. London: Taylor and Francis, 1996.

Philip, Marlene NourbeSe. "The Absence of Writing or How I Almost Became a Spy." In *A Geneology of Resistance and Other Essays*, edited by Marlene NourbeSe Philip, 41–56. Toronto: Mercury Press, 1997.

Pierson, Ruth Roach. *Canadian Women and the Second World War.* Ottawa: Canadian Historical Association, 1983.

—. "Experience, Difference, Dominance and Voice in the Writing of Canadian Women's History." In *Writing Women's History: International Perspectives*, edited by Karen Offen, Ruth Roach Pierson and Jane Rendall, 79–106. Bloomington: Indiana University Press, 1991.

Poulantzas, Nicos. *Political Power and Social Classes.* London: Verso, 1978.

Prince, Tracy. "The Post of Colonial in the Works of Pratibha Parmer: *Kiss My Cuddies."* In *Women Filmmakers: Refocusing,* edited by Jacqueline Levitin, Judith Plessis, and Valerie Raoul, 291–298. Vancouver: UBC Press, 2003.

Quandt, Tarel. "Does the Goddess Have a Hidden Agenda?" *Kinesis* (May 1990): 15–16.

Rebick, Judy. "Where Are Women's Voices?" *Canadian Forum* (April 1997): 24.

Rich, Adrienne. "Towards a Woman-Centered University (1973–74)." *On Lies, Secrets, and Silences: Selected Prose, 1966–1978.* New York: W.W. Norton, 1979.

Rich, B. Ruby. *Chick Flicks.* Durham, NC: Duke University Press, 1998.

—. "Anti-Porn: Soft Issue, Hard World." In *Gendering the Nation: Canadian Women's Cinema*, edited by Kay Armatage, Kass Banning, Brenda Longfellow and Janine Marchessault, 62–75. Toronto: University of Toronto Press, 1999.

Rosen, Marjorie. *Popcorn Venus: Women, Movies and the American Dream.* New York: Avon Books, 1973.

Ross, Becky. "A Lesbian Politics of Erotic Decolonization." In *Painting the Maple: Race, Gender, and the Construction of Canada,* edited by Veronica Strong-Boag, Sherrill Grace, Avigail Eisenberg, and Joan Anderson, 187–214. Vancouver: University of British Columbia Press, 1998.

Rowbotham, Sheila. *Women's Consciousness, Men's World.* Harmondsworth, UK: Penguin Books, 1973.

Rundle, Lisa Bryn. "Who Needs NAC?" *This Magazine* (March/April 1999): 24–29.

Scherbarth, Chris. "Studio D of the National Film Board of Canada: Seeing Ourselves through Women's Eyes." MA thesis, Carleton University, 1986.

—. "Why Not D? An Historical Look at the NFB's Women's Studio." *Cinema Canada* 139 (1987): 9–13.

—. "Canada's Studio D: A Women's Room with an International Reputation." *Canadian Woman Studies/les cahiers de la femme* 8, no. 1 (1987): 24–27.

Scott, Joan Wallach. *Gender and the Politics of History*. 2nd ed. New York: Columbia University Press, 1999.

—. "Women's Studies on the Edge, Introduction." *differences: A Journal of Feminist Cultural Studies* 9, no. 3 (1997): i–v.

Sexton, Anne. *Transformations.* Boston: Houghton Mifflin, 1971.

Shannon, Kathleen. "'D' is for Dilemma." *Herizons* (Summer 1995): 24–29.

—. "Real Issues in a Reel World." *Media & Values* (Winter 1989): 14–15.

—. "Women Making Films: Kathleen Shannon." *Pot Pourri* (June 1974): 2–6.

Skeggs, Beverley, ed. *Feminist Cultural Theory: Process and Production.* Manchester: Manchester University Press, 1995.

Smelik, Anneke. "Feminist Film Theory." In *The Cinema Book*, edited by Pam Cook and Mike Berniuk, 353–365. London: British Film Institute, 1999.

Soper, Laurie. *"Long Time Comin'." Herizons* (Spring 1994): 44–45.

Strong-Boag, Veronica, Sherrill Grace, Avigail Eisenberg, and Joan Anderson, eds. *Painting the Maple: Essays on Race, Gender, and the Construction of Canada.* Vancouver: University of British Columbia Press, 1998.

Suleri, Sara. "Woman Skin Deep: Feminism and the Postcolonial Condition." In *The Post-Colonial Studies Reader*, edited by Bill Ashcroft, Gareth Griffiths and Helen Tiffin, 273–282. London: Routledge, 1995.

Sussex, Elizabeth. *The Rise and Fall of British Documentary: The Story of the Film Movement Founded by John Grierson.* Berkeley: University of California Press, 1975.

Sweet, Lois. "Studio D Faces Big Job Small Budget." *Toronto Star*, 4 May 1987: C1.

Taylor, Anita. "The National Film Board of Canada's Studio D: Feminist Filmmakers." In *Women and Media: Content/Careers/Criticism*, edited by Cynthia M. Lont, 293–306. Belmont, CA: Wadsworth, 1995.

Thiele, Beverly. "Vanishing Acts in Social and Political Thought: Tricks of the Trade." In *Defining Women: Social Institutions and Gender Divisions*, edited by Linda McDowell and Rosemary Pringle, 26–35. London: Polity Press in association with Open University Press, 1992.

Thornham, Sue, ed. *Feminist Film Theory: A Reader.* New York: New York University Press, 1999.

Turner, Graeme. *National Fictions: Literature, Film and the Construction of Australian Narrative*. 2nd ed. St. Leonards, Australia: Allen and Unwin, 1993.

Verduyn, Christl. "Reconstructing Canadian Literature: The Role of Race and Gender." In *Painting the Maple: Essays on Race, Gender, and the Construction of Canada*, edited by Veronica Strong-Boag, Sherrill Grace, Avigail Eisenberg and Joan Anderson, 100-112. Vancouver: University of British Columbia Press, 1998.

Vickers, Jill. "The Intellectual Origins of the Women's Movements in Canada." In *Challenging Times: The Women's Movement in Canada and the United* States, edited by Constance Backhouse and David H. Flaherty, 39–60. Montreal: McGill-Queen's University Press, 1992.

Vickers, Jill, Pauline Rankin, and Christine Appelle, eds. *Politics as if Women Mattered: A Political Analysis of the National Action Committee on the Status of Women.* Toronto: University of Toronto Press, 1983.

—. "The Intellectual and Political Context for the Development of NAC." In *Open Boundaries*, edited Barbara A. Crow and Lise Gotell, 111–133. Toronto: Prentice Hall, 2000.

Waldman, Diane, and Janet Walker, eds. *Feminism and Documentary*. Minneapolis: University of Minnesota Press, 1999.

Warren, Ina. "Future Bleak for Famed Studio D." *Globe and Mail*, 30 July 1986: C8.

—. "Head of Women's Film Unit Faces Big Task." *Ottawa Citizen*, 20 June 1987: C6.

—. "NFB Disbands Women's Studio." *Ottawa Citizen*, 13 February 1989: C6.

White, Patricia. "Feminism and Film." In *The Oxford Guide to Film Studies*, edited by John Hill and Pamela Church Gibson, 117–134. New York: Oxford University Press, 1998.

Williams, Linda. *Hard Core: Power, Pleasure and the "Frenzy of the Visible."* Berkeley: University of California Press, 1989.

Winston, Brian. "The Tradition of the Victim in Griersonian Documentary." In *Image Ethics: The Moral Rights of Subjects in Photographs, Film, and Television*, edited by Larry Gross, John Stuart Katz and Jay Ruby, 34–57. New York: Oxford University Press, 1988.

Yi, Sun-Kyung. "Trouble in Paradise or Testing the Limits at Studio D." *Take One* 5 (Summer 1991): 40.

Zeleke, Centeme. "That's a Cut: Feds Close Women's Studio." *Herizons* (Summer 1996): 9.

INDEX

Other titles from The Women's Issues Publishing Program

Trans/forming Feminisms: Transfeminist Voices Speak Out
Edited by Krista Scott-Dixon

Remembering Women Murdered by Men: Memorials Across Canada
The Cultural Memory Group

Growing up Degrassi: Television, Identity and Youth Cultures
Edited by Michele Byers

Feminism, Law, Inclusion: Intersectionality in Action
Edited by Gayle MacDonald, Rachel L. Osborne and Charles C. Smith

Troubling Women's Studies: Pasts, Presents and Possibilities
Ann Braithwaite, Susan Heald, Susanne Luhmann and Sharon Rosenberg

Doing IT: Women Working in Information Technology Krista Scott-Dixon

Inside Corporate U: Women in the Academy Speak Out
Edited by Marilee Reimer

Out of the Ivory Tower: Feminist Research for Social Change
Edited by Andrea Martinez and Meryn Stuart

Strong Women Stories: Native Vision and Community Survival
Edited by Kim Anderson and Bonita Lawrence

Back to the Drawing Board: African-Canadian Feminisms
Edited by Njoki Nathane Wane, Katerina Deliovsky and Erica Lawson

Cashing In On Pay Equity? Supermarket Restructuring and Gender Equality
Jan Kainer

Double Jeopardy: Motherwork and the Law Lorna A. Turnbull

Turbo Chicks: Talking Young Feminisms
Edited by Allyson Mitchell, Lisa Bryn Rundle and Lara Karaian
Winner of the 2002 Independent Publishers Award

Women in the Office: Transitions in a Global Economy Ann Eyerman

Women's Bodies/Women's Lives: Women, Health and Well-Being
Edited by Baukje Miedema, Janet Stoppard and Vivienne Anderson

A Recognition of Being: Reconstructing Native Womanhood Kim Anderson

Women's Changing Landscapes: Life Stories from Three Generations
Edited by Greta Hofmann Nemiroff

Women Working the NAFTA Food Chain: Women, Food and Globalization
Edited by Deborah Barndt, Winner of the 2000 Independent Publishers Award

Cracking the Gender Code: Who Rules the Wired World?
Melanie Stewart Millar, Winner of the 1999 Independent Publishers Award

Redefining Motherhood: Changing Identities and Patterns
Edited by Sharon Abbey and Andrea O'Reilly

Fault Lines: Incest, Sexuality and Catholic Family Culture Tish Langlois